WHAT COMES AFTER MONEY?

WHAT COMES AFTER MONEY?

ESSAYS FROM
REALITY SANDWICH
ON TRANSFORMING
CURRENCY & **COMMUNITY**

EDITED BY
DANIEL PINCHBECK
& **KEN JORDAN**

EVOLVER
EDITIONS

Berkeley, California

Published by Evolver Editions

Evolver Editions' publications are distributed by
North Atlantic Books
P.O. Box 12327
Berkeley, California 94712

Art Direction, Design, and Photography by michaelrobinsonnyc.com
Illustrations on pages v and viii by Micah Lidberg
Printed in the United States of America on 30% post-consumer-waste paper

Chapter 14, "An Army of Jacks to Fight the Power," first appeared in *Fifth Estate* magazine (www.fifthestate.org). Chapter 20, "Local Control of Credit: The Foundation of Economic Democracy," is reprinted from *The End of Money and the Future of Civilization,* copyright 2009 by Thomas Greco and used with the permission of Chelsea Green Publishing (www.chelseagreen.com).

What Comes After Money? is sponsored by the Society for the Study of Native Arts and Sciences, a nonprofit educational corporation whose goals are to develop an educational and cross-cultural perspective linking various scientific, social, and artistic fields; to nurture a holistic view of arts, sciences, humanities, and healing; and to publish and distribute literature on the relationship of mind, body, and nature.

North Atlantic Books' publications are available through most bookstores. For further information, visit our website at www.northatlanticbooks.com or call 800-733-3000.

Library of Congress Cataloging-in-Publication Data

What comes after money? : essays from Reality sandwich on transforming currency and community / edited by Daniel Pinchbeck and Ken Jordan.
    p. cm.
 Summary: "A collection of twenty-two essays from the web magazine Reality Sandwich that discuss alternatives to the current systems of bank-financed currency and global capitalism"—Provided by publisher.
 ISBN 978-1-58394-349-6
 1. Money. 2. Economic development—Social aspects. 3. Community development.
I. Pinchbeck, Daniel. II. Jordan, Ken. III. Reality sandwich.
 HG221.W347 2011
 332.4—dc22
                    2011012690

1 2 3 4 5 6 7 8 9 SHERIDAN 16 15 14 13 12 11

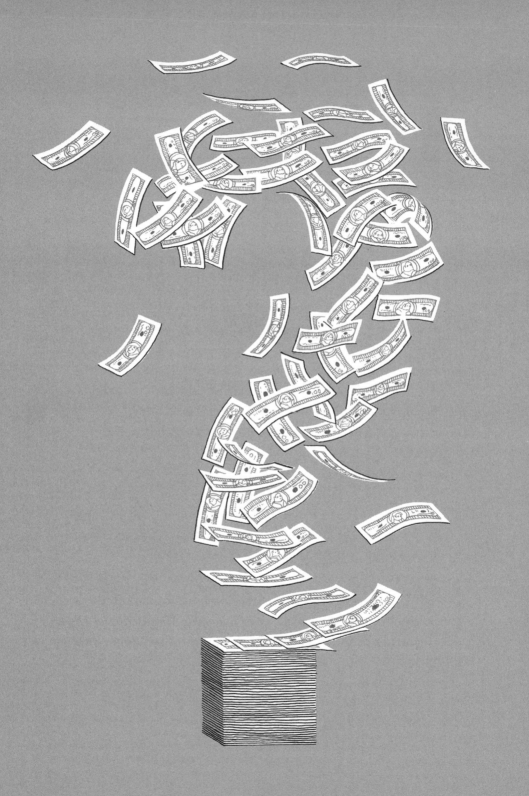

THE IMPOSSIBLE ALTERNATIVE

DANIEL PINCHBECK

The money game … We are all forced to play it, whether we like it or not. A few leap across the Monopoly board with great gusto, building or toppling companies, gobbling up futures on resources and minerals, speculating on currencies. Some market new cultural products—images, memes, books, lines of software code, musical jingles—as their gambits and dice throws in the global casino. Others, dealt a worse hand, play a more brutal version of the game in the back alleys of third world cities, begging for baksheesh, selling their sex for a meager sum, sending their children to work in factories or collect bits of nickel and aluminum from toxic trash heaps. Simply by virtue of being born into this single global system, this omni-oppressive world order, we are all conscripted into a relentless contest, a ceaseless tumult.

Ever since the mangling of his ideas led to horrific dictatorships and genocidal regimes over the last century, the philosopher Karl Marx has been out of fashion, neglected and suppressed. This is understandable but unfortunate, as many of his insights into the mythic dimensions of money and the workings of capital deserve reconsideration. In the *Economic and Philosophic Manuscripts of 1844*, Marx describes money as "the visible divinity" in our capitalist world: "By possessing the property of buying everything, by possessing the property of appropriating all objects, money is thus the object of eminent possession. The universality of its property is the omnipotence of its being. It therefore functions as almighty being.

Money is the pimp between man's need and the object, between his life and his means of life. But that which mediates my life for me, also mediates the existence of other people for me. For me it is the other person." Since birth, we have been trained like performing seals to accept the spiteful conjuror's trick that transmutes any and all qualities into quantities—into bigger or smaller piles of cash. Seemingly without an alternative, most of us accept a system in which everything and everyone has its price, and beneath every celebration lies a cynical calculation.

Hypnotized by our culture, most people believe that our current form of money is the only rational way to exchange value—that a debt-based currency, detached from any tangible asset, is something as organic and inevitable as carbon molecules, ice, or photosynthesis. We forget that money, in its current form, is just a tool. Humans created money to perform certain functions and satisfy certain needs. But just as engineers and computer programmers drop cruder, out-of-date tools and pick up better ones as soon as they become available, we might also switch to more sophisticated instruments for transferring goods and services that function more efficiently and equitably. We could implement new mechanisms and platforms for exchanging value that we have designed to prevent the destructive social and ecological feedback loops produced by our current financial system. As an operating system for society, money needs a major upgrade. This upgrade will not just happen on its own; we need to apply our intelligence and creativity to make it happen.

This requires an act of will, and a leap of faith, from many of us. Personally, I grew up with an artistic New York background and, until a few years ago, I never gave much thought to economics, considering it incredibly boring, useless, and the opposite of anything cool. About five years ago, I began to comprehend that the underlying logic of our economic system was inciting a systemic crash—that our model of endless growth on a finite planet was bringing about mass species extinction, mass pollution, and was somehow linked to a nihilistic value system that mortgaged the future of the planet for the instant gratification of the lucky few. When we launched our web magazine Reality Sandwich, we made alternative approaches to our economy one of our areas of focus, and a priority. First appearing in Reality Sandwich, the essays included in this book present a range of perspectives on the problems endemic to our current financial system, and propose tangible ways to change it. For those who are not used to this type of discussion, it takes a while to familiarize yourself with the issues and the terminology, but the effort is worth it, as the subject is of critical importance.

Over the last half-century, the mainstream culture institutionalized hipster rebellion and integrated it within the corporate mainstream, which constantly instructs us to "Just Do It," "Think Different," "FCUK," and the like. Corporations took our innate impulse toward dissent and our desire for meaningful change, and transmuted them into effective sales tools for their products. The new counterculture, which I believe Reality Sandwich represents, goes beyond easily assimilated gestures of rebellion to interrogate and analyze the underpinnings of our current destructive social order. We believe it is no longer enough to propose alternatives— we need to implement them, instead of waiting around, expecting that someone else is going to do it for us. For this reason, along with Reality Sandwich, we launched a social network, Evolver.net, which provides the organizing hub for what we call the Evolver Social Movement. The ESM brings together local communities that share a vision of how society could be transformed under a global umbrella, and promotes initiatives in permaculture, public performance, local currencies, and viable alternatives in many areas. Evolver actively seeks to collaborate with other movements and organizations that employ DIY tactics to revitalize civil society, such as Transition Town, the Zeitgeist Movement, Iraq Veterans Against the War, Burners Without Borders, etcetera. We propose that reimagining and reinventing society through conscious collaboration is the avant-garde art form of our time.

While rarely discussed in the mainstream media, an awakening is currently underway: More and more people are coming to realize that what we use as money is not some natural force or omnipotent being, but a magic spell. This spell is maintained by the oracles and high priests of finance from their well-guarded temples—the banks and treasuries—where they alchemically transmute little bits of paper or blips of data into valuable artifacts, using occult symbol, incantation, and numerical abracadabra. Indeed, what the financial sorcerers fear more than anything is a collective loss of faith in the abstruse and arcane instruments they use to bind the great human mob in invisible chains of debt, servitude, and scarcity.

The political philosopher Antonio Negri demystified "capital" by defining it, simply, as a "social relation." What does this mean? When a billionaire walks into the room, everyone reacts as though the intangible assets circulating as data streams in his investment portfolio are as real as the armor that Tony Stark puts on when he becomes Iron Man. These streams of virtual data permit the tycoon to control servants, private security forces, mansions, yachts, Picassos, and whatnot. In actual fact, the extraordinary superpowers ascribed to such a personage exist only in the mind.

If a sudden pulse of solar radiation wiped out our hard drives, everyone would quickly see that stored capital was merely a cultural convention, a belief system. The billionaire would lose all of his perceived superpowers and, like an incredible shrinking magnate, retract back to modest size. The vast apparatus of contemporary media and the sleek glass architecture of corporate skyscrapers are designed to reinforce unquestioning obedience and faith in this belief system of capitalism, which gives the privileged few the power of life and death over the multitudinous many.

Antiglobalization activists often proclaim that another world is possible. They declare their faith that the current, tragically unjust orchestration of capital is not the only way we can organize our planetary community, even at our current level of size and complexity. Most people find it almost impossible to imagine a systemic alternative. This seeming impossibility of envisioning and then constructing a viable alternative is an illusion. The corporate media constantly imprints and indoctrinates us into the unquestioning belief that the way it is now is the only way it can be. The system keeps our consciousness trapped within a particular set of beliefs, a certain frequency of awareness and closed framing of our reality. The media ignores the alternatives that already exist, and constantly amps up people's fear of losing what little they have. For those who see beyond these prison walls, it is not enough to insist upon the possibility of another world. We need to understand how we can construct the alternative, and then work together to bring it about.

There was a time before our current monetary system existed, and there will be a time after it is gone. We can look, without sentimentality or nostalgia, at the practices of premodern indigenous cultures that didn't need lawyers, accountants, Swiss bank accounts, or land that could be owned. These cultures organized themselves around gift exchange rather than financial transaction. For indigenous people in Australia or South America, power is not something that can be hoarded; power can only be expressed in the living present, through ceremony, initiation, and action. As anthropologist Pierre Clastres discusses in *Society Against the State,* the tribal chief is generally the one who owns the least, as he gains respect by giving away everything that comes to him to maintain harmony and balance among his people. His generosity is a source of power. These cultures may provide keys for us, models to make use of as we go forward, reinventing our institutions and technologies so they support long-range prosperity for everyone on earth.

When the Thai baht suddenly ceases to function, when the Mexican peso bites the dust, these devastating traumas have nothing to do with the productivity of the local lands or the skills of the people. Neither their houses and farms nor the machines in their factories suddenly molt or liquefy; the abstract data flows manipulated by the financial elites are all that shift. For some reason, we have vested a small coterie of avaricious speculators with the ability to dismantle a nation's economy in a matter of hours, as they follow flickering tugs of fear and greed.

Our current monoculture of money enforces aggressive, competitive, and unsustainable patterns of behavior by creating artificial scarcity. When you get a loan from a bank, the bank gives you the principle, but does not create the interest. Therefore, you are forced to go out into society and compete against everyone else to bring back the interest that accrues. Publicly traded corporations, similarly, are forced to maximize profits to satisfy their shareholders, and therefore must use the most expedient methods to create revenue, even when this means sabotaging environmental safeguards or depriving local communities of their fair share. "Free market" capitalism guarantees there will be big winners, and bigger losers. The biggest loser, alas, is the earth itself. As long as our technological powers increase within a system of domination and exploitation, more catastrophes like the Gulf oil spill and the Chernobyl and Bhopal disasters are essentially guaranteed. As technology becomes more powerful, these calamities will only get more horrifying, until the rotting foundations of our social order are exposed and addressed.

Our currency is not a neutral tool, but a crystallized belief system. "Money" is an expression of ideology, the blinkered reasoning or "irrational rationality" that mortgages the present moment for a future payoff that never arrives. In the interim, the laboring multitudes grind it out, hour by hour, day by day. As we reconsider the meaning of money and the true nature of value, our society will also reconceive our approach to work; eventually, we will change our ideas of what progress means, and even our relationship to time.

Once "time" is no longer "money," we may transform the way we choose to live in time.

Many progressives and social crusaders argue that unemployment is a major social problem. They call for more jobs, "green jobs," or guaranteed employment. This focus on employment is also a misconception based on a limited reasoning. In actual fact, it is not unemployment but work that is the problem. Deep down, nobody wants a job to occupy his or her time. We want a mission that inspires us.

As the design scientist Buckminster Fuller noted, most of the work that our society creates produces no real benefit for the earth, and in fact subtracts from it. Most of the work we do requires pointless expenditures of energy and makes more waste. Rather than having people drive to jobs and use up endless Styrofoam containers and toner cartridges, it would be cheaper—in the real terms of the vitality and thrive-ability of the earth—to subsidize them to remain in their home communities, support them to grow their own food, foster permaculture projects to increase biodiversity, and encourage them to educate themselves and their children, to make art and perform ritual if they felt so inclined, and to generally celebrate the sacred mystery of being with a minimum of interference.

Without idealizing the past, we know that many indigenous people did not "work" in the way we now understand it. Colonialists were outraged that native peoples only spent a few hours a day doing those activities necessary to support life, such as hunting and gathering, building their temporary habitats, and so on. While zealous application of the Protestant ethic brought the benefits of Western medicine and technology to the human community, it also had the unfortunate result of turning our world from a garden into a gulag.

The human-devised concept that "time is money" has created a wasteland of boredom and nihilism where many of us are forced, as the critic Lewis Mumford cunningly observed, to look into the mirror each morning and ask ourselves what part of our personality we can sell today. Given such a system, some of the most successful manipulators are those natural sociopaths who feel no compunction about thieving from the masses to line their own pockets—think the "smartest guys in the room" from the bygone Enron days; or complacent CEOs like Tony Hayward of BP, happy to attend yachting races while his company's activities terminated entire undersea ecosystems; or all the "masters of the universe" not yet exposed, let alone brought to justice. Modern capitalism makes sociopathic behavior humdrum and routine. What else can we make of a corporation like Walmart, which takes out secret life insurance policies on its harassed and humiliated employees, utilizing statistical "quant" analysis to cash in on their aggravated death rates?

Our current economic system is institutionalized psychopathology, a parasitic virus, and its perpetuation would likely lead to the termination of the human experiment in an accelerating series of catastrophes, as climate change accelerates and the exploitation of resources and technological domination of nature intensify. The alternative is extremely difficult to imagine, until we realize it. Albert Einstein once noted that a problem is never solved by the same level of consciousness that created it, but can be superseded once a new level of consciousness is attained. We rapidly approach an exciting threshold where breakdown and breakthrough could happen almost simultaneously.

The good bad news is that we are witnessing the collapse of the current financial order, a bit like watching a multi-car collision take place in sickening slow motion. While vast amounts of intangible finance capital continue to amass, the real assets of the earth are in rapid decline, and this growing gap between the abstract and the real is bringing on an inevitable crash, one in which the delusions of finance capital can no longer be maintained. The global system has revealed itself as a massive Ponzi scheme, a debt pyramid, and we are reaching that thrilling, terrifying precipice where maintaining the fiction is no longer possible.

Nobody has ever been in this situation before. What happens next is anyone's guess, but a few alternatives seem most plausible. Over the last decades, wealth has been concentrated in fewer and fewer hands. According to a recent study, fewer than seven hundred billionaires have a combined net worth of more than $2 trillion. At the same time, an estimated 2.8 billion people survive on less than $2 a day, and 1.2 billion live on less than $1. Here in the United States, fewer than 7,500 individuals out of 300 million control "almost three-quarters of the nation's industrial (nonfinancial) assets, almost two-thirds of all banking assets, and more than three-quarters of all insurance assets," notes political scientist Thomas Dye in *Who's Running America?* Members of this small group can be found in the top tiers of the most exclusive law firms, investment banks, federal government posts, and military commands, where they can control the herd.

As the superstructure of the financial system melts down, it is unlikely that this small coterie of the world's financial elite will choose, in a great heartfelt conversion, to democratize wealth and share resources equitably. They will, more likely, seek to grasp onto their privilege and keep their stranglehold over resources, potentially creating an increasingly authoritarian state apparatus in which the divide between the haves and have-nots becomes ever greater. As social pressure builds, draconian restrictions based on trumped-up fears of terrorists, immigrants, and other bogeymen may supplant democratic freedoms. The corporate oligarchy has spent decades mastering techniques of getting uninformed and ignorant people to act against their own best interests, and will continue to foster stupefaction and mob rule. As increasing constraints are placed on us, as security forces patrol the perimeter and drone helicopters circle overhead, as basic necessities like drinking water are sold back to us, as hyperinflation leaves only a few megabanks still standing, we will be told—over and over again—that this culture is still the greatest thing ever, that the evil others are to blame, and that it is all being done for our own good.

The other option is the one discussed, from various angles, in the essays collected in this book: the prospect that the rapidly deepening, globally systemic, economic-ecological collapse will provide the necessary ground for a mass awakening, and for the reinvention of our economic system in accord with a design science that follows nature's operating principles. As the economist Bernard Lietaer has noted, what we require is a shift from a fragile monoculture based on one form of money to a diversified offering of many currency tools, providing a variety of ways for human beings to exchange value. The current form of Yang currency that supports masculine competition and aggression must be complemented, perhaps superseded, by Yin currencies that foster collaboration and cooperation.

More fundamental than any new currency is the shift in awareness, the change of consciousness, necessary before a truly equitable global society can emerge. This change is already occurring on many levels, some visible and some subliminal, throughout our increasingly interconnected world. We are developing a thoroughly evolutionary perspective, one that sees human cultures, relationships, and social systems as expressions of an evolution of life and of a consciousness that is perpetually ongoing. We are not passive observers of this process, but active participants. We are the coming-into-consciousness of the Gaian mind, and our actions and intentions—as individuals and communities—determine the trajectory of our future culture.

From this evolutionary viewpoint, we can see the development of capitalism over the last few hundred years as a necessary phase, but not a final endpoint, toward the inception of a planetary community. Capitalism drove technological innovation and a melding of the world's cultures, but kept us locked in an adolescent state of mind. Communications technologies such as the internet have now linked humanity into a global tribe, able to communicate instantaneously and experience simultaneously. The intensifying economic and ecological meltdown is akin to the process that occurs when a caterpillar morphs into a butterfly: There is, first of all, a disintegration of the caterpillar form and the emergence of imaginal cells that direct the process of transmutation into a new form of life. To the old system, this appears as danger, as death, but to the new emergent form, it is necessary as an aspect of the birthing process.

We are inexorably moving toward the realization of humanity as a unified being, a singular organism, meshed with the delicate planetary ecology that nurtures us. As Bruce Lipton and Steven Bhaerman discuss in their book *Spontaneous Evolution,* the cells in the human body have developed to work together in perfect symbiosis, sharing resources equitably. You don't find one cell hoarding masses of energy while another cell is left utterly deprived and gasping. If individual humans are akin to cells in a greater Gaian organism, we could similarly reach a point at which sufficient energy is provided to all, for everyone's benefit, to ensure the effective functioning of the whole.

The essays in *What Comes After Money?* are thought experiments that explore our current economic predicament and reveal the path to a new economy, biospherically balanced and equitably attuned. For many people, the idea that our global capitalist system could make a quantum jump into a new systemic paradigm will initially seem impossible and outlandish. However, human culture can change with remarkable speed when necessary. Before 1989, among all the highly paid think tank analysts and political specialists, nobody predicted that the Berlin Wall would be taken down, piece by piece, through a euphoric civilian uprising, while the military stood down—that East would reunite with West without nuclear conflict or vast loss of life. This happened because, on a secret and subliminal level, the consciousness of people operating under that old oppressive order could no longer tolerate a barricade created by ideology and maintained through domination. Today, Wall Street and its "banksta" allies in foreign capitals control the movements of capital and the destiny of people and nations. Is it possible that a civil society upsurge could tear this conceptual barricade down as well? If something like this were to take place, the best-case scenario would be that we would have a new paradigm, a working operating system for exchanging goods and services using different principles, ready for rollout *before* social chaos could lead to the imposing of authoritarian controls.

Personally, I agree with the visionary thinker José Argüelles, who proposes that time is not money: time is art. The next phase of human development should be one of conscious evolution and co-creative collaboration, when we recognize that society is, in itself, an art project. We have the power to use our intelligence and imagination to reinvent society's operating system so that it fulfills humanity's highest hopes and age-old aspirations. If we can develop and construct a new economic foundation that strikes a balance between the gift exchanges of the archaic past and our modern system of swift global transactions, we might manifest a magnificent art project, an ever-evolving social sculpture, together. Such an expression of our collective human genius will benefit our kin and our descendants, and support the greater web of life. Facing a crisis unleashed by human greed and ignorance, we have an extraordinary opportunity to bring about a new—or renewed—society that is far more comfortable, harmonic, relaxed, peaceful, and humane. My hope is that this book offers a set of helpful tools for thinking through this extraordinary process, and that it inspires you to collaborate on the great co-creative experiment that lies ahead.

1

MONEY AND THE CRISIS OF CIVILIZATION

CHARLES EISENSTEIN

Suppose you give me a million dollars with the instructions, "Invest this profitably, and I'll pay you well." I'm a sharp dresser—why not? So I go out onto the street and hand out stacks of bills to random passersby: ten thousand dollars each. In return, each scribbles out an IOU for twenty thousand dollars, payable in five years. I come back to you and say, "Look at these IOUs! I have generated a 20 percent annual return on your investment." You are very pleased, and pay me an enormous commission.

Now I've got a big stack of IOUs, so I use these "assets" as collateral to borrow even more money, which I lend out to even more people, or sell them to others like myself who do the same. I also buy insurance to cover me in case the borrowers default—and I pay for it with those selfsame IOUs! Round and round it goes, each new loan becoming somebody's asset against which to borrow yet more money. We all rake in huge commissions and bonuses, as the total face value of all the assets we've created from that initial million dollars is now fifty times that.

Then one day, the first batch of IOUs comes due. But guess what? The person who scribbled his name on the IOU can't pay me back right now. In fact, lots of the borrowers can't. I try to hush up this embarrassing fact as long as possible, but pretty soon you get suspicious. You want your million-plus dollars back—in cash. I try to sell the IOUs and their derivatives that I hold, but everyone else is suspicious too, and no one buys them. The insurance company tries to cover my losses, but it can only do so by selling the IOUs I gave it.

So finally, the government steps in and buys the IOUs, bailing out the insurance company and everyone else holding the IOUs and the derivatives stacked on them. Their total value is way more than a million dollars now. I and my fellow entrepreneurs retire with our lucre. Everyone else pays for it.

This is the first level of what has happened in the financial industry over the past decade. It is a huge transfer of wealth to the financial elite, to be funded by U.S. taxpayers, foreign corporations and governments, and ultimately the foreign workers who subsidize U.S. debt indirectly via the lower purchasing power of their wages. However, to see the current crisis as merely the result of a big con is to miss its true significance.

I think we all sense that we are nearing the end of an era. On the most superficial level, it is the era of unregulated casino-style financial manipulation that is ending. But the recent efforts of the political elites to fix the crisis at this level only reveal its deeper dimensions. In fact, the crisis goes all the way to the bottom. It arises from the very nature of money and property in the world today, and it will persist and continue to intensify until money itself is transformed. A process centuries in the making is in its final stages of unfoldment.

Money as we know it today has crisis and collapse built into its basic design. That is because money seeks interest, bears interest, and indeed is born of interest. To see how this works, let's go back to some finance basics. Money is created when somebody takes out a loan from a bank (or more recently, a disguised loan from some other kind of institution). A debt is a promise to pay money in the future in order to buy something today; in other words, borrowing money is a form of delayed trading. I receive something now (bought with the money I borrowed) and agree to give something in the future (a good or service which I will sell for the money to pay back the debt). A bank or any other lender will ordinarily only agree to lend you money if there is a reasonable expectation you will pay it back—in other words, if there is a reasonable expectation you will produce goods or services of equivalent value. This "reasonable expectation" can be guaranteed in the form of collateral, or it can be encoded in one's credit rating.

Any time you use money, you are essentially guaranteeing, "I have performed a service or provided a good of equivalent value to the one I am buying." If the money is borrowed money, you are saying that you will provide an equivalent good or service in the future.

Now enters interest. What motivates a bank to lend anyone money in the first place? It is interest. Interest drives the creation of money today. Any time money is created through debt, a need to create even more money in the future is also created. The amount of money must grow over time, which means that the volume of goods and services must grow over time as well.

If the volume of money grows faster than the volume of goods and services, the result is inflation. If it grows more slowly—for example through a slowdown in lending—the result is bankruptcies, recession, or deflation. The government can increase or decrease the supply of money in several ways. First, it can create money by borrowing it from the central bank, or in the United States, from the Federal Reserve. This money ends up as bank deposits, which in turn give banks more margin reserves on which to extend loans. You see, a bank's capacity to create money is limited by margin reserve requirements. Typically, a bank must hold cash (or central bank deposits) equal to about 10 percent of its total customer deposits. The other 90 percent it can loan out, thus creating new money. This money ends up back in a bank as deposits, allowing another 81 percent of it (90 percent of 90 percent) to be lent out again. In this way, each dollar of initial deposits ends up as nine dollars of new money. Government spending of money borrowed from the central bank acts a seed for new money creation. (Of course, this depends on banks' willingness to lend. Since 2008, banks have hoarded excess reserves, so that repeated injections of government money have had little effect.)

Another way to increase the money supply is to lower margin reserve requirements. In practice this is rarely done, at least directly. However, in the recent past, various kinds of nonbank lending skirted the margin reserve requirement, through the alphabet soup of financial instruments that haunted the news and the public imagination during the 2008 financial crisis. The result is that each dollar of original equity is leveraged not to nine times its original value, as in traditional banking, but to seventy times or even more. This allows returns on investment far beyond the 5 percent or so available from traditional banking, along with "compensation" packages beyond the dreams of avarice.

Each new dollar that is created comes with a new dollar of debt—more than a dollar of debt, because of interest. The debt is eventually redeemed either with goods and services, or with more borrowed money, which in turn can be redeemed with yet more borrowed money ... but eventually it will be used to buy goods and services. The interest has to come from *somewhere*. Borrowing more money to make the interest payments on an existing loan merely postpones the day of reckoning by deferring the need to create new goods and services.

The whole system of interest-bearing money works fine as long as the volume of goods and services exchanged for money keeps growing. The crisis we saw in 2008 was in part because new money was created much faster than goods and services were, and much faster than has been historically sustainable. There are only two ways out of such a situation: inflation and defaults. The rescue packages that followed the crisis basically came down to an attempt to prevent both. Superficially successful, actually they only kicked the problem into the future. The mortgage-backed securities were bailed out and morphed into sovereign debt, and more and more of society's wealth concentrated in the hands of the creditors, as is inevitable when interest rates exceed economic growth.

There was a much deeper crisis at work as well, a crisis in the creation of goods and services that underlie money to begin with, and it was this crisis that gave birth to the real estate bubble everyone blamed for the 2008 crisis. To understand it, let's get clear on what constitutes a *good* or a *service*. In economics, these terms refer to something that is exchanged for money. If I babysit your children for free, economists don't count it as a service. It cannot be used to pay a financial debt: I cannot go to the supermarket and say, "I watched my neighbor's kids this morning, so please give me food." But if I open a day care center and charge you money, I have created a service. Gross domestic product (GDP) rises and, according to economists, society has become wealthier.

The same is true if I cut down a forest and sell the timber. While it is still standing and inaccessible, it is not a good. It only becomes a good when I build a logging road, hire labor, cut it down, and transport it to a buyer. I convert a forest to timber, a commodity, and GDP goes up. Similarly, if I create a new song and share it for free, GDP does not go up and society is not considered wealthier, but if I copyright it and sell it, it becomes a good. Or I can find a traditional society that uses herbs and shamanic techniques for healing, destroy their culture and make them dependent on pharmaceutical medicine which they must purchase, evict them from their land so they cannot be subsistence farmers and must buy food, clear the land and hire them on a banana plantation—and I have made the world richer. I have brought various functions, relationships, and natural resources into the realm of money. In *The Ascent of Humanity* I describe this process in depth: the conversion of social capital, natural capital, cultural capital, and spiritual capital into money.

Essentially, for the economy to continue growing and for the (interest-based) money system to remain viable, more and more of nature-and-human relationship must be monetized. For example, thirty years ago most meals were prepared at home; today some two-thirds are prepared outside the home, in restaurants or super-market delis. A once unpaid function, cooking, has become a service. And we are the richer for it. Right?

Another major engine of economic growth over the last three decades, child care, has also made us richer. We are now relieved of the burden of caring for our own children. We pay experts instead, who can do it much more efficiently. Even if we don't want to become "richer" in this way, the destruction of social structures like tight-knit neighborhoods and extended families gives most people little alternative. Community has been converted to a paid service.

In ancient times entertainment was also a free, participatory function. Everyone played an instrument, sang, participated in drama. Even seventy-five years ago in the United States, every small town had its own marching band and baseball team. Now we pay for those services. The economy has grown. Hooray.

The crisis we are facing today arises from the fact that there is almost no more social, cultural, natural, and spiritual capital left to convert into money. Centuries—millennia—of near-continuous money creation have left us so destitute that we have nothing left to sell. Our forests are damaged beyond repair, our soil depleted and washed into the sea, our fisheries fished out, the rejuvenating capacity of the earth to recycle our waste saturated. Our cultural treasury of songs and stories, images and icons, has been looted and copyrighted. Any clever phrase you can think of is already a trademarked slogan. Our very human relationships and abilities have been taken away from us and sold back, so that we are now dependent on strangers, and therefore on money, for things few humans ever paid for until recently: food, shelter, clothing, entertainment, child care, cooking. Life itself has become a consumer item. Today we sell away the last vestiges of our divine bequeathment: our health, the biosphere and genome, even our own minds. This is the process that is culminating in our age. It is almost complete, especially in the United States and the "developed" world. In the developing world there still remain people who live substantially in gift cultures, where natural and social wealth is not yet the subject of property. Globalization is the process of stripping away these assets, to feed the money machine's insatiable, existential need to grow. Yet this strip-mining of other lands is running up against its limits too, both because there is almost nothing left to take, and because of growing pockets of effective resistance.

The result is that the supply of money—and the corresponding volume of debt—has for several decades outstripped the production of goods and services that it promises. It is deeply related to the classic problem of oversupply in capitalist economics. The Marxian crisis of capital can be deferred into the future as long as new, high-profit industries and markets can be developed to compensate for the vicious circle of falling profits, falling wages, depressed consumption, and overproduction in mature industries. The continuation of capitalism as we know it depends on an infinite supply of these new industries, which essentially must convert infinite new realms of social, natural, cultural, and spiritual capital into money. The problem is, these resources are finite, and the closer they come to exhaustion, the more painful their extraction becomes. Therefore, contemporaneous with the financial crisis we have an ecological crisis and a health crisis. They are intimately interlinked. We cannot convert much more of the earth into money, or much more of our health into money, before the basis of life itself is threatened.

Faced with the exhaustion of the nonmonetized commonwealth that it consumes, financial capital has tried to delay the inevitable by cannibalizing itself. The dot-com bubble of the late '90s showed that the productive economy could not longer keep up with the growth of money. Lots of excess money was running around frantically, searching for a place where the promise of deferred goods and services could be redeemed. So, to postpone the inevitable crash, the Fed slashed interest rates and loosened monetary policy to allow old debts to be repaid with new debts (rather than real goods and services). The new financial goods and services that arose were phony, artifacts of deceptive accounting on a vast, systemic scale.

Various pundits have observed that the Bernard Madoff Ponzi scheme was not so different from the financial industry's pyramid of mortgaged-based derivatives and other instruments, which themselves formed a bubble that, like Madoff's, could only sustain itself through an unceasing, indeed exponentially growing, influx of new money. As such, it is a symbol of our times—and even more than people suppose. It is not only the Wall Street casino economy that is an unsustainable pyramid scheme. The larger economic system, based as it is on the eternal conversion of a finite commonwealth into money, is unsustainable as well. It is like a bonfire that must burn higher and higher, to the exhaustion of all available fuel. Just as fire breaks existing chemical bonds and frees heat, so does our economy break the bonds of community, nature, and culture, liberating free energy—called money—in the process. Only a fool would think that a fire can burn ever higher when the supply of fuel is finite. To extend the metaphor, the recent deindustrialization and financialization of the economy amounts to using the heat to create more fuel. It says, "We will use more money, rather than goods and services, to redeem the promise of money." According to the second law of thermodynamics, the amount created is always less than the amount expended to create it. Obviously, the practice of borrowing new money to pay the principal and interest of old debts cannot last very long, but that is what the economy as a whole has done for ten years now.

Yet even abandoning this folly, we still must face the depletion of fuel (remember, I mean not literal energy sources, but any bond of nature or culture that can be turned into a commodity). Most of the proposals for addressing the present economic crisis amount to finding more fuel. Whether it is drilling more oil wells, paving over more green space, or spurring consumer spending, the goal is to reignite economic growth: that is to expand the realm of goods and services. It means finding new things for which we can pay. Today, unimaginably to our forebears, we pay even for our water and our songs. What else is left to convert into money?

A collapse is coming, unavoidably; indeed, we are in the midst of it. The first government response to the 2008 crisis, the bail-out, was an attempt to uphold a tower of money that is far beyond the total value of real goods and services it promises to redeem. Unless economic growth brings us more new goods and services, this measure can only delay the inevitable. That is what economic stimulus, such as Obama's 2009 package, is designed to do. But it too is doomed to fail—for a different and much deeper reason. It will fail because we are maxed out: maxed out on nature's capacity to receive our wastes without destroying the ecological basis of civilization; maxed out on society's ability to withstand any more loss of community and connection; maxed out on our forests' ability to withstand more clear-cuts; maxed out on the human body's capacity to stay viable in a depleted, toxic world. That we are also maxed out on our credit only reflects that we have nothing left to convert into money. Do we really need more roads and bridges? Can we sustain more of them, and more of the industrial economy that goes along? Government stimulus programs will at best prolong the current economic system for a few more years, with perhaps a brief period of tepid growth as we complete the pillage of nature, spirit, body, and culture. When these vestiges of the commonwealth are gone, then nothing will be able to stop an economic collapse on a global scale.

The persistent economic crisis of recent years is actually the final stage of what began in the 1930s. Successive solutions to the fundamental problem of keeping pace with money that expands with the rate of interest have been applied, and exhausted. The first effective solution was war, a state that has been permanent since 1940. Unfortunately, or rather fortunately, nuclear weapons and a shift in human consciousness have limited the solution of endless military escalation. Other solutions—globalization, technology-enabled development of new goods and services to replace human functions never before commoditized, technology-enabled plunder of natural resources once off limits, and finally financial auto-cannibalism— have similarly run their course. Unless there are realms of wealth I have not considered, and new depths of poverty, misery, and alienation to which we might plunge, the inevitable cannot be delayed much longer.

In the face of an impending crisis, people often ask what they can do to protect themselves. "Buy gold? Stockpile canned goods? Build a fortified compound in a remote area? What should I do?" I would like to suggest a different kind of question: "What is the most beautiful thing I can do?" You see, the gathering crisis presents a tremendous opportunity. Deflation, the destruction of money, is only a categorical evil if the creation of money is a categorical good. However, you can see from the examples I have given that the creation of money has in many ways impoverished us all. Conversely, the destruction of money has the potential to enrich us. It offers the opportunity to reclaim parts of the lost commonwealth from the realm of money and property.

We actually see this happening every time there is an economic recession. People can no longer pay for various goods and services, and have to rely on friends and neighbors instead. Where there is no money to facilitate transactions, gift economies reemerge and new kinds of money are created. Ordinarily, though, people and institutions fight tooth and nail to prevent that from happening. The habitual first response to economic crisis is to make and keep more money—to accelerate the conversion of anything you can into money. On a systemic level, the debt surge is generating enormous pressure to extend the commodification of the commonwealth. We can see this happening with the calls to drill for oil in Alaska, commence deep-sea drilling, and so on. The time is here, though, for the reverse process to begin in earnest—to remove things from the realm of goods and services, and return them to the realm of gifts, reciprocity, self-sufficiency, and community sharing. Note well: This is going to happen anyway in the wake of a currency collapse, as people lose their jobs or become too poor to buy things. People will help each other and real communities will reemerge.

In the meantime, anything we do to protect some natural or social resource from conversion into money will both hasten the collapse *and* mitigate its severity. Any forest you save from development, any road you stop, any cooperative playgroup you establish; anyone you teach to heal himself, or to build her own house, cook his own food, make her own clothes; any wealth you create or add to the public domain; anything you render off-limits to the world-devouring Machine, will help shorten the Machine's lifespan. Think of it this way: if you already do not depend on money for some portion of life's necessities and pleasures, then the collapse of money will pose much less of a harsh transition for you. The same applies to the social level. Any network or community or social institution that is not a vehicle for the conversion of life into money will sustain and enrich life *after* money.

There exist today, in theory and increasingly in practice, alternative money systems, based on mutual credit and demurrage, that do not drive the conversion of all that is good, true, and beautiful into money. These enact a fundamentally different human identity, a fundamentally different sense of self, from what dominates today. No more will it be true that more for me is less for you. On a personal level, the deepest possible revolution we can enact is a revolution in our sense of self, in our identity. The discrete and separate self of Descartes and Adam Smith has run its course and is becoming obsolete. We are realizing our own inseparateness, from each other and from the totality of all life. Interest belies this union, for it seeks growth of the separate self at the expense of something external, something other. Many in the West are now coming to agree with the principles of interconnectedness, whether from a Buddhistic or an ecological perspective. The time has come to live it. It is time to enter the spirit of the gift, which embodies the felt understanding of nonseparation. It is becoming abundantly obvious that less for you (in all its dimensions) is also less for me. The ideology of perpetual gain has brought us to a state of poverty so destitute that we are gasping for air. That ideology, and the civilization built upon it, is what is collapsing today.

Individually and collectively, anything we do to resist or postpone the collapse will only make it worse. Let us stop resisting the revolution in human beingness. If we want to survive the multiple crises unfolding today, let us not seek to *survive* them. That is the mindset of separation; that is resistance, a clinging to a dying past. Instead, let us shift our perspective toward reunion, and think in terms of what we can give. What can we each contribute to a more beautiful world? That is our only responsibility and our only security.

More concretely, let us engage in conscious, purposeful money destruction in place of the unconscious destruction of money that happens in a collapsing economy. If you still have money to invest, invest it in enterprises that explicitly seek to build community, protect nature, and preserve the cultural commonwealth. Expect a zero or negative financial return on your investment—that is a good sign that you are not unintentionally converting even more of the world to money. Whether or not you have money to invest, you can also reclaim what was sold away by taking steps out of the money economy. Anything you learn to do for yourself or for other people, without paying for it; any utilization of recycled or discarded materials; anything you make instead of buy, give instead of sell; any new skill or new song or new art you teach yourself or another, will reduce the dominion of money and grow a gift economy to sustain us through the coming transition. The world of the gift, echoing primitive gift societies, the web of ecology, and the spiritual teachings of the ages, is nigh upon us. It tugs on our heartstrings and awakens our generosity. Shall we heed its call, before the remainder of earth's beauty is consumed?

2

THE CAPITAL IS PERSONAL

ANYA KAMENETZ

I was talking on the phone to a friend about the plight of unhappily single women in New York. "They just don't give themselves the right value in the dating market," I said. "Hey, we were just talking about the banking crisis. Look how these capitalist phrases have taken over our language!" he replied. "You're right. I shouldn't use these bankrupt expressions." We both laughed when we realized I had inadvertently repeated my mistake.

As my friend pointed out, capitalism has colonized our words, our identities, and our minds. The habit of thinking of people, ideas, and relationships as commodities has been pervasive. We are collectively guilty of extreme reification—treating the abstraction of money as if it were the only real thing. We have constructed an idol out of our own adornments—pulling our very teeth to do it—and in the process subjected our innate divinity to the inert form.

And then, in late 2008, American-style free market capitalism, the single dominant human system of the last century or so, underwent a bloodless, swift, and absolute coup. The king was dead. The golden calf had been melted back down into dross. This event would be even harder to believe if the exact same thing hadn't happened to capitalism's doppelganger, totalitarian socialism, just a decade before. This time, we didn't topple any walls or statues, but a set of powerful illusions fell nevertheless. The crisis will take time to fully be absorbed into our culture.

What illusions have sustained capitalism, and what has been the consequence? Our democratically elected leaders, with the collaboration of thousands of business oligarchs and wealthy financiers, have refused to put our country's vast resources to use to feed the hungry, lift up the destitute, provide care to the sick, or protect the planet from degradation—even now that it's widely acknowledged that the future of the species is at stake. The argument was always that "the market," with its unique capacity to produce "economic growth," was too sacrosanct to be subject to the "distortions" of government intervention, whether in the form of taxes or regulation. No human need or desire was deemed as important as the interests of the market: not the survival of innocent children and not the health of the air we breathe.

But when the market itself was in danger of collapse, Congress acted within days, authorizing taking $700 billion in bad debt off the hands of troubled banks and investment firms. This desperate rescue operation exposed market fundamentalism as just another form of false, extremist religion. When banks, financial institutions, and corporations failed, the power to respond rested with the United States government. Clearly, then, government intervention is not detrimental to the market. Government intervention makes the market possible.

Anarchist anthropologist David Graeber writes about the history of systems of value within different cultures. In *Toward an Anthropological Theory of Value,* he summarizes the views of Hungarian economist Karl Polanyi thus: "The state and its coercive powers had everything to do with the creation of what we now know as 'the market'—based as it is on institutions such as private property, national currencies, legal contracts, credit markets. ... 'Market behavior' would be impossible without police."

Legal scholar Cass Sunstein makes a related point in his book *The Second Bill of Rights: FDR's Unfinished Revolution and Why We Need It More Than Ever.* He points out that our Constitution happens to guarantee the right to the abstraction of private property, but not the right to the necessities of life such as food, clothing, or shelter. That means that the police are empowered to cast out someone who is hiding from the rain, if the roof he or she is huddling under happens to technically "belong" to someone else. The choice to defend one principle over the other is not always in line with our acknowledged moral values, as in the case of the starving man who steals a loaf of bread. (In the time of the New Deal, Sunstein argues, FDR identified "Freedom from Want" as a new American right, and created new social institutions to try to protect it, but failed to enshrine it in the Constitution—thus, an unfinished revolution.)

The relationship between markets and government coercion may be felt most keenly when it comes to the institution of debt. Graeber points out the inextricable historical link between debt, violence, and enslavement. In eighth-century Germanic law, the concept of wergild replaced the older, biblical idea of "an eye for an eye." *Wergild* translates as "man" (*wer,* as in werewolf) plus "gold" *(gild).* Wergild was the substitution of a fixed sum of money or some other substance of value to compensate for a death, whether murder or accidental. On one hand, the payment of blood money was a moral advance because it stopped a cycle of violence. On the other hand, it was a step down the path of reducing a human life to a sum of money and an exchange delineated and enforced by courts and governments. Besides blood debts, some of the earliest debts were also calculated as terms of indentured servitude. And everywhere and always debt has tended to be wielded by the rich and powerful over the poor and powerless, from the "company store" at a mining camp on America's frontier, to the payday lending and pawnshops that fill low-income neighborhoods today, to the massive debts imposed as "aid" on the world's poorest countries by the International Monetary Fund.

It's no coincidence that the enormous increase in debt, the

most coercive and oppressive of market institutions, caused the recent financial crisis. The amount of consumer debt doubled between 1997 and 2007. For those who wanted to participate in the so-called American dream—a house, a car, a college education for one's children, and an ever-increasing array of material comforts—the ubiquitous result was a pile of student loan, credit card, and mortgage debt. This house of cards collapsed when people who had higher and higher debt and flat incomes could no longer keep up the payments.

Indebted people tend to be submissive and restricted in their choices, not strong and free citizens. Soon after the 2008 financial crisis, Graeber wrote: "What is debt, after all, but imaginary money whose value can only be realized in the future: future profits, the proceeds of the exploitation of workers not yet born. Finance capital in turn is the buying and selling of these imaginary future profits. ... Freedom has become the right to share in the proceeds of one's own permanent enslavement." But I believe freedom is not so fragile or limited as all that. The state, like the market, is nothing more than a human creation. And as human creations, they ought to be within our collective power to transform. The bursting of the debt bubble has provided a once-in-a-lifetime opening to begin.

Consider the ongoing interventions by the Federal Reserve and the Treasury Department to keep interest rates low and try to encourage recovery. By what mechanism is the U.S. government able to set interest rates and control the money supply? Because it issues Treasury bonds backed with the "full faith and credit" of the U.S. government. What backs that full faith and credit? To put it another way, why do buyers of Treasury bonds believe that they'll get their money back within ten, twenty, or fifty years? Because of the long-term social stability of our nation, as partially guaranteed by our powerful military. And who's to say that our military will remain powerful and our nation stable? To the extent that we do believe it, this is ensured in turn by the continuing faithful contributions of the U.S. taxpayer—generations of average people working for a living and cooperating with their obligations. Our time, the connections holding together the American community—it is not an exaggeration to say our love—is what ultimately backs up the greenback.

Over the long term, human relationships ultimately control the market, and over the short term, human emotions do the same thing. In early 2009, a college friend of mine was in town for business, so we invited her to stop by for dinner. She revealed that since I had last seen her almost a year ago, she had gone from doing international aid work in Afghanistan to working as the special assistant to Treasury Secretary Tim Geithner. She told us that as she sat in meetings with the Nobel Prize winners and the financial mandarins, the foremost factor in the minds of the elite group managing America's way out of the financial crisis is nothing less than the esoteric phenomenon of collective consciousness. "The most important thing is to avoid a market panic," she said. "It's all about the state of people's minds—captured in phrases like 'consumer confidence.'"

So, even in the world's most developed and sophisticated market economy, it is ultimately human emotions and relationships that hold sway, not some abstract coercive power of the state. Markets exist because of people, not the other way around; the economy exists to fulfill human needs and serve human desires. This may be a truism, but we don't act as if we really believe it. When we put the sanctity of the "free market" ahead of human freedom and social relations, as we can see everywhere we look, we're falling prey to a fallacy. The same failing happens in our personal lives when we act more directly and more often as consumers or producers than as citizens and family members, or when like the woman on the dating "market," we submit ourselves and others to commodification.

So now that the abject and pathetic nature of the commodification fallacy has been conclusively demonstrated, it is up to us as the participants in, fools of, and creators of this ongoing illusion to carefully examine our words and our actions for signs of error, to try to make whole what has been broken, and to embark on a new way of living.

Here are three contemporary models for how to do that:

- In Judaism, this process is prescribed annually and is called *teshuvah*—translated as repentance, it literally means return, as to a native state of wholeness and holiness.
- In the addiction recovery movement, four of the famous twelve steps consist in performing a "searching and fearless moral inventory" and in making amends to those we have wronged.
- And for nations that have undergone a severe collective trauma such as civil war, apartheid, or genocide, a truth and reconciliation commission attempts to accomplish a similar task by drawing testimony from the oppressors and the oppressed.

What would truth, reconciliation, repentance, and amends look like for the market system? First of all, it is incumbent upon each of us to look within our own words and actions. I can't blame an outside force such as "the corporations" or "the bankers" when I act greedy or when I objectify another human being with a glance or a word. We have to hold each other and ourselves accountable.

Second, it is appropriate for us all to engage in mourning and symbolic expressions of regret for the degree to which we have allowed the market to usurp our humanity. The Homo economicus model of human behavior is false and limited. Whether we are working, borrowing, buying, or selling, we are also thinking, breathing, loving, and hating. When we do things just for the money, we feel sick and greedy and fake because we are contributing to the oppressive ubiquity of the market.

Finally, now that we have been forced to recognize that the

economy is a human creation, we should be re-empowered and freed to imagine an alternative to the oppression of market fundamentalism—to remake a system that serves humanity.

To do so, we could look outside mainstream Western culture at the way other societies and subcultures are organized. In *Toward an Anthropological Theory of Value,* Graeber writes, "In most societies, [market] institutions did not exist. … one has to … examine the actual process through which the society provides itself with food, shelter, and other material goods, bearing in mind that this process is entirely embedded in society and not a sphere of activity that can be distinguished from, say, politics, kinship, or religion."

A famous example of a society without a market is the potlatch cultures of the Native Americans of the Pacific Northwest. To simplify, say there are two clans. One fishes on the seashore and one hunts inland. When the fish are running, the first clan catches more than it can eat, and feasts the second. When the buffalo are running, the second clan returns the favor. In this way, both clans eat year-round, strengthen their social ties, celebrate, worship, and make peace. Redistribution of resources happens across time and across social hierarchies as well. For chieftains, skilled hunters, and anyone who manages to accumulate excess, the best way to raise their social standing in a potlatch society is to share their wealth and display generosity. This way, everyone shares and everyone eats without the need for a formal market or redistributive taxation.

If you need a less exoticized example of an alternative economy than a Native American tribe, consider the "reputation economies" of the internet. Wikipedia, YouTube, and open-source software projects like Mozilla are valuable common resources. The platform—servers for storage and networks for transmission—must be subsidized by advertising or donations. But the highly valuable content is created, sustained, and used by people for free. Why do we do it? The phrase "reputation economy" suggests that we do it to raise our social standing, but really it's more than that. I do it and I think other people do too because it feels good to create, to connect, to make the world a better place, and to be recognized for doing so.

So to make amends in the wake of the financial crisis, the path is toward healing the separation between our "economics" and our politics, our morality, our friendships, our earth, our family, and our spirituality. Rather than attempt to destroy or abolish the formal market, we can enrich it by bringing more of ourselves to it. We can think in terms of creating alternative forms of exchange and integrating our other human values along with economic value—putting our money where our heart is. For example, you can look for work that expresses your creativity or makes the world a better place. Even if our jobs are less than ideal, most people can still find opportunities to express their highest values at work like honesty, integrity, and kindness. You can consume mindfully—buy well-crafted, meaningful objects that connect you to other people, to the earth, and to your local community. You can reduce your consumption in order to avoid the perpetuation of enslavement in the form of debt. You can invest your money in socially responsible businesses and projects that help society. You can attempt to fulfill more of your material needs outside the formal market and thus reduce its impact on your life by salvaging, thrifting, creating, swapping, or otherwise reducing waste, improving creativity, and strengthening social ties. Like the potlatch societies, you can practice giving away money, goods, and time to those more needy, in order to demonstrate and manifest abundance.

And, we all can take political action to transform some of the government rules of the market game. The current world recession won't lift by resuming the path of endless growth and mounting debt. A profound global reorganization has to take place so that we put a fair value on the natural resources that underlie our unprecedented prosperity. The leap toward a sustainable economy will be realized when each of us wakes up to the reality that you are the economy, and the economy is you.

3

THE ARITHMETIC OF COMPASSION

DAVID ULANSEY

Ever since I was a child, I have been searching for a certain number: namely, the figure for the annual Gross World Product (GWP). The GWP is the value of all goods and services produced each year by the entire human species, and the reason I was searching for this number as a child is that I wanted to take it and divide it by the number of people in the world, so that I would know what each human being was actually entitled to if the world's resources were divided fairly and equitably.

I finally ran into this number recently, and I have now performed the simple arithmetic of compassion. It turns out that the Gross World Product is now roughly $70 trillion. It is important to note that this figure of $70 trillion—arrived at independently by the World Bank, the International Monetary Fund, and the CIA—has been adjusted in advance to take into account what is called "purchasing power parity" (PPP): which means that the figure is 70 trillion units, each unit of which (sometimes called an "international dollar") represents what one U.S. dollar will currently buy *in the United States.* (The PPP adjustment eliminates from the very start any strategies of denial such as, "Oh, that doesn't mean anything—you can live like a king in India for $5,000 a year." No. Wrong. You *can't* live like a king on what 5,000 U.S. dollars will currently buy *in the United States.*) [1]

Now to the arithmetic of compassion:

Since the GWP is roughly 70 trillion U.S. dollars, if we divide that figure by the number of people in the world—approximately

7 billion—we get a rough estimate of the maximum annual income that anyone in the world is morally entitled to (assuming that it is moral to strive for an equitable distribution of the world's resources to all of humanity).

So, dividing $70 trillion by 7 billion we get about $10,000 per year (again, that's already adjusted for purchasing power parity: it's 10,000 units, each unit of which is what one U.S. dollar will currently buy *in the United States*). That's what each of us is actually entitled to $10,000 a year—and any more than that represents institutionalized and socially sanctioned armed robbery: indeed, every additional increment of $10,000 (beyond the maximum moral income of $10,000 a year) represents one slave somewhere in the world whose entire life, birth to death, is completely devoted to getting us our "stuff."

And unfortunately we can't "grow" our way beyond this $10,000 a year figure, since at the current level of $70 trillion GWP we have already *overshot by 50 percent* what the earth actually produces.[2] That is, it now requires one year and six months for the earth to replenish what humans consume in a year. This unsustainable 50 percent "overshoot," in which we are temporarily consuming 150 percent of what the earth produces, is only possible because we are metaphorically "liquidating" the earth—i.e., spending its capital rather than living on its interest.

The fact that the human species is already in 50 percent overshoot means that not only can we not "grow" our way beyond the $10,000 maximum moral income level, we actually need to *shrink* that by one-third (50 percent is one-third of 150 percent)—down to below $7,000—just to come back to a level where humanity is merely using 100 percent of everything the earth produces (rather than using 150 percent of what the earth produces, as we are very temporarily doing). This is especially the case since the world population is due to increase by almost 50 percent—to more than nine billion people—by 2050.

Of course a $7,000 a year income may sound rather frightening to those of us who have become accustomed to the "American standard of living."

However, to place this figure in its proper perspective, it is helpful to keep in mind that according to the World Bank, at this very moment almost half of the people in the world (3 billion people) live on less than $2.50 (PPP) a day—*$912 a year*—and a quarter of the world's population (1.4 billion people) live below the official world poverty level of $1.25 a day—*$456 a year.*[3]

In fact, in 2005 the World Bank chief economist Nicholas Stern estimated that on average each European *cow* receives $2.50 a day in government livestock and dairy subsidies, while 75 percent of African *people* live on less than $2 a day.[4]

So although $7,000 a year may sound disturbing to us, for the majority of the people in the world it would literally constitute wealth beyond their wildest dreams.

Finally, it is crucial to realize that $7,000 a year per person is actually still far too high to be sustainable, even if there were no population growth ahead at all. This is because at the level of $7,000 a year per person for 7 billion people, we would still be consuming 100 percent of what the earth can produce, and would thus be doing absolutely nothing to prevent the two greatest threats facing us in our own lifetimes: (1) a mass extinction of the earth's biodiversity resulting from habitat destruction, pollution, invasive species, and overharvesting, and (2) catastrophic climate change that could render the earth uninhabitable for much of higher life including our own species.

The solution is clear: we must immediately and drastically reduce our levels of consumption. Something like $5,000 a year per person (PPP) is probably in the right ballpark for what is ecologically possible and morally justifiable. Again, that may be difficult for many of us to hear, but remember that $5,000 a year is more than *five times* the amount that half of the people in the world live on (or below) at this very moment ($2.50 a day = $912 a year). In fact, according to the World Bank, 95 percent of all people in developing countries, which means almost *80 percent of all human beings,* are living at this very moment on less than $10 a day—which, of course, is well below $5,000 a year.[5]

Of course then the question is: how can we in the "developed" world accomplish such a reduction? One common answer to this question—namely, "It's impossible!"—is obviously absurd, since *right now* 80 percent of the people in the world are living *below* the necessary level of reduction. Whenever I find that answer spontaneously rearing its ugly head in my own imagination, I like to remind myself that Eskimos live in houses made of ice, but their lives are filled with just as much love and beauty, and their children laugh and play with just as much joy—perhaps more!—as our own.

Beyond all its other characteristics, Homo sapiens is a species capable of extreme adaptability. The time has at last arrived for us to become actual human beings, and to allow compassion—and celebration—to guide us into a radically new world: a world where we experience "*quality* of life" for ourselves as being indistinguishable from "*equality* of life" for all.

4

PROGRAM YOUR OWN MONEY

DOUGLAS RUSHKOFF

The credit crunch may actually be good for business.

No, not in the short term. When money becomes more expensive, it is harder for most businesses to get the capital they need to conduct their most basic operations. Even successful companies borrow money to buy materials, pay employees, and cash in on invoices that have yet to be paid. Without the cash flow provided by banks, it is a lot harder for many companies to function—much less expand.

With any luck, however, the future of business will be less dependent on banks and the currency they lend into existence. The Fortune 500 will become something other than brand names on piles of debt, and business operations will be characterized more by what companies produce than by how much credit their "stories" can earn them on one of the stock exchanges.

Yes, we are watching something melt down. But I'd argue that the thing that's dying is not business itself, but a financial parasite—a speculative marketplace that no longer funds business but instead seeks to extract value from healthy commerce. More a funds vampire than an infuser of needed capital, the investment industry has been exposed as a drag on business. The future of commerce looks bright to me because it may be unencumbered by the weight of this nonproductive capital.

This all began back in the Renaissance, when a waning monarchy was looking for ways to preserve its power in the face of a rising merchant class. The merchants were becoming richer than the royals. So the monarchs came up with an idea: chartered monopolies. By granting one of these new companies exclusive province over a particular industry or region, monarchs earned their undying loyalty—as well as a generous portion of shares in the enterprise. They began to write laws that favored their chartered companies, such as preventing inhabitants of colonies from creating any value for themselves; they had to ship raw resources back to the mother country, where they were processed into clothes or other finished goods.

This model of business-by-extraction carried over to finance as well. European towns had used local currencies for centuries. Farmers would bring their wheat to a grain store, which would in turn give them receipts for the amount of grain the store was keeping for them. These receipts served as local currency. The system was so efficient, and people were living so well, that people of this era were taller than at any time before the last few decades. By making local currency illegal, a monarch could force people to use his own more expensive "coin of the realm" instead. Instead of being earned into existence, this money was *borrowed* into existence.

Over the next four hundred years, the business of money slowly grew bigger than business itself. A central bank creates money and charges interest to the next bank down the line, and so on, until it gets to the business that needs it to do something useful. The problem is, more value is being extracted on each level than businesses can produce. There are simply too many institutions—too many lenders—to be paid.

As the banking industry grew bigger and less regulated, institutions consolidated, making the notion of a local lender obsolete, as well. Loans are centrally processed by bankers who have little knowledge of the companies or people to whom they are lending—and little reason to learn about them, since they are simply packaging and selling the loans, anyway.

The house of cards had to fall eventually. The truly amazing thing is how long it lasted. And as our attempts to prop it back up continue to fail us, we might consider whether there is a better way to do business. I think there is.

The beauty of this era—this networked, high-tech, and decentralized world—is that we no longer have to do everything from the center. The laws and regulations requiring us to run our finances and resources through tremendous industrial age corporations are more obsolete than ever. And real people are beginning to catch on to how inefficient and risky it is to conduct their transactions in this way. They are starting to trust the real world around them more than the mythologies created by the public relations departments of distant corporations.

Moneys are programmed. They behave in certain ways because they have been embedded with certain biases. The United States mortgage and banking crisis of 2008, for example, was no more the fault of particular bankers' behaviors than the underlying biases of the centralized, monopoly currencies we use. This is why bailouts of those banks have not led to any broader economic recovery. At least that's the opinion of a growing population of citizens and businesses turning to the use of what they call "complementary currencies"—alternative, net-enabled, bottom-up money systems that let them accomplish what money loaned out by the Fed just isn't letting them do anymore.

Complementary currencies treat money as a utility, rather than an asset class. Their bias is toward functionality instead of savings, transaction instead of speculation. And they are spreading quickly across America—not just in the crunchy progressive Northwest (where people have been working on local currencies for decades) but the dying industrial towns of the rust belt, the inner city of the New York metropolitan area, and the nonlocal business-to-business transactions of strapped corporations themselves.

In 1995, as recession rocked Japan, unemployment rose and

currency became scarce. This made it particularly difficult for people to continue to take care of their elderly relatives, who often lived in distant areas. The Sawayaka Welfare Foundation developed a complementary currency by which a young person could earn credits for taking care of an elderly person, and then spend them on the care of their own relatives in distant towns. At last count, the alternative currency was accepted at 372 health centers throughout Japan, and all administered by a simple piece of software. Close to a thousand alternative currencies are now in use in Japan.

In October 2008, as the U.S. credit crisis paralyzed business lending, companies started signing onto barter networks in droves. One system called ITEX, which allows businesses to trade merchandise, reported a 37 percent increase in registrations for the month of October alone. Utilizing more than 250 exchange services now available through the internet, companies can barter directly with each other, or earn U.S.-dollar-equivalent credits for the merchandise they supply to others. This bartering already accounts for $3 billion of exchanges annually in the United States.

Complementary currencies hearken back to an earlier form of money—the local, grain-based currencies in wide use throughout Late Middle Ages Europe before Renaissance corporatism and centralized money schemes were invented by monarchs. Local currencies were earned—not borrowed—into existence. They reflected the abundance of the season's grain, and did not depend on artificial scarcity for their value.

Local currencies actually lost value over time. The grain store needed to be paid, and some grain was always lost to moisture or rats. This meant people wanted to spend the money as quickly as possible, rather than holding onto it. So towns spent and reinvested their money constantly. People did preventative maintenance on their equipment, and paid their workers well. They worked less and ate better than we do today. People had so much extra wealth that they invested in their futures by building cathedrals.

That's right—the cathedrals of Europe were not built with Vatican dollars, but local currency. The people of these towns were looking for ways to help their grandchildren profit off current wealth. Cathedrals attracted pilgrims and tourists, and have kept many towns profitable to this day.

By making local currencies illegal, monarchs were able to monopolize money, and tilt investment and wealth toward the center. People could no longer earn money into existence—they would have to borrow it from a central bank, at interest. While this kind of money worked great when it was allowed to function alongside a local currency, it was not particularly well suited for local transactions. It was just too expensive and too scarce. It did not reflect the needs or bounty of a town, but the needs and artificial scarcity of a market created by a monarch. Going into business meant borrowing from the central bank—and then paying it back, at interest. And where did the extra money come from? Someone else who borrowed it and would necessarily go bankrupt.

Either that, or borrow more money. And thus, the requirement of a central bank–dominated economy for infinite expansion—often at the expense of the environment and labor. But most importantly, the new economic scheme was designed to drain wealth from the periphery—such as colonies, territories, and rural areas—and pay it back to the middle. And it's the way banks work to this day, each borrowing from a higher, more centralized authority.

Internet-enabled complementary currencies breathe life into the *decentralized* marketplace of real businesses. Our networks give us a way to verify transactions and develop trust. Second, perhaps more importantly, they help us see the way many of the tools we use are the result of programs. Where availability of printing presses may have encouraged counterfeiting of official currencies, the availability of computers and networks is encouraging the creation of altogether new ones. We are proving more likely to treat our money as software, and to write our own.

Local currencies have spread far beyond the experimental fringe to over four thousand U.S. towns at last count, because of both the new scarcity of dollars and the availability of software and tools. Beginning a local currency requires no store of capital—it is as easy as visiting the websites for local economic transfer systems (LETS) or Time Dollars.

In my own town, for example, there's a tiny organic cafe called Comfort that is seeking to expand. John, the owner, secured a second location for a sit-down restaurant, but doesn't have enough money to renovate the space. Although he has great credit, he cannot get a loan from any of the banks in town. Even though the bankers know him, they don't have lending authority from the conglomerates that own them. So what's John to do?

John has turned to the community for help. He invented "Comfort Dollars" that people can buy at a discount of 20 percent. If you spend $1,000, you receive $1,200 in Comfort Dollars that can be spent at the restaurant. John gets the cash infusion he needs to complete his expansion—and for cheaper than the bank would charge him. The local community gets a 20 percent discount on food they would be buying anyway, as well as the chance to invest in making their town better. This is a 20 percent return on investment, payable as fast as the investor and his family can eat.

The Comfort Dollars scenario reveals just how much of the mess of the recent economic crisis resulted from the way we "outsourced" our finances to begin with. The real problem underlying the global financial meltdown had much less to do with low efficiency, bad labor, or poor innovation than it did with the decreased utility of the financial industry itself. Money has stopped working properly—at least in its capacity to lubricate transactions. The sad part is that money is working exactly as it was designed to.

Once we accept the fact that the money and banks we have grown accustomed to using are not the only ways to generate capital, we liberate ourselves and our businesses from a finance industry that has enjoyed a monopoly over our commerce for far too long. They have not only abused our trust through corrupt self-dealing, but abused their privilege through systemic usury. Businesses are only obligated to support their employees, owners, and customers—not an entire finance industry.

The financial meltdown will help many businesses realize that their priorities have been artificially skewed toward making bankers and investors happy—and their own communities less so. As we start to finance locally or from our own nonlocal communities, our services will become more finely tuned toward them as well. We will get better at what we do, rather than obsessed with growth (to pay back lenders) or financing (to achieve that growth through acquisition).

This is all good—at least for businesses that have any remaining connection to a community or core competency. It will be possible to scale companies appropriately rather than to infinite expansion. It will be easier to take and share profits rather than watch them be extracted by last year's lenders. It will favor local and connected businesses instead of big chains operated from afar by corporations behaving as if it were still the 1500s and they had a royal imprimatur on their business license.

The future of business—real business—is bright, as it has been for close to a millennium. It just might not be reflected in the Dow Jones Industrial Average for quite some time, if ever. That's because instead of earning money, we'll be creating value.

5

MONEY AS A ZERO-SUM GAME

DALE PENDELL

In game theory, zero-sum games are those where one person's gain is another's loss. A poker game is zero-sum. Those busy accumulating hoards of money try to hide its zero-sum nature by saying that the "pie" is getting bigger. Prosperity is not a zero-sum game, though "prosperity" is too easily conflated with monetary wealth, which is not the same thing at all. Clearly, quality of life is not a zero-sum game—quite the contrary. The whole bodhisattva impulse of Mahayana Buddhism stems from recognizing that individual nirvana is incomplete until everyone is liberated.

$ $ $

All of the things that we might call true wealth: health, enough to eat, shelter, meaningful work, diverse habitats and resources, natural and artistic beauty around one—none are diminished by all having more.

But this is not true of money. If everyone had a million dollars, what would a million dollars be worth? Money is a usurper; it pretends to be wealth. And its pretension is backed up by force, creating a new type of slave: the mercenary. And most conveniently, the mercenary, truly the oldest profession, is paid in the money he protects. Money has power because of scarcity, and the threat of scarcity. Without money you will starve and die, even if there is food around. Without money you will become homeless, sleeping in the rain and shivering in the cold. Therefore when I say I need some dirty work done, you say yes. I say yes. We say yes.

Money is coercive, seductive, corrupting, and exploitative, hence often linked with diabolical power. "The love of money is the root of all evil," suggests Paul's first letter to Timothy. Or, as amended by George Bernard Shaw, "The lack of money is the root of all evil." Both sayings seem true: greed for more in the already-haves wreaks destruction on a scale order of magnitude beyond the petty crimes of the indigent. Still, lack of money, need for money, loads my soul with care.

$ $ $

Money seems like a natural and necessary part of the world, but, actually, it is neither. Money has a history and a biography. It had a childhood and an adolescence. No one knows if it has an old age and senility, unless that is now. No one really understands money, and certainly no one, not even the governments that print money, controls it, despite the best efforts of so many.

In some ways money is the ultimate pyramid scheme—its value is surprisingly sensitive to human attitudes.

"Your money's no good here."

Others make money their god, their master. Pragmatic. Realist.

"Money will win. Trust me. And either you are with the haves or you are with the have-nots."

But how much "have" is enough? There seems no limit.

$ $ $

I hear arguments against copyright laws—yet the first copyright law is against counterfeiting. No one is talking about doing away with that law! If money were a "natural" item of value, why not produce it?

Actually, this is done all the time. Corporations create new stock, and governments create bonds. Moe Moskowitz, the late owner of Moe's Books, a used bookstore in Berkeley, California, printed trade slips that looked like dollar bills, with a cartoon picture of Moe in the center and the words *In Moe We Trust.* On the back the clerks would write how much trade you had left and initial it. Moe's Money even had an exchange rate with U.S. dollars—on Telegraph Avenue one could get 50 percent of its marked value in "real" money.

The monopolistically inflated value of the money of national governments such as that of the U.S. Treasury is protected by armies and prisons. The coercive, zero-sum quality of money is nowhere more apparent. If counterfeiting money were not a criminal matter, but only one of public acceptance, "official" currencies would find their true social value. It is no coincidence that the corporate economy evolved along with the debtors' prison.

$ $ $

Because most of us exchange work for money, money pretends to be a measure of work, of one's contribution to society. This is of course ludicrous. In the twenty-first century the connection of money to productive work is secondary or accidental. In a money economy, one can work hard for a lifetime and still be poor, while another can be rich by having money to start with, or by a few vagaries of fortune. Fortune. And everything in between.

$ $ $

Fortune is a gamble, and the big money is in gambling. Nothing is being produced: it's a game.

"Made a fortune betting against Wall Street."

"Made a fortune betting with the big money."

"Here's a million dollars: double it."

"Lost a fortune."

High risk: betting the dark horse, but with other people's money. Dark horse lost this time. Hmmm. National disaster. International crisis. And the government as insurance: "too big to fail."

Send the bill to those who work. Otherwise money will be seen as a sham. There will be a collapse. And hey, nobody wants that. Charge all the workers a year's wages, then get tough on "welfare."

$ $ $

The head of Tyche, goddess of fortune, is stamped on a gold stater minted in Smyrna in the first century BCE. On Tyche's head are miniature walls and guard towers: the walls of the city, the walls of the state. Or walls of a prison. Or the vault of a bank. On the reverse there is a statue of Aphrodite, one breast exposed. Security and pleasure. Part lottery token, part whorehouse pass.

$ $ $

Maybe the two dollar bill should be given yet one more chance. Actresses and other celebrities could pose nude, artistically of course. Certain bills might even appreciate beyond their minted value. Trade a Cindy for a Clara, a Greta for a Marilyn. Or a Burt for a Tom or a Brad. Whole exchanges could develop. There could be a futures market. Money could be lent on the future value, and bundles of the loans could themselves be considered capital credit and marketed to pay off the national debt.

$ $ $

For love or money. Will do. Won't do.
"Not without money, honey."
"I love you darling, but this other man has money."
All of us whores.
"Need somebody killed? Call Mack."

$ $ $

Herodotus credits the Lydians with the invention of money, of first coining gold and silver and electrum. The Lydians are also noted as being the first to trade items not of their own manufacture, to have the custom of prostituting their daughters, and to arouse the wrath of the Persians.

The Chinese began using paper money in the Sung. Kublai Khan forbade the circulation of metal coinage, though (as reported by Marco Polo) his notes were redeemable in metal at his mint by metal smiths and jewelers. Exchanging worn and tattered bills for fresh printings cost 3 percent.

In the West, the first circulating paper money was created in Sweden in 1661 by Johan Palmstruch, who got government backing by promising half of the profits to the crown. He did well for a while, but printed too many bills. His bank collapsed. As an act of mercy, he was allowed to go to prison rather than being executed. Fifty years later the Scotsman John Law made a deal with the government of France to give his bank a monopoly in printing government money, promising to pay off the national debt. Law's scheme also worked for a while: trade soared, new industries were given low interest loans, and Law's bank financed road building and other infrastructure projects. Then his bubble burst, and he died penurious in exile. Neither Law nor Palmstruch was evidently "too big to fail."

The first issue of paper currency by a government in the West was in Massachusetts in 1690, to finance a military expedition. Banks, states, and wars.

> War is the parent of armies; from these proceed debts and taxes; and armies, and debts, and taxes are the known instruments for bringing the many under the domination of the few.
>
> —James Madison, April 20, 1795

Wars, states, banks. The eternal triangle.

$ $ $

Alexander Hamilton thought a national debt would be a national blessing, not only binding the people together but also creating a need for taxation that would force people to work harder: "We labour less now than any civilized nation of Europe, and a habit of labour in the people is as essential to the health and vigor of their minds and bodies as it is conducive to the welfare of the State." Of course, Hamilton was a banker, and stood to make a bundle.

Julius Caesar borrowed large sums of money from his officers. Not only did this enable him to pay off his mutinous troops, but it insured that the future success and prosperity of his officers depended on his own.

$ $ $

Paper money is revolutionary. Printing presses (such as Benjamin Franklin's) financed the revolution in America, and later the revolutions in France, Russia, and China. Inflation caused by the promiscuous printing of money tends to favor debtors—it has an equalizing effect. The United States was born from hyperinflation. The biggest debtor, of course, was the government itself.

$ $ $

Edward Gibbon, writing at the dawn of the age of imperialism, said that money was a stimulant—the drug that got us off our asses to rise above "barbarism." So we run around on speed, inventing new doodads to sell, and suffering the lash of withdrawal if we fall behind. Economists talk of "injecting" money into the economy: stimulus. Like freebase cocaine. Hooked on money, then held hostage. "I'm the pusher, if I fall, you'll be cut off cold turkey. So you pay my bail, my tickets, and my lawyer."

Money as a drug: if the right dosage can be found—printing just enough, not too much—it's like magic. As long as people keep buying things they don't need. As long as those in the business don't hoard too much—which is of course their only reason for being in the business. As long as the real resources don't dry up, the illusion of prosperity can be maintained with more and more IOUs. To the future. To the earth. Like all stimulants, money steals from tomorrow.

$ $ $

A shrine to money in a place of business is wholly appropriate: the first dollar bill framed on the wall by the cash register. Let's keep it straight. Let's keep it clear. Commerce flows through here. Banks don't do that, though, nor brokerage houses. It would be too obvious. Overstated. Money is our business but let's say, instead, that it's about your future: a warm beach, your money for nothing and your chicks for your money.

Success counselors say you have to attract money with your attitude and your mantras. Repeat every morning: "I admire the rich. I want to be like them." Surely you don't want to be one of the have-nots. I, too, wish to be paid. Will I get paid for this? Shall I dance? May this be my mantra, a spell: "Money, money, money." Maybe just writing the word will be enough. Invocation. Makes the world go round.

> It is more easy to write on money that to obtain it; and those who gain it jest much at those who only know how to write about it.
> —Voltaire

Sigh.

$ $ $

Perhaps Jesus does smile on wealth, in spite of his sandals. The Calvinists thought worldly success a mark of the elect, and made hoarding a virtue. Hoarding, of course, is anal. The fecal, excremental nature of money has been analyzed by Norman O. Brown:

> Until the advent of psychoanalysis and its doctrine of the
> anal character of money, the profoundest insights into the
> nature of the money complex had to be expressed through
> the medium of myth—in modern times, the myth of the
> Devil. The Devil, we said in our chapter on Luther, is the
> lineal descendant of the Trickster in primitive mythologies;
> the evolution of the Trickster, through such intermediary
> figures as the classical Hermes, into the Christian Devil
> reflects the history of anality.
> —*Life Against Death,* 301

My grandmother, a woman who always liked to carry a wad of
bills, taught me that money was dirty and that you had to wash your
hands after counting it. Which is really pretty obvious.

$ $ $

And yet there is a Dionysian quality to money, or at least to spending it. Burning money would be very Dionysian. "His alternative
worship is war." Norman O. Brown. War or potlatch: the dilemma
of late capitalism.

$ $ $

Burning money. Art project for Burning Man—an offering to
Dionysus, a superstitious rite to avert bloodshed and cataclysm, to
bring true prosperity, peace. A large cage, the metal rods plated
with gold and silver, set atop a wooden pyre. Everyone contributes
a dollar bill. Thousands. Large blowers whirl the bills in a vortex,
then it's burned. Gas cannons. Flame throwers.

People dance.

$ $ $

Aristotle said that money was meant to be used in exchange, but
not to increase at interest. He called the ability of money to engen-

der itself usury (τόκος), the birth of money from money, and called it the most hated sort of moneymaking.

> They have brought whores for Eleusis
> Corpses are set to banquet
> at behest of usura
> —Ezra Pound, "Canto XLV"

$ $ $

Is money the best system? That lack of certain pieces of paper can condemn ordinary people to misery and early death does not seem "best" in any way. Yet as globalization seeks out and destroys the last vestiges of the old economy—based on barter and networks of reciprocal obligations—poverty will be the inevitable result. A few, of course, will find new power and privilege, and lots of new gadgets. Everyone, in fact, will have new gadgets, even the poor. The poor may no longer have gardens or a pasture held in common or their own fishing boats, but they will have new gadgets.

Money is about poverty, and the threat of poverty. It is poverty that gives money value. By threat of poverty, one must not only work—which people have always done—but must work *for money*, even if that work has no value or is destructive. And money is about power—power backed up by arms and prisons. Poverty, power, and prison are money's soul, flesh, and bones.

$ $ $

Do I have a better idea? No, but that doesn't change my analysis. Still, just for fun, let's remove one leg of the tripod: legalize counterfeiting. Would the world be better or worse? Would there be less poverty, or more? Less crime, or more crime?

"Oh, Moe's Money, sure, I'll take that."

"Treasury note? Hmmm. You got anything else?"

One could carry around whole rolls of money in case one got mugged. Counterfeiting would naturally prey on the big currencies. Local scrips would acquire a new respect. And while the paper value of the tycoons would drop, they would still be tycoons— they've been printing money for years. For everybody else, actually, life would go on just fine. Maybe there would be more trading. And maybe you'd want to know the person you were working for, and whose money it was you were taking.

But paper money is a relic anyway. Money today is mostly a web of interlocking databases. There have been proposals in the government to phase out the hundred-dollar bill, to curb the black market. Even the writing of checks has declined. More and more financial transactions are electronic and invisible: card swipes, bits shifting on a hard drive. Little fees can be sliced off, the house take at the gaming table.

And the "house" can create more money whenever it wants to—a note of obligation—which can then be bundled and sold. Who needs a Fed? Get the U.S. out of the money business. Leave it to private businesspeople, who know what they are doing and have such a great record. Like banks, or insurance companies. Ha Ha. We take your money and then we're gone.

$ $ $

Burned.
Burned me.
Caesar burned me.
My partner burned me.
I'm busted.
I need a hundred dollars.
Now gimme money.
Brother, can you spare a dime?

$ $ $

Back to metal? An ounce of gold for a couple of pounds of laptop? Or further back, before money. There are still things of value—cowrie shells, strings of dentalium, beaten sheets of copper, herds of cattle or horses. "Big men," those with much, give feasts, and thereby earn prestige. Ordinary people get by. Maybe a young man has to take risks to earn the bride price if he's in love with a girl from a big house.

$ $ $

It's a question of scale and edge: before money, subsistence level was the poorest one could be, and it was the way most people lived. Money has created a poverty *below* subsistence. Today some "earn" enough money in one hour to feed and shelter one hundred people for a whole year, or to pay twenty thousand people minimum wage, or to pay almost five thousand people twenty dollars an hour and still leave two hundred dollars an hour for oneself.

Milton Friedman's grandfatherly voice tells us that those women in the sweatshop aren't being exploited, they are being given a chance—they are working their way up. After all, when they lived on farms they didn't have any money at all. Now they can buy things. Now she'll do a strip tease. Now she'll let me fuck her.

Perhaps the bottom of the scale is a better measure of the wealth of a society than the gold and jewels at the top. We need something better than the silly and wholly self-serving Gross Domestic Product (GDP), which really has nothing to do with "product." A country that destroys its farming soil to force out three record yields isn't making itself richer, it is impoverishing itself. We can save money by not dealing with our trash—better bottom line. Put the trash in the water. Put the trash in the air. Plastic in the oceans. Save money. Write another IOU. Maybe deserts aren't so bad. I'll be dead. But hey, I'm rich now. Money defines only itself as "capital," excluding air, water, forests, and the health, happiness, and harmony of citizens.

The first duty of every citizen is to insist on having money on reasonable terms; and this demand is not complied with by giving four men three shillings each for ten or twelve hours' drudgery and one man a thousand pounds for nothing. The crying need of the nation is not for better morals, cheaper bread, temperance, liberty, culture, redemption of fallen sisters and erring brothers, nor the grace, love and fellowship of the Trinity, but simply for enough money.
—George Bernard Shaw, preface to *Major Barbara*, 1907

One of eleventh-century Chinese statesman Wang An-Shih's reforms was to make low interest government loans available to farmers, to undercut usurious loan-sharking.

Any of the recent U.S. bailouts would have been better served by giving the money to the people: $5,000 per person, $10,000 per person, $20,000 per person. Thousands of new businesses spring up; there is money in circulation, new joint ventures, new banks, education in neighborhood collectives—a chance to break out of the cycle of poverty. Who knows better what is good for the people than the people? Not Papa Banker and his cronies at the Treasury.

The single most successful issue of paper money in the colonies, in Maryland, was given directly to the taxpayers.

How to play the game? Let's be rational, think this through. Cooperate or double-cross? Tit for Tat or Screw 'em all the Time? Actually, let's cheat: collude, merge, monopolize the market and then split the take. That's win-win. Let's bankrupt the company, pocket the money, pay a couple of fines, then retire. Rational.

They dance, out of sight, and play muted tambourines, all the way to the bank. We would like to quiet their laughter and wipe the smirks from their faces, perhaps call them philistines, but they own the speakers and the paper. A mass of cold air is pouring through the mountain passes: I need a jacket. No money. Zen Roshi Robert Aitken once opined, somewhat enigmatically, that it is easier to practice "true poverty" if you own your own home.

$ $ $

Money, you must realize, is a dharma. Like all things—pickup trucks, loaves of bread, flashy jewelry—money is a part of the Buddha's body, and therefore just as precious and as deserving of respect, as a bucket of water. "It dazzles, and it slips us by," writes Gary Snyder in "Money Goes Upstream." That which seeks to own the source: winged Hermes, god of commerce and thieves.

6

ALL MY RELATIVES:
THE BINARY FRACTALS OF THE GIFT ECONOMY

BARBARA ALICE MANN

One of the most successful cons in modern history has people—intelligent people, educated people—believing that capitalism is the only "realistic" economic system to support complex, sophisticated cultures. There are intrepid iconoclasts out there, refusing to reify capitalism, but they are typically waved off as fantasy-prone, Marxist, or unemployed. Most Westerners sadly accept that the only alternative to capitalism ever attempted was the "failed" Soviet experiment. Thus has future economic discussion been ceded to the realm of Western imagination, where one idiosyncratic dys/u/topia after another is proposed only to be dashed. Before we all jump off the utopian pier into rippling delusion, however, let us try quizzing the original premise.

Is capitalism the only system ever to support large-scale, sophisticated cultures?

Hell, no! Gift economies have been doing that splendidly, throughout history.

Around the world, both historically and into the present, gift economies have thrived. In Native North America, they were the right hand of our constitutional democracies, and still flourish underground. The gift economy of the magnificent Iroquois League supported five nations from the year 1142 on, adding the sixth nation in 1712, and including another sixty or so affiliated nations along the way.[1] The Lahu, or mountain people of southern

China, have survived both colonial capitalism and Maoism into the present, their gift culture battered but intact.[2] The Berber women in Kabylia continue to manage abundance without capitalism in the unforgiving lands of North Africa.[3] The Minangkabau of Sumatra do just fine without capital; indeed, their gift culture weathered the 2005 tsunami.[4] The Sami ("Laplanders") of Finland are emerging from centuries of oppression, by both Soviets and Western Europeans, with their gift economies alive.[5] These are just *some* of the gift economies extant in the world, and the list does not even scratch the surface of the theoretical work that has been done on the economics of the gift.[6]

Why, then, the steady, determined gaze away from these healthy alternatives, all of them with economic histories longer and more robust than that of capitalism?

Part of the determined oblivion has to do with ignoring the competition so it will go away. Obviously, the West's Cult of Capitalism—and it *is* a faith system—does not wish to lose converts. The rest of the oblivion has to do with the structure of gift-giving cultures: they are all matriarchies. Indeed, the gift economy is the one, constant characteristic that all matriarchies, worldwide, hold in common. You, the reader, do not know about this, because, in the West, these facts are taboo, forbidden knowledge.

The hatchet job that Western patriarchy has done on matriarchy is a masterpiece. As a silencer, the fiat worked fine in academia, where, until the last quarter of the twentieth century, anthropology and history flatly forbade matriarchies to exist. No one got a PhD by noting that they did. Marija Gimbutas study groups were banished to a moldy corner of the gym. The male-run, raiding economies of Western Europe were officially billed as The Way It Is *and Always Has Been,* SINCE THE BEGINNING OF TIME!

Elsewhere, Western law declared women nonpersons, while in religion, that companion-in-chief of capitalism, desert monotheism, spent two thousand years blackening the eye of every woman from Eve on, while insisting implausibly that men had birthed everything in sight. That last violation of common sense worked because people had grown accustomed to swallowing at least three impossibilities before breakfast: denial of death ("Jesus lives"—and so can you!), denial of woman-worth (Adam's rib, Eve's sin, Lilith's nonexistence), and denial of compassion (everlasting hellfire, Armageddon).

Clearing away the underbrush for a plain discussion of gift economies requires us first to look away from Western culture, a task that most Westerners have an awfully hard time managing. Even when they *think* they are discarding Western ideas, they continue Euro-forming the data with energy.[7] This is because the most basic concepts of any birth culture seed themselves so deeply into the consciousness of their members that pulling them into the light for rational evaluation is a time-consuming, emotionally unpleasant, readily sacrificed chore.

The first, serious error that Westerners make in looking at, specifically, Native American cultures: the assumption that their own base number of One is the base number of all cultures.[8] It certainly is not. Native American cultures use a base number of Two. Western cultures use linear math; Native American cultures use binary math. In Native American math, the base unit consists of two equal halves, which are immediately replicated (so that the first unit has a twin), resulting in what looks like a base four to users of Western linear math. In fact, it is just a binary set.

This accounts for the very common "plus sign" symbol so common to Native American iconography. It connects with the cardinal directions of Breath (Sky) and Blood (Earth). When Breath, they are the Four Winds; when Blood, they become the Four Serpents or the Four Mothers. Just to keep life interesting, Native groups tilt the plus sign ╬ into an **X,** so that it is the interstices, not the lines, that matter. We are big on in-between spaces. When everything is a middling, nothing can be an outlier. Figure 1 shows the standard colors and cardinal conceptions of the Iroquois. Note the traditional, tilted concept of the Twinned Direction of the Sky (E↔W) and Split Sky (N↔S). White (E↔S) wampum and purple (N↔W) wampum are referenced by the background colors.

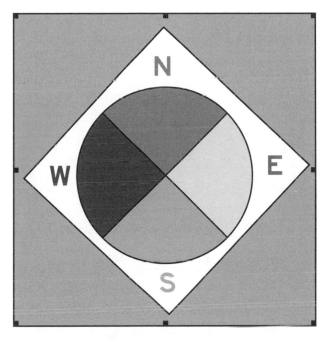

Figure 1. The Breath and Blood of the cardinal directions.

Translating all of this into an economic system requires something beyond basic math, however. Human interaction is much more involved than simplistic linear probabilities suggest, which is usually what Westerners try to slap over economics as predictors. Yes, diagrams of probabilities *look* complex at first blush (see figure 2), but they are really just accreted, either-or propositions, following the standard Manichean list of choices: good or bad, light or dark, yes or no, up or down, as though such a list *really* covered all possibilities. (Figure 2 represents the line of a happy simplist, walking cheerfully along, until confronted with a yes-no proposition. Each answer follows its own potential direction, with more yes-no choices at intervals. The circles represent the nodes where the either-or choices live.) Worse, we are assured that none of the previous outcomes affect future outcomes. I remember arguing in my college math class the improbability of the first decision not affecting the second, whereas my professor categorically refused to accept my proposition, replying that it represented fuzzy thinking. It was not fuzzy thinking, however, but just Native American thinking.

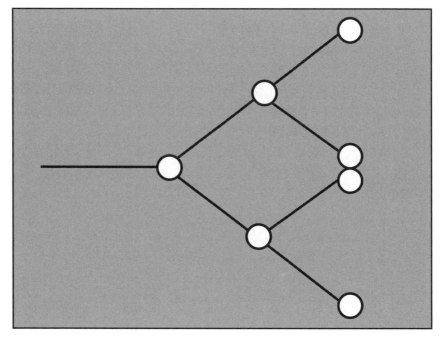

Figure 2. Standard probability chart.

What is needed to describe gift economies is a complex form of representation that takes into account interactive binaries as mass in motion. This is because, in the world of the gift economy, every-thing influences the outcome of everything else, a primary impli-cation of the Native American commonplace reference to "All My Relatives." Nothing Native is a freestanding, once-and-for-all, over-

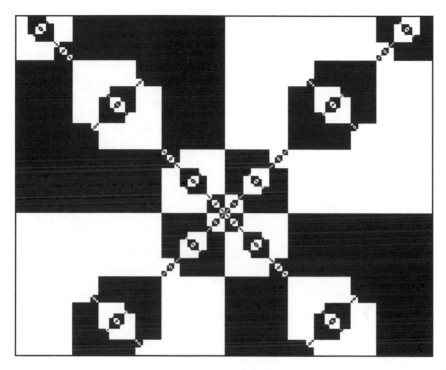

Figure 3. A binary fractal. Image courtesy of Mark Dow.

and done-with proposition, as each transaction is represented as being in exchange economics. Instead, there is a constant motion, in which every action is implicated in every other action.

I have seen this idea represented in spiderweb format, which is not bad for a two-dimensional impression of what All My Relatives are doing. The underlying mechanism of this spiderweb image is fractal geometry, which offers representations much more complex and fitting than a two-dimensional spiderweb.[9] The idea of fractals is a set of images, repeating endlessly, each repetition, no matter how large or small, a perfect replica of the original impetus.

At this point, the limitations of paper, not to mention my own inadequacies in computer graphics, prevent any three-dimensional, let alone, moving mass of imagery, but the reader should try to imagine just that. Neither do fractals *have* to go binary, but the most convincing ones do. The limitation of fractal representations is that each is a perfectly measured increment, so that the only distinction is in the largeness or smallness of any given detail. The irregular regularities, such as compose nature, do not come through. Nevertheless, the basic idea does get across. See, for instance, figure 3, which is a nice fractal vision of the nearly seventy groups (the six nations plus the sixty-some affiliated nations) of the Iroquois League. Notice the plus sign ⫟ rotated into an **X,** with the fractal repetitions mimicking chaos. The figure even includes the light-dark contrast so common to League conceptions, for instance, white and "black" (blue purple) wampum.

Gift economics start with the Mother, herself the initial gift of the cosmos. She gives to her child, who remains attached, setting up the prototype of gifting. Traditional gift economies focus on *communities,* not individuals, though, while needs are defined both materially and spiritually. The idea is to jump into a self-replicating process that is already in motion. The size of the gift is immaterial, since the process, itself, is repeated. Any gift expresses a need. Thus, all of our prayers give thanks, without asking for anything, yet the output of energy in the gift of thanks creates a vacuum that sucks in new energy, the two halves completing one repetition (which, naturally, needs a twin). Since the action is no good unless communal, gifting happenings multiply, among All My Relatives, human and nonhuman alike. Energy is constantly in motion, so that no one can hoard, constipating the works.

Gift economics tend to confuse and surprise Westerners, who keep trying to interpret them in terms of their One-base culture with its exchange-based economics. The sheer idea of giving away one's goods and energy as a means of replenishing one's store of goods and energy seems counterintuitive to Europeans, who give only on pain of death or, maybe, on threat of IRS audit. Consequently, extensions of gifting, such as gambling, just look bizarre to Europeans.

In fact, gambling is an honorable expression of gift economics,

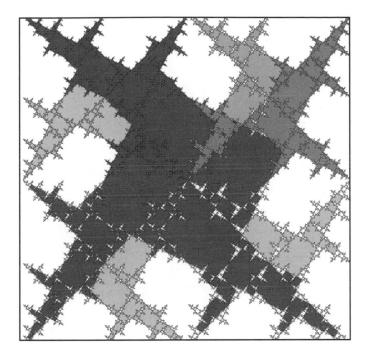

Figure 4. The binary fractal of the gift economy. Image courtesy of Mark Dow.

and one that makes full use of fractals to replicate chaos, the sacred action. Gambling only appears "immoral" to Westerners because they saddle it with the consequences of their own exchange economy in its most brutal form, and then blame the loser, of course. In a gift culture, however, where it is not possible to "lose everything," gambling becomes what it essentially is, an act of fractal spirituality, i.e., the making of the heavy medicine of chaos. The energy that compulsive gamblers so love is spread over the whole community, which then mutually enjoys it, as well as any goods involved.

The best, two-dimensional representation I have found for the gift economy is in figure 4. It honors the twinship principal, whereby one consists of its two halves, replicated in mirror image. The overall effect looks haphazard and unsustainable, but the gift keeps on giving, in actions writ large or small. The gift economy is a perpetual motion machine, collapsing only when the known universe collapses, or when Europeans arrive on the continent, with their raiding economy, to gut the gift and still the motion.

I do not know how to reinstate gift economics worldwide; that will take a total do-over of culture, I fear—but then again, a do-over is what the prophecies are promising. For the record, it is only the Mayas who quote the 2012 date, and it is only Europeans who turn the prospect of 2012 into their own doomsday. Among the Iroquois, prophecy gives the date as 2010, and it indicates a process, not a solitary event.[10] This prophecy connects with the original Peacemaker's prophecy from the twelfth century, in which he predicted the coming of The White Panther of Discord, when the children's faces would be ground into the dirt and heads would roll west.[11] Once the invader had taken all the land from the Indians, even ripping off the scalp of Mother Earth for the scalp bounty, then Great Grandmother Turtle, who carries us all on her back, would begin to rock the edges of her carapace, brushing off the annoyances. Finally, she would pitch, rolling over completely in the waves. When she righted herself again as Turtle Island, only the Shining People (indigenous people) would be left, to start again.[12]

7

THE TWILIGHT OF MONEY

JOHN MICHAEL GREER

One of the least constructive habits of contemporary thought is its insistence on the uniqueness of the modern experience. It's true, of course, that fossil fuels have allowed the world's industrial societies to pursue their follies on a more grandiose scale than any past empire has managed, but the follies themselves closely parallel those of previous societies, and tracking the trajectories of these past examples is one of our few useful sources of guidance if we want to know where the current versions are headed.

The metastasis of money through every aspect of life in the modern industrial world is a good example. While no past society, as far as we know, took this process as far as we have, the replacement of wealth with its own abstract representations is no new thing. As Giambattista Vico pointed out back in the eighteenth century, complex societies move from the concrete to the abstract over their life cycles, and this influences economic life as much as anything else. Just as political power begins with raw violence and evolves toward progressively more subtle means of suasion, economic activity begins with the direct exchange of real wealth and evolves through a similar process of abstraction: first, one prized commodity becomes the standard measure for all other kinds of wealth; then, receipts that can be exchanged for some fixed sum of that commodity become a unit of exchange; finally, promises to pay some amount of these receipts on demand, or at a fixed point in the future, enter into circulation, and these may end up largely replacing the receipts themselves.

This movement toward abstraction has important advantages for complex societies, because abstractions can be deployed with a much smaller investment of resources than it takes to mobilize the concrete realities that back them up. We could have resolved the 2008 debate about who should rule the United States the old-fashioned way, by having McCain and Obama call their supporters to arms, march to war, and settle the matter in battle amid a hail of bullets and cannon shot on a fine September day on some Iowa prairie. Still, the cost in lives, money, and collateral damage would have been far in excess of those involved in an election. In much the same way, the complexities involved in paying office workers in kind, or even in cash, make an economy of abstractions much less cumbersome for all concerned.

At the same time, there's a trap hidden in the convenience of abstractions: the further you get from the concrete realities, the larger the chance becomes that the concrete realities may not actually be there when needed. History is littered with the corpses of regimes that let their power become so abstract that they could no longer counter a challenge on the fundamental level of raw violence; it's been said of Chinese history, and could be said of any other civilization, that its basic rhythm is the tramp of hobnailed boots going up stairs, followed by the whisper of silk slippers going back down. In the same way, economic abstractions keep functioning only so long as actual goods and services exist to be bought and sold, and it's only in the pipe dreams of economists that the abstractions guarantee the presence of the goods and services. Vico argued that this trap is a central driving force behind the decline and fall of civilizations; the movement toward abstraction goes so far that the concrete realities are neglected. In the end the realities trickle away unnoticed, until a shock of some kind strikes the tower of abstractions built atop the void the realities once filled, and the whole structure tumbles to the ground.

We are uncomfortably close to such a possibility just now, especially in our economic affairs. Over the last century, with the assistance of the economic hypercomplexity made possible by fossil fuels, the world's industrial nations have taken the process of economic abstraction further than any previous civilization. On top of the usual levels of abstraction—a commodity used to measure value (gold), receipts that could be exchanged for that commodity (paper money), and promises to pay the receipts (checks and other financial paper)—contemporary societies have built an extraordinary pyramid of additional abstractions. Unlike the pyramids of Egypt, furthermore, this one has its narrow end on the ground, in the realm of actual goods and services, and widens as it goes up.

The consequence of all this pyramid building is that there are not enough goods and services on earth to equal, at current prices, more than a small percentage of the face value of stocks, bonds, derivatives, and other fiscal exotica now in circulation. The vast majority of economic activity in today's world consists purely of exchanges among these representations of representations of representations of wealth. This is why the real economy of goods and services can go into a free fall like the one we have seen in recent years, without having more than a modest impact so far on an increasingly hallucinatory economy of fiscal abstractions.

Yet an impact it will have, if the free fall proceeds far enough. This is Vico's point, and it's a possibility that has been taken far too lightly both by the political classes of today's industrial societies and by their critics on either end of the political spectrum. An economy of hallucinated wealth depends utterly on the willingness of all participants to pretend that the hallucinations have real value. When that willingness slackens, the pretense can evaporate in record time. This is how financial bubbles turn into financial panics: the collective fantasy of value that surrounds tulip bulbs, or stocks, or suburban tract housing, or any other speculative vehicle, dissolves into a mad rush for the exits. That rush has been peaceful to date; but it need not always be.

The industrial age is in some sense the ultimate speculative bubble, a three-century-long binge driven by the fantasy of infinite economic growth on a finite planet with even more finite supplies of cheap abundant energy. Still, I am coming to think that this megabubble has spawned a second bubble on nearly the same scale. The vehicle for this secondary megabubble is money—meaning here the entire contents of what I've called elsewhere the tertiary economy, the profusion of abstract representations of wealth that dominate our economic life and have all but smothered the real economy of goods and services, to say nothing of the primary economy of natural systems that keeps all of us alive.

Speculative bubbles are defined in various ways, but classic examples—the 1929 stock binge, say, or the 2005–2008 housing bubble—have certain standard features in common. First, the value of whatever item is at the center of the bubble shows a sustained rise in price not justified by changes in the wider economy, or in any concrete value the item might have. A speculative bubble in money functions a bit differently than other bubbles, because the speculative vehicle is also the measure of value; instead of one dollar increasing in value until it's worth two, one dollar becomes two. Where stocks or tract houses go zooming up in price when a bubble focuses on them, then, what climbs in a money bubble is the total amount of paper wealth in circulation. That's certainly happened in recent decades.

A second standard feature of speculative bubbles is that they absorb most of the fictive value they create, rather than spilling it back into the rest of the economy. In a stock bubble, for example, a majority of the money that comes from stock sales goes right back into the market; without this feedback loop, a bubble can't sustain itself for long. In a money bubble, this same rule holds good; most of the paper earnings generated by the bubble end up being reinvested in some other form of paper wealth. Here again, this has certainly happened; the only reason we haven't see 1,000 percent inflation as a result of the vast manufacture of paper wealth in recent decades is that most of it has been used solely to buy even more newly manufactured paper wealth.

A third standard feature of speculative bubbles is that the number of people involved in them climbs steadily as the bubble proceeds. In 1929, the stock market was deluged by amateur investors who had never before bought a share of anything; in 2006, hundreds of thousands, perhaps millions, of people who previously thought of houses only as something to live in came to think of them as a ticket to overnight wealth, and sank their net worth in real estate as a result. The metastasis of the money economy, which I have written about as well, is another example of the same process at work.

Finally, of course, bubbles always pop. When that happens, the speculative vehicle du jour comes crashing back to earth, losing the great majority of its assumed value, and the mass of amateur investors, having lost anything they made and usually a great deal more, trickle away from the market. This has not yet happened to the current money bubble. It might be a good idea to start thinking about what might happen if it does so.

The effects of a money panic would be focused uncomfortably close to home, I suspect, because the bulk of the hyperexpansion of money in recent decades has focused on a single currency, the U.S. dollar. That bomb might have been defused if 2008's collapse of the housing bubble had been allowed to run its course, because this would have eliminated no small amount of the dollar-denominated abstractions generated by the excesses of recent years. Unfortunately the U.S. government chose instead to try to reinflate the bubble economy by spending money it doesn't have through an orgy of borrowing and some very dubious fiscal gimmickry. A great many foreign governments are accordingly becoming reluctant to lend the United States more money, and at least one rising power—China—has been quietly cashing in its dollar reserves for commodities and other forms of far less abstract wealth.

Up until now, it has been in the best interests of other industrial nations to prop up the United States with a steady stream of credit, so that it can bankrupt itself filling its self-imposed role as global policeman. It's been a very comfortable arrangement, since other nations haven't had to shoulder more than a tiny fraction of the costs of dealing with rogue states, keeping the Middle East divided against itself, or maintaining economic hegemony over an increasingly restive third world, while receiving the benefits of all these policies. The end of the age of cheap fossil fuel, however, has thrown a wild card into the game. As world petroleum production falters, it must have occurred to the leaders of other nations that if the United States no longer consumed roughly a quarter of the world's fossil fuel supply, there would be a great deal more for everyone else to share out. The possibility that other nations might decide that this potential gain outweighs the advantages of keeping the United States solvent may make the next decade or so interesting, in the sense of the famous Chinese curse.

Over the longer term, on the other hand, it's safe to assume that the vast majority of paper assets now in circulation, whatever the currency in which they're denominated, will lose essentially all their value. This might happen quickly, or it might unfold over decades, but the world's supply of abstract representations of wealth is so much vaster than its supply of concrete wealth that something has to give sooner or later. Future economic growth won't make up the difference; the end of the age of cheap fossil fuel makes growth in the real economy of goods and services a thing of the past, outside of rare and self-limiting situations. As the limits to growth tighten, and become first barriers to growth and then drivers of contraction, shrinkage in the real economy will become the rule, heightening the mismatch between money and wealth and increasing the pressure toward depreciation of the real value of paper assets.

Once again, though, all this has happened before. Just as increasing economic abstraction is a common feature of the history of complex societies, the unraveling of that abstraction is a common feature of their decline and fall. The desperate expedients now being pursued to expand the American money supply in a rapidly contracting economy have exact equivalents in, say, the equally desperate measures taken by the Roman Empire in its last years to expand its own money supply by debasing its coinage. The Roman economy achieved very high levels of complexity and an international reach; its moneylenders—we would call them financiers today—were a major economic force, and credit played a sizeable role in everyday economic life. In the decline and fall of the empire, all this went away. The farmers who pastured their sheep in the ruins of Rome's forum during the Dark Ages lived in an economy of barter and feudal custom, in which coins were rare items more often used as jewelry than as a medium of exchange.

A similar trajectory almost certainly waits in the future of our own economic system, though what use the shepherds who pasture their flocks on the Mall in the ruins of a future Washington DC will find for vast stacks of Treasury bills is not exactly clear. How the trajectory will unfold is anyone's guess, but the possibility that we may soon see sharp declines in the value of the dollar, and of dollar-denominated paper assets, probably should not be ignored, and cashing in abstract representations of wealth for things of more enduring value might well belong high on the list of sensible preparations for the future.

8

CHANGE YOUR TIME ZONE, CHANGE YOUR MIND

ELLEN PEARLMAN

In three hours I will be rich.
In five hours I can only eat out once a month.
In thirteen hours I can buy myself an apartment paying full cash.
But right now, in this moment I could face foreclosure on my home.

During the next twenty-four hours nothing will have changed in my life. The only difference is the how long it takes for me to arrive in a new time zone or country.

Travel and globalization have shown the relativity of worth, value, and wealth. I know I speak from a perceived privileged position. Not all the world's people can just hop on an airplane and zip off to destinations known or unknown. There are undeniably serious problems with poverty, dislocation, and starvation. What I am referring to here is more subjective. It is the perception behind what we desire, not the immutability and direness of critical sustainability.

I am a white, funky fringe American urbanite barely hanging onto my status as a middle-class creative arts professional. In my home country I have adapted myself to the considerable economic restrictions that come with my trade; cabs are taken only to get to the airport, and my car is sixteen years old. I survive on thrift store expeditions and lots of Craigslist forays. For the past few years I have been living inside artist villages that surround the outer rings of Beijing, China. Before that it was Latin America, and before that, Europe. I have outsourced my heath care to the most modernized, lowest cost places I could find (Argentina, Mexico, now looking at India), been able to take cabs everywhere (China), and only been able to afford to go out for coffee and barely even that (London). All of this is not new news for anyone who has traveled or sprung for a vacation.

What has not changed under any of these myriad circumstances is who I am and what I aspire to. My values, spirituality, and outlook remain the same—simple living, remaking and reusing most things, public transportation if available, vegetarianism, abstaining from luxury or brand name items at least on a first-pass basis (though I don't mind the quality if it's used). Yes, I have a laptop computer, but my TV is only thirteen inches wide and it is secondhand. I Dumpster dive when I have money and I Dumpster dive when I don't. No difference. I have earned $100,000 a year and I have earned nothing.

What makes this wide discrepancy in my material circumstances is money, whether it is pesos, euros, renminbi, or dollars. It is various colored pieces of paper with intricate layered graphics issued and handled by hoards of international monetary traders who set my worth relative to where I stand on the planet at any given instant. The value of that paper, as everyone knows, can fluctuate tremendously. In China, I am perceived as a wealthy Westerner—no questions asked. That perception gains me entrée into the highest levels of society; I mean lunch with millionaires, powerbrokers, diplomats and even representatives to the National People's Congress, levels that in my own country are not a daily staple of my life. It's easy to say it is because I am a foreigner, but that's not entirely true. It is also because of my perceived monetary value.

I am poor in Dubai and London, but I can be middle class or even rich depending on the location of my plane on the tarmac.

What does this say about the value of money and self-worth? It's not that money is not real, and its not that money doesn't make a difference, but it does say that money is highly perceptual. The value of that perception, which many people base their worth upon, is skewed. I admit I get skewered by it as well, especially when there is not enough of it. For instance, to stretch the analogy, say you have purchased a new BMW car. As soon as you purchase it, it immediately loses a percentage of its value, even if you drive it a hundred miles for just one week. In real terms as the supposed newest model it's probably still as valuable as it was the week before, but its worth has changed considerably because now there is a little dirt on the tires.

It's certainly a more enviable position to be wealthy, or at least perceived as wealthy. The reasons are, besides material possessions, access, mobility, respect, and opportunity. Wanting these things allows one to develop potential, and enjoying the "better" things in life, although what is better does not share an across the board cultural consensus. Some people think bigger is better, and base their lives on that premise. It's the pursuit of that premise that leads to the successful Ponzi schemes that frequently make it into the news. However, severe lack of money does restrict survival levels and growth—there can be no doubt about that.

Another way to look at this issue of worth is from a Buddhist perspective. Any phenomenon experienced is experienced only in the mind. The fact that things change is proof that they are transient and not as real as they appear. For instance, if pleasure truly existed it could never change into pain. You would experience nonstop pleasure. The truth is you cannot hold onto change. But where do experiences really originate? They emanate from your own mind.

Mind is powerful. For example if you imagine or dream that you are burning in a fire, you might break out in a real sweat, even though there is no actual fire anywhere. Buddhists say there is no object and no perceiver of the object and it is the mind that solidifies things. Still, believing in objective reality is very helpful when you look both ways while crossing a busy street so you don't get hit by a car. But getting back to the analogy of the fire, as soon as you imagine the idea of flames you name it—fire. Names, in fact, are also imaginary. Think about all the languages in the world and the all the words for "fire." What you are actually doing is connecting a sound or guttural utterance to a nonexistent image according to a set of strange, grammatical rules. That is an issue of perception. So is money.

Value arises from mutual consensus. In China, the cold green translucent stone jade is highly valued. The deeper green it is, the more expensive it gets. I personally think jade is an ugly polished stone. It holds no value for me, yet this view is at odds with an entire nation and five thousand years of its history. That is what I mean by perceived value. I am not talking about the next hot meal on the table, which is clearly necessary for survival.

What happens in times of economic meltdown is partially about perceived value; what got us into the 2008 mess in the first place was betting on the nonexistent value of imaginary future assets called CDMOs. That formerly illegal speculation was made legal again in the year 2000 by an act of Congress allowed trading concrete assets (homes) for imaginary scenarios based on vague future predictions. This is the mass hallucination that has produced crippling consequences. It sprung from perceived, imaginary value.

Now SUVs are out. Credit card debt is out. Spending beyond your means is out. Living on borrowed funds is out. Acquiring what you can't afford is out. Recycling plastic bags is in and carrying fiber or woven shopping bags is in. Because of rapid globalization I can clearly see my relative worth radically shift in the blink of an eye. I see it when I land in a foreign country. I see it in my own neighborhood.

In three hours I will be rich. In five hours I can only eat out once a month. In thirteen hours I can buy myself an apartment paying full cash. But right now, in this moment I could face foreclosure on my home. Which one of these scenarios is real?

9

REINVENTING MONEY:
AN ECOSYSTEMATIC APPROACH

BERNARD LIETAER, ROBERT ULANOWICZ
& SALLY GOERNER

CRISIS OF 2008

By now, everybody knows that we are still experiencing the ramifications of the biggest global financial crisis since the 1930s. The
causes of this crisis will be debated for years to come. Some are
blaming unrestrained greed; others a "sorcerer's apprentice" problem in which financial engineering created products too complex
even for their creators; still others condemn excessive financial
deregulation, incompetence by bankers and/or regulators, or even
willful manipulation. However, all policy debates focuses typically
on how to limit the excesses laid bare by the last financial crisis,
as if this crisis is the only systemic one that has taken place so far.
While the 2007–08 crisis was the biggest, the International Monetary Fund (IMF) has identified no less than 122 systemic banking
crashes preceding this one since the 1970s![1] To this, they add 208
monetary crashes and 72 sovereign debt crises. By now, such systemic crises have hit more than three-quarters of the 180 countries
that are members of the IMF. If we want to ensure that "it never
happens again" as all policy makers ritually claim after each crash,
would it not make sense to start looking at the whole forest, rather
than any specific tree?

From our perspective, what all this means is that we have now entered the period of unprecedented convergence of four planetary problems—climate change, financial instability, high unemployment, and the financial consequences of an aging society (as predicted in 1999 in Lietaer, *The Future of Money*). The ensuing crisis is playing out (and will continue to play out) in a classic two or three steps downward for every step upward pattern. Every small step upward (i.e., any temporary improvement) is predictably hailed as the end of the crisis. The same thing happened throughout the 1930s, and it is only after World War II that the expression "Great Depression" got used to refer back to that whole decade.[2] It is quite understandable—then as now—why governments, banks, and regulators make such statements, simply because, then as now, saying otherwise would only make the situation worse.

The next logical phase in this systemic crisis keeps unfolding as if on automatic pilot. Whatever governments do, the banks and other financial institutions will want to cut back drastically on their loans portfolios wherever possible, in order to rebuild their balance sheets after huge financial losses. Thus, while cutting back on its loan portfolio is a logical reaction for each individual bank, when they all do it simultaneously, it deepens the hole that is being collectively dug for the world economy and ultimately for the financial system itself.

> The second stage [of this economic crisis] is an attempt by the banks to cut their leverage and reduce their lending, so helping to drive the economy into recession. That will then feedback via bad debts in non-subprime lending and impact the capital strength of the banks. So we will see an adverse vicious circle of weak banks creating a weak economy which creates more weak banks.
> —Charles Goodhart, professor emeritus, London School of Economics

There is a super bubble that has been going on for twenty-five years or so that started in 1980 when Margaret Thatcher became prime minister and Ronald Reagan became president. That is when the belief that markets are best left to their own devices became the dominant belief. Based on that, we had a new phase of globalization of financial markets and liberalization of financial markets. The idea is false. Markets do not correct towards equilibrium. … the whole construct, this really powerful financial structure, has been built on false grounds. For the first time, the entire system has been engaged in this [economic] crisis.

—George Soros, global financier and philanthropist

The Economist editorialized in its lead story on October 11, 2008, "Confidence is everything in finance … With a flawed diagnosis of the causes of the crisis, it is hardly surprising that many policymakers have failed to understand its progression."[3] This chapter will show that this is indeed the case, although in a deeper way than *The Economist* itself believes.

The last time we dealt with a crisis of this scale, the 1930s, it ended up creating widespread totalitarianism and ultimately World War II. The trillion dollar questions are:

How can we do better this time?

What are the strategies that will prevent us getting caught in an economic tailspin?

What are *all* the available options for dealing with large-scale systemic banking crises?

WHY SAVE THE BANKS?

Since governments' initial response has been to bail out banks and other financial institutions, the first question must be: why should governments and taxpayers get involved in saving banks in the first place? After all, when a private business fails, it is considered part of the "creative destructiveness" that characterizes the capitalist system.[4] But when large banks fail, somehow that doesn't seem to apply, as shown again in the 2008 scenario.

The short answer to why banks are being saved is fear. Since banks enjoy the monopoly on creating money through providing loans, bankrupt banks means reduced credit, which in turn results in a lack of money for the rest of the economy. Without access to capital, most businesses contract, which causes mass unemployment and a host of collateral social problems. Thus, when banks are in trouble, they can trigger what is known as a "second wave" crisis, through a ferocious circle making a victim of the real economy: bad balance sheets in banks => credit restrictions => recession => worse bank balance sheets => further credit restrictions and so the spiral downward goes …

It is to avoid such a tailspin that governments feel the need to prop up the banks' balance sheets. The next logical step is also formulaic. Whenever a bank or group of banks is "too big to fail" and gets in trouble, the taxpayers end up footing the bill, so that they can start all over again. In the latest banking crisis, exactly as in the previous 122 major banking crises preceding it, taxpayer bailouts have been the answer in every instance. Central banks will help by providing an interest yield curve that makes it easy for financial institutions to earn a lot of money at no risk, and in some cases by buying back bad assets.[5]

Among earlier examples, the United States government, which funded Reconstruction Finance Corporation during 1932–53 period, repeated the exercise with the Resolution Trust Corporation for the Savings and Loan crisis in the 1989–95 period, and again with the Troubled Asset Relief Program (TARP) of 2008. Other examples include the Swedish Bank Support Authority (1992–96) and the Japanese Resolution and Collection Corporation since 1996. For the 2008 international crisis, the amounts involved are unprecedented. Usually, the costs of the U.S. bailout refer to the $700 billion of the emergency Troubled Assets Relief Program (TARP) that was spectacularly squeezed through Congress during the last months of the administration of President George Bush. In reality, the actual cost to the American taxpayer of the bailout exceeds $4.616 trillion![6] This includes the direct loans to Wall Street companies and banks, purchases of toxic assets, and support for the mortgage and mortgage-backed securities markets through federal housing agencies. This is an astonishing 32 percent of our GDP (2008), 130 percent of the 2009 federal budget.

Bloomberg, which went to court to obtain the numbers from the administration, concludes with an amount at $7.4 trillion.[7] The most comprehensive estimate was performed by an ex–Wall Street insider. Before becoming a journalist, Nomi Prins worked on Wall Street as a managing director at Goldman Sachs, and running the international analytics group at Bear Stearns in London. Her estimate includes all the types of supports provided by both the U.S. Treasury and the Federal Reserve and comes up with a mind-boggling total of $14.4 trillion![8]

To put things into perspective, even the lowest of these estimates ($4.6 trillion) is greater than the entire inflation adjusted costs of World War II borne by the United States. Indeed, WWII cost the U.S. at the time $288 billion, which adjusted for inflation would amount to $3.6 trillion today. It is even harder to believe, but true, that $4.6 trillion is higher than the inflation adjusted costs of the Louisiana Purchase, the New Deal and the Marshall Plan, the Korean and Vietnam Wars, the S&L debacle, and the NASA race to the moon combined![9]

This begs the question: at what point do the costs for rescuing the bank system become unbearable? Governments learned in the 1930s that they can't afford to let the banking system go under, as this brings down the entire economy. What they may learn in our times is that they can't afford to save the banking system.

REREGULATION OF THE FINANCIAL SECTOR

As after every crisis, the political leitmotiv is to "ensure that it never happens again," and the solution that is invariably proposed is to tighten regulations on banks to plug the holes through which the latest problem showed up. History shows, however, that we have engaged in the same cat-and-mouse game between regulators and banks for several centuries, actually since the beginning of handing the money issuance function to the private banking system. To be precise, while such reregulation may avoid the repetition of the identical traps and abuses next time, over time, new loopholes will be discovered or created, resulting in a new variation of the same type of banking crisis.[10]

In addition, massive and very sophisticated lobbying is mobilized to reduce the scope of reregulation, or to provide useful loopholes from the beginning. Let us take the example of Washington, because it is one of the few places where we do have relatively reliable numbers on lobbying. During the debate on reregulation of the U.S. banking system, more than three full-time lobbyists were working for the banks for every elected official! Is it surprising that all the talk ended up with relatively marginal changes in the system?

CONVENTIONAL SOLUTIONS: NATIONALIZATIONS

There are two conventional ways for governments to prop up the banks' balance sheets, both involving a form of nationalization. The first is nationalizing what Ben Bernanke called in his presentation to the U.S. Congress the banking system's "toxic assets." The second is nationalizing the banks themselves. Let's briefly explore the advantages and disadvantages of both.

NATIONALIZING THE TOXIC ASSETS

This solution is invariably preferred by the banks themselves. It consists of either the government (in the initial Paulson bailout plan, for example, it is the U.S. Treasury Department) or a specially created institution funded by the government buying assets from the banks that they now want to jettison. Of course, determining the price at which these assets are purchased is a very tricky issue, particularly when a liquid market for such assets has dried up completely, as was the case in 2008.

Buying the toxic assets clearly doesn't convince everybody as an appropriate remedy.[11] It is also by far the most expensive solution, because it doesn't take advantage of the leveraging factor available in the banking system. Consequently, the injection of money by the government as capital directly to the banks is a lot more effective financially.

NATIONALIZING THE BANKS

The second way to buttress the banks is by governments providing capital directly to banks themselves, either by buying stocks or by acquiring a newly issued preferred stock. In Europe, governments have typically taken the bank nationalization road: it was the option taken for instance in Sweden in 1992; and in 2008, first for Northern Rock in the UK, and then for a wide range of banks in all countries by mid-October.

There are two advantages in this approach compared to the previous one of nationalizing the toxic assets. First, thanks to the fractional banking system by which all money is created, when banks make loans to customers, they can create new money at a multiplier of the amount of capital they actually have. Consequently, if a bank's "leveraging factor" is 10, then injecting $1 billion in the bank's capital makes it possible for it to create at least $10 billion in new money, or carry $10 billion in problem assets. In fact, the multiplier is typically much higher. For instance, Lehman Brothers's and Goldman Sachs's ratio of assets to capital were respectively 30 and 26, before they both disappeared. Some European banks have had an even higher leverage: BNP Parisbas at 32; Dexia's and Barclays's both estimated at about 40; UBS's at 47; and Deutsche Bank's at a whopping 83.17.[12] Therefore, very conservatively put, it is ten times more financially effective for governments to bolster the balance sheets of the banks directly than to buy toxic assets.

The second advantage to buying bank shares instead of toxic assets is that there is generally a market that indicates some relative value between different banks. In contrast, when the market for toxic assets has dried up, there is no such indication, and the decisions can be quite arbitrary.

The banks themselves, of course, prefer to avoid the dilution of bank equity and control that this approach implies. Politically, nationalizing the banks also sounds like the "socialization" of the economy, since the former communist states nationalized their banks. This ideological taint may explain why this approach was not initially considered in Washington.

UNRESOLVED PROBLEMS

The first objection to nationalizing banks or their toxic assets is the well-known "moral hazard" problem. If banks know that they will be saved when in trouble, they may be tempted to take higher risks than otherwise prudent. When these risks pay off, the profits are held privately and translated into generous dividends for the banks' shareholders and extraordinary bonuses to management. But when they fail, the losses end up being absorbed by the taxpayers. The current salvage programs confirm that this problem hasn't gone away and is unavoidably further strengthened by new bailouts. Christine Lagarde, minister of economic affairs, finances, and industry in France, stated, "Moral hazard has to be dealt with later … Maintaining the functioning of our markets is the top priority."[13]

This is exactly the argument that pops up at every systemic crisis.

Secondly, even if both strategies—bailing out the banks and reregulation of the financial sector—were implemented reasonably well, neither resolves the "second wave" problem: The banking system will get caught in a vicious circle of credit contraction that invariably accompanies the massive deleveraging that will be needed. Depending on how the reregulation is implemented, it may actually inhibit banks from providing the finances needed for a reasonably fast recovery of the real economy. In any case, given the size of the losses to be recovered, it will take many years, in the order of a decade, certainly more than enough time to bring the real economy into real trouble.

In practice, this means we are only at the beginning of a long, drawn-out economic unraveling. The social and political implications for such a scenario are hard to fathom. The last time we faced a problem of this size and scope was in the 1930s, and that event resulted in social and economic problems that ended up manifesting violently in a wave of fascism and ultimately World War II. Still, there are important differences vis-à-vis the situation of the 1930s. So far, the situation is less extreme economically, in unemployment and business bankruptcies, than what happened in the 1930s. On the other hand, governments are now a lot more indebted than was the case at the beginning of the Great Depression, and today's crisis is a lot more global than was the case then.

More important still, a financial/banking issue isn't the only one we have to deal with. It happens to coincide with several major global challenges, by now generally accepted: climate change and mass species extinction, the increase of structural unemployment, and the financial consequences of unprecedented aging in our societies. In some respects, therefore, today's crisis is less dramatic, and in others far worse than what the previous generation had to face.

NATIONALIZING THE MONEY CREATION PROCESS

Nationalizing the money creation process itself is an old proposal; though a less conventional approach, it reappears periodically in the "monetary reform" literature, particularly during periods of major banking crises such as the 2008 crisis. For historical reasons, the right to create money was transferred to the banking system as a privilege, originally to finance wars during the seventeenth century. So, contrary to what some people believe, our money isn't created by the governments or the central banks: it is created as bank debt. When banks are private, as they are in most of the world, the creation of money is therefore a private business. If the banking system abuses this prerogative, this privilege could or should be withdrawn. The logic is not new: money is a public good, and the right of issuing legal tender belongs at least theoretically to governments.

So, while bailing out the banking system through nationalizing banks or nationalizing the problem assets is the classical policy choice, it can also be expected that proposals for nationalizing the money creation process itself will reemerge, as they have in previous predicaments, including the 1930s. Under a government-run monetary system, the governments would simply spend money into existence without incurring interest at its creation; banks would become only brokers of money they have on deposit, not creators of money, as is the case now.

This would definitely make systemic banking crises a problem of the past. It would also make it possible to relaunch the economy through a large-scale Keynesian stimulus at a much lower cost to the taxpayers, given that the money thus created wouldn't require interest payments to be reimbursed in the future.

One objection to a government managing the monetary system is that governments may abuse this power, issue more money than is appropriate, and thereby create inflation. That argument is valid. However, given that the current method of creating money through bank-debt made the twentieth century one of the highest inflationary centuries on the historical record, inflation is obviously not a problem specific to the process of money issuance by governments. Furthermore, there is no reason that Milton Friedman's proposal for the issuance of money by the central banks couldn't be applied to governments as well: put in place a rule that obliges the issuing body to increase spending by no more than a fixed 2 percent per year, reflecting the improvements of productivity in the economy.

The most important reason that this solution is unlikely to be implemented is that it will be doggedly resisted by the banking system itself. The financial system has always been and remains today a powerful lobby, and losing the right to create money would hit it at the core of its current business model.[14]

Our own objection to this solution is that, even if governments were to issue the money, while that might protect us from banking crises, it would nevertheless not solve the core systemic problem of the instability of our money system. In short, it might protect us from banking crises, but not from monetary crises.

UNDERSTANDING SYSTEMIC STABILITY AND VIABILITY

The solution we propose below is new, and relates to the identification of the fundamental systemic reason for our monetary and financial instability. Understanding this solution, however, requires that we review some evidence as to why a systemic problem is likely, that we develop a scientifically sound understanding of its nature, and, finally, that we identify effective ways to address the trouble.

The good news now is that we know a lot more than in the 1930s, and that we have many more tools available than even a decade ago. Consequently, it is now possible to identify the deeper underlying systemic causes as well as a new way to deal with them.

Furthermore, this new way is one that governments can afford, and that actually addresses a number of other social and economic issues that exist even when there is no financial crisis.

At first sight, it may not be the bankers' preferred solution, but it would actually stabilize their own portfolios while structurally stabilizing the economies of the world. It would also give them a whole new line of business, in activities that would be particularly attractive for local and regional banks. Introducing such a systemic solution is the only way to avoid periodically repeating the banking crisis exercise, which all conventional approaches are condemned to do because they deal only with some of the symptoms, and not the cause.

BEYOND THE BLAME GAME

A lot of energy and ink have been spent trying to allocate the blame for this disaster. Greed in the financial sector, lack of oversight by regulators, policies that overemphasize deregulation, and incompetence at various levels have all become favorite targets. Our view is that any or all of these may indeed have played a role, but at the core we are dealing, as already stated, with a much deeper systemic issue.

Floating exchanges rates, introduced by President Nixon in 1971, were the last structural change introduced into the global monetary architecture, and are increasingly being blamed as another cause for the instabilities. However, even before this period, boom-and-bust cycles involving banking and monetary crises were, in Charles Kindleberger's words, a remarkably "hardy perennial." Kindleberger inventories no less than forty-eight massive crashes, ranging from the 1637 tulip mania in Holland to the 1929 crash on Wall Street.

Such repeated financial breakdowns, in very different countries and times, under different regulatory environments, and in economies with very different degrees of development, should be seen as a first telltale symptom of some underlying systemic or structural problem.

If such a deeper issue is involved, it would explain why each new set of regulations achieves, at best, a reduction in the frequency of banking and monetary crises, without getting rid of them or their horrific economic and socio-political costs. If such a deeper structural problem exists, it would also explain why even some of the brightest and best-educated people on the planet have not been able to avoid major financial catastrophes, however diligently they do their work, whether on the regulatory or on the financial services side. Finally, if our money system is indeed a structural "accident waiting to happen," then even if it were possible to perfectly control greed through innovative, tight regulations, this could only defer when the next disaster would hit.

STABILITY AND SUSTAINABLE VIABILITY IN COMPLEX FLOW SYSTEMS

We now have scientific evidence that a structural issue is indeed involved. The theoretical origin of this evidence may be surprising to the economic or financial community, although it wouldn't be such a surprise for scientists familiar with natural ecosystems, thermodynamics, and complexity or information theory. The science that explains this issue rests on a thermodynamic approach with deep historical roots in economics.[15]

In this view, complex systems, such as ecosystems, living organisms, and economies, are all seen as matter-, energy-, and information-flow systems. For example, the famous food chain is actually a matter-/energy-/flow-network built of complex relationships among organisms. Plants capture the sun's energy with photosynthesis; animals eat the plants; species then eat each another in a chain to top predator; only to have all organisms die, decompose, and have their energy/matter be recycled by bacteria. Similarly, economies are circulation networks consisting of millions of businesses and billions of customers exchanging different products and services, which when taken as a whole, are supposed to meet the needs of all participants.

For the past twenty-five years, major progress has been made on understanding what makes natural ecosystems sustainable or not. This work is the natural extension of Nobel Prize–winning chemist Ilya Prigogine's and Club of Rome cofounder Erich Jantsch's work with self-organizing energy-flow systems. In fact, according to Kenneth Boulding, many early economists held energy-based views of economic processes. This changed when those who favored Newtonian mechanics during the late nineteenth century (such as Léon Walras and William Stanley Jevons) turned economics into today's familiar views on the mechanics of "rational actors" and the reliable self-restraint of general equilibrium theory, an approach which completely dominates not only practically all of today's mainstream academic economic literature, but also the boardrooms and political venues of the world.[16]

A growing body of empirical and theoretical work, published under different academic banners such as self-organization theory, universality theory or nonlinear dynamics, shows that all flow systems follow certain universal principles and patterns.[17] Consequently, as Sally Goerner says about universality: "all [flow] systems, no matter how complex, fall into one of a few classes. All members of a class share certain common patterns of behavior." Similarly, Predrag Cvitanovic explains, "The wonderful thing about this universality is that it does not matter much how close our equations are to the ones chosen by nature; as long as the model is in the same universality class … as the real system, both will undergo a period-doubling sequence. That means that we can get the right physics out of very crude models."[18]

The existence of parallel patterns and dynamics explains why similar energy-flow concepts and analysis methods apply to economic systems as well as natural ones. Decades of studying natural ecosystems, in particular, have led to very sophisticated mathematical understandings of how a network structure affects an ecosystem's long-term viability, as judged by its balance between efficacy and resilience. Efficacy measures the ability of a system to process volumes of the relevant matter-, energy- and/or information-flow.

Resilience measures the ability of a system to recover from a disturbance. These variables have been more formally defined as follows:

1. Efficacy: a network's capacity to perform in a sufficiently organized and efficient manner as to maintain its integrity over time;[19] and
2. Resilience: a network's reserve of flexible fallback positions and diversity of actions that can be used to meet the exigencies of novel disturbances and the novelty needed for ongoing development and evolution.[20]

Two key structure-related variables—diversity (the existence of different types of agents acting as "nodes" in the network) and interconnectivity (number of pathways between agents)—play a central role in both efficacy and resilience but in the opposite direction. In general, a system's resilience is enhanced by more diversity and more connections, because there are more channels to fall back on in times of trouble or change. Efficacy, on the other hand, increases through streamlining, which usually means reducing diversity and connectivity.

The main point is that nature never selects for maximum efficacy, but for an optimal balance between the two opposing poles of efficacy and resilience. Because both are indispensable for long-term sustainability and health, the healthiest flow systems are those that maintain an optimal balance between these two opposing pulls. Conversely, an excess of either attribute leads to systemic instability. Too much efficacy leads to brittleness and too much resilience leads to stagnation: the former is caused by too little diversity and connectivity, and the latter by too much diversity and connectivity.

Sustainability of a complex flow system can therefore be defined as the optimal balance between efficacy and resilience of its network. With these distinctions we are able to define and precisely quantify a complex system's sustainability in a single metric. Indeed, we now have a way of quantitatively measuring all the relevant components separately: total throughput, efficacy, and resilience. Furthermore, the underlying mathematics are well behaved enough so that there exists only one single maximum for a given network system. The generic shape of the relationships between sustainability and its constituent elements is such that there is an asymmetry: optimality requires more resilience than efficacy!

Until recently, total throughput and efficacy have been the only means for us to identify the relative success of a system, whether in nature or in economics. For example, in ecosystems, as in economies, size is generally measured as the total volume of system throughput/activity. Gross Domestic Product (GDP) measures size this way in economies, while Total System Throughput

(TST) does so in ecosystems. Many economists urge endless growth in size (GDP) because they assume growth is a sufficient measure of health. GDP and TST, however, are poor measures of sustainable viability because they ignore network structure. They cannot, for example, distinguish between a resilient economy and a bubble that is doomed to burst—or between healthy "development," as Herman Daly describes it, and explosive growth in monetary exchanges simply due to runaway speculation.

Now, however, we can distinguish whether a particular increase in throughput and efficacy is a sign of healthy growth or just a relatively short-term bubble that is doomed to collapse. Over time, nature must have solved many of the structural problems in ecosystems (otherwise, these ecosystems simply wouldn't exist today.)

APPLICATION TO OTHER COMPLEX SYSTEMS

The question will undoubtedly be raised whether what we learn from ecosystems still makes sense when applied to other systems, such as economic communities. It is critical to understand that the findings described so far arise from the very structure of a complex system, and therefore that they remain valid for any complex network with a similar structure, regardless of what is being processed in the system: it can be biomass in an ecosystem, information in a biological system, electrons in an electrical power network, or money in an economic system. This is precisely one of the strong points of using a weblike network approach instead of machine-like metaphor.

The fields of engineering, business, and economics have all been focusing almost exclusively on efficacy, and therefore constitute a wide open field to explore the validity of the proposed metrics to improve sustainability. For example, electrical power grids have been systematically optimized for decades toward ever-greater technical and economic efficacy. It has come as a surprise to many engineers that, as they have approached higher efficiencies, suddenly large-scale blackouts have been breaking out with a vengeance "out of nowhere." For instance, large-scale blackouts have hit huge areas of the United States and Northern Germany. Among the famous ones, we should mention the 1965 blackout in New York, or the Northeastern United States blackout of 2003, and the November 2006 blackout hitting much of Western Europe. But, even excluding lightings and other catastrophic natural events, on the average every four months a power outage large enough to darken at least five million American homes occurs. The data should be available to model these systems as networks because that is what they literally are. One can then quantify their efficacy and resilience. The solution on how to rebalance such a system to make it less brittle, and to determine its optimal sustainability, would be an obvious "hard science" test application of the metrics described here.

The point being made here is truly profound and has wide-reaching implications for all complex systems, natural or human-made, including our worldwide financial and monetary system.

Placing too much emphasis on efficacy tends to automatically increase size and consolidation at the expense of diversity, connectivity, and resilience until the entire system becomes unstable and collapses. In short, excessive focus on efficacy tends to create exactly the kind of bubble economy that we have been able to observe repeatedly in every boom-and-bust cycle in history, including the biggest bust of them all, the 2008 crisis and its aftermath.

APPLICATION TO FINANCIAL/MONETARY SYSTEMS

Viewing economies as flow systems ties directly into money's primary function as a medium of exchange. In this view, money is to the real economy like blood is to your body: it is an essential vehicle for catalyzing processes, allocating resources, and generally allowing the exchange system to work as a synergetic whole. The connection to structure is immediately apparent. In economies, as in ecosystems and living organisms, the health of the whole depends heavily on the structure by which the catalyzing medium, in this case, money, circulates among businesses and individuals. Money must continue to circulate in sufficiency to all corners of the whole because poor circulation will strangle either the supply side or the demand side of the economy, or both.

Our global monetary system is itself an obvious flow network structure, in which monopolistic national currencies flow within each country (or group of countries in the case of the euro), and interconnect on a global level. The technical justification for enforcing a monopoly of national currencies within each country was to optimize the efficacy of price formation and exchanges in national markets. Tight regulations are in place in every country to maintain these monopolies. In his seminal 1955 paper on this topic, Milton Friedman proposed that letting markets determine the value of each national currency would further improve the overall efficacy of the global monetary system. This idea was actually implemented by President Nixon in 1971, to avoid a run on the dollar at that time. Since then, an extraordinarily efficient and sophisticated global communications infrastructure has been built to link and trade these national currencies. According to the Bank of International Settlements (BIS), the trading volume in the foreign exchange markets reached an impressive $4 trillion per day in 2007, and the derivatives are not included in that statistic! Nobody questions the efficacy of these markets, but many people are now coming to question their resilience.

The global network of our monopolistic national moneys has evolved into an overly efficient and dangerously brittle system. This system's lack of resilience, however, shows up not in the technical field of the computer networks (which all have backups), but clearly in the financial realm. This fact has been spectacularly demonstrated by the large number of monetary and banking crashes over the past thirty-five years. Such crises—particularly a combined monetary and banking crash—are, other than war, the worst thing that can happen to a country.

Even more ironically, whenever a banking crisis unfolds, governments invariably help the larger banks to absorb the smaller ones, under the logic that the efficacy of the system is thereby further increased.

Today's global monetary ecosystem is significantly overshooting the optimal balance, because of its exclusive emphasis on efficacy. It is careening toward brittleness and collapse because a general belief prevails that all improvements need to go further in that the same exclusive direction of increasing growth and efficacy. For instance, the global monoculture of bank-debt money as legal tender is technically justified on the basis of efficacy of price formation and exchanges within each country. Internationally, floating exchanges were also justified because they make the foreign exchange markets "more efficient." An overly efficient system is an accident waiting to happen. In observing the dynamics of an artificially enforced monoculture in a complex system where efficacy is the only criterion considered relevant, we find that the only possible outcome is systemic collapse.

As stated earlier, nature has over billions of years selected the conditions under which complex ecosystems are sustainable; otherwise they wouldn't exist today. In contrast, humanity still struggles with the issue of how to create sustainable economies. We know that the theoretical framework applies to both natural and man-made complex systems. Has the time not come to learn in this domain from nature?

THE SYSTEMIC SOLUTION

The systemic solution to our monetary crisis, therefore, is to increase the resilience of the monetary system, even if at first sight that may be less efficient. Conventional economic thinking assumes the de facto monopolies of national moneys as an unquestionable given. The logical lesson from nature is that systemic monetary sustainability requires a diversity of currency systems, so that multiple and more diverse agents and channels of monetary links and exchanges can emerge.

This is the practical lesson from nature: allow several types of currencies to circulate among people and businesses to facilitate their exchanges, through the implementation of complementary currencies. These different types of currencies are called complementary because they designed to operate in parallel with, as complements to, conventional national moneys. The problem is the monopoly of one type of currency, and replacing one monopoly with another isn't the solution.

As Edgar Cahn's work on Time Dollars demonstrates,[21] whenever complementary currencies begin flowing through the mainstream, the degree of diversity and interconnectivity in the system will increase, due to their ability to catalyze business processes and individual efforts that are too small or inefficient to compete for national currencies in a global marketplace. This approach will certainly appear unorthodox to conventional thinking, but conventional thinking is precisely what got us into this trouble to begin with. This tactic can also resolve the dilemma of what to do now about today's systemic banking crisis.

OUR PROPOSAL

Our proposal focuses here on what can and should be done most urgently to reduce the impact of the financial crisis on the "real" economy, the one where businesses produce and sell nonfinancial goods and services. It involves three components: (a) actions by the private business sector, (b) decisions by national governments, and (c) decisions by city and local governments.

THE BUSINESS SECTOR

The "real" economy is predictably becoming the biggest victim of the ongoing financial crisis. Whatever governments do for the banks, credit will be a lot harder for companies to obtain from banks for years to come. However, there is something that companies can do themselves to avoid the worst aspects of this problem. It is possible for companies to lead themselves out of this crisis.

THE WIR IN SWITZERLAND: A CASE STUDY

Once upon a time, during a crisis similar to the one in which we are now mired, sixteen businessmen got together to decide what they could do among themselves. They or their clients had each received a notice from their respective banks that their credit line was going to be reduced or eliminated; hence bankruptcy was only a question of time. They realized that business A had needed the bank loan to buy goods from business B, which in turn needed money to buy stuff from its own suppliers. So they decided to create a mutual credit system among themselves, inviting their clients and suppliers to join. When business A bought something from B, A got a debit and B the corresponding credit. They created their own currency, whose value was identical to the national money, but with the interesting feature that it didn't bear interest.

The country's banks mounted a massive press campaign to try to squelch this revolutionary idea. Miraculously, that campaign failed, and this little system saved the businesses involved at the time. A cooperative was set up among the users to keep the accounts dealing with that currency. Soon participants could also borrow from that cooperative in that currency at the remarkably low interest rate of 1 percent. All such loans needed to be backed by inventory or other assets. Over time, the system grew to include up to one-quarter of all the businesses of the entire country.

Sixty-five years later, James Stodder from Rensselaer Polytechnic Institute performed an econometric study proving that the secret for the country's legendary economic stability was that strange little unofficial currency, circulating among businesses in parallel with the national money. That well-known economic resilience was usually credited to some mysterious and unknown national characteristic. Stodder's remarkable quantitative study used more than sixty years of high quality data to prove the points made in this story.[22]

Whenever there was a recession, the volume of activity in this unofficial currency would expand significantly, thereby reducing the recession's impact on sales and unemployment. Whenever there was a boom, business in national currency expanded, while activity in the unofficial currency proportionally dropped back again. The surprising implication of this study is that the spontaneous counter-cyclical behavior of this little "unorthodox" system actually helped the central bank of the country in its efforts to stabilize the economy.

This is not a fairy tale, but the true story of the WIR system in Switzerland; the sixteen founders met in Zurich in the year 1934, and the system is still operating today. The annual volume of business in the WIR currency is now about $2 billion per year. The WIR system is also now accepting deposits and making loans in Swiss francs as well as in WIR. The biggest limitation of the WIR system is that WIR are not convertible into national money. Therefore, credits earned in WIR need to be spent on good and services of other members of the same network. That limitation has now been resolved thanks to another complementary currency innovation called the Commercial Credit Circuit (C3).

COMMERCIAL CREDIT CIRCUITS (C3)

It is also a well-known fact that the vast majority of private jobs (between 80 and 90 percent) are provided by small and medium sized enterprises (SMEs). And the survival of many such firms is now increasingly at risk because of cash flow problems.

SMEs are being pressured by suppliers for prompt payments, say within thirty days, while their larger customers pay them only in ninety or more days. This becomes a deadly cash flow trap whenever banks refuse to provide bridge financing, or do so at steep conditions. This problem has become more critical recently in developed countries under the impact of the financial crisis, but it has long been an endemic issue in developing countries.

The Social Trade Organisation (STRO), a Dutch research and development NGO, has successfully developed business models over the past decade in several Latin American countries which culminated with a financial innovation that structurally addresses this precise challenge. The process uses insured invoices or other payment claims as liquid payment instruments within a business-to-business clearing network. Each recipient of such an instrument has the choice to either cash it in national money (at a cost), or directly pay its own suppliers with the proceeds of the insured invoice. This is achieved via the following six steps:

1. Participating businesses start by securing an invoice insurance up to a predetermined amount, based on the specific credit worthiness of their own business and of the claims they obtain on third parties.

2. The business that has obtained such an insurance (hereafter referred to as business A) opens a checking account in the clearing network, electronically exchanges the insured invoice for clearing funds, and pays its supplier (business B) immediately and fully with those clearing funds via the clearing network.

3. To receive its payment, business B only needs to open its own checking account in the network. Business B has now two options: either cashing it in for conventional national money (at the cost of paying the interest for the outstanding period, e.g., ninety days, plus banking fees); or pay its own suppliers with the corresponding clearing funds (at no cost).

4. Whatever the timing of the payment is to business A, business B is in a position to use the positive balance on its account in the network, for instance to pay its supplier, business C.

5. Business C only needs to open an account in the network. It has then the same two options as business B: cash it in for national money, or spend it in the network. And so on ...

6. At maturity of the invoice, the network gets paid the amount of the invoice in national money, either by business A or by the insurance company (in case of default of business A). Whoever owns at that point the proceeds of the insured invoice can cash them in for national money without incurring any interest costs.

The implementation of a C3 a system has distinct benefits for businesses, governments, and banks.

Businesses increase their access to short-term credit as needed to improve their working capital and the use of their productive capacity. The size of this credit can be built up to a stable level between a quarter (covering therefore up to an average of ninety days of invoices) and half of annual sales, at a cost substantially lower than what is otherwise possible. Suppliers are paid immediately, regardless of the payment schedule of the original buyer, injecting substantial liquidity at very low cost in the entire SMEs network. The approach provides a viral spreading of participation to the C3 networks from clients to suppliers. The technology is a proven one, doesn't require any new legislation or government approvals, and the necessary software is available in open source.[23] Only invoices that are 100 percent guaranteed, and 100 percent computerized, are acceptable in a C3 system. C3 thereby encourages the generalization and more efficient use of IT infrastructure among SMEs, including the opening of new markets and marketing channels through e-commerce.

Governments, particularly regional governments, will also benefit. Notice that the most effective way for governments at any level to encourage the implementation of the C3 strategy is for them to accept payment of taxes and fees in the C3 currency. This encourages everybody to accept the C3 currency in payment, and provides additional income to the government from transactions that otherwise wouldn't take place. Furthermore, that additional income becomes automatically available in conventional national currency at the latest ninety days after the payment, thereby not upsetting any existing procurement policies. The first country that has followed this strategy is Uruguay.

The C3 approach is also a dependable way to systemically reduce unemployment. Governments at different levels (EU, national, regional) can contribute to a joint guarantee mechanism.

Such a guarantee mechanism is considerably cheaper to fund than subsidies or other traditional approaches to reduce unemployment. C3 helps shift economic activities from the black or grey economy into the official economy, because SMEs need to be formally incorporated to participate, and all exchanges are electronic and therefore traceable.

C3 systems are best organized at a regional level, so that each network remains at a manageable scale. Businesses with an account in the same regional network have an incentive to spend their balances with each other, and thus further stimulate the regional economy. C3 provides a win-win environment for all participants, and therefore promotes other collaborative activities among regional businesses. Each C3 network should use the same insurance standards and compatible software so that they can interconnect as a network of networks to facilitate exchanges internationally.

The win-win approach of C3 also benefits banks and the financial system. As the entire C3 process is computerized, it significantly streamlines the lending and management for the insurance and loan providers. SMEs can therefore become a more profitable sector for banks, because the credit lines are negotiated with the entire clearing network, providing the financial sector with automatic risk diversification among the participants in the network. In the upcoming surge of new competitors in the market—such as Facebook, Google, or Tesco currencies and banks—this monetary innovation provides an additional window for banks to sell their core activities. Most banks are also involved in providing insurance services. C3 opens for them a whole new market for insurances and credit, all the way down to services for microfinance enterprises. As C3 is completely computerized, even such individually small-scale entities can now be serviced at a very low cost. Finally, the C3 mechanism systemically contributes to the stability of employment and of the entire economy, which is helpful for the overall solidity of the banks' portfolios.

We propose that businesses take the initiative of creating such business-to-business (B2B) systems at whatever scale makes most sense to them.

There is one more thing that the businesses that get involved in such systems should consider doing: lobbying their respective governments to have them accept their B2B currency in payment of business taxes. This could apply only temporarily, i.e., for the period during which the banking system will not be in a position to fulfill its traditional role of financing the "real" economy to the extent that is necessary. The lobbyists have a simple but powerful argument: it doesn't cost the government any money, will actually increase tax revenue, and is the best systemic way to reduce unemployment.

GOVERNMENTS

Governments will not be willing or able to force banks to lend out to the "real" economy, any more than you can push on a string. Therefore, in addition and parallel to accepting the usual bank-debt conventional money, accepting some complementary currency for payment of taxes makes a lot of sense. Which currencies should be acceptable for payment of what types of taxes is a political question that remains open for each government to decide.

They also have a built-in interest in receiving payments in a robust currency. It is obvious that the existence of such a currency facilitates exchanges that otherwise wouldn't happen, while conventional money or credit are difficult to obtain. These additional exchanges, in turn, increase the taxable income of the businesses involved, thereby starting a virtuous loop that counteracts the credit reductions by the banking system.

When people and businesses are strangled by lack of money, taxable income is automatically squeezed as well. By accepting some payments in currencies other than bank-debt money, by definition more governmental income is possible.

CITIES AND LOCAL GOVERNMENTS

There are two reasons why we recommend allowing cities and local governments to choose their own complementary currencies to implement this strategy. First, cities and local governments will be the first governmental entities to get into still deeper trouble than they are today; and second, they represent diversity and resilience at work. Given that this approach is radically new, it is simply safer to test out a new system as a pilot at a city or local level, rather than directly on a larger scale at the national level.

Indeed, cities and other local government entities will find themselves in the first line to bear the brunt of the social effects of the looming recession, while at the same time they will see their tax revenue shrink, and conventional financing through debt become much harder to obtain. This kind of problem is not going to be limited only to the United States.

The London-based *Observer* asks, "What could possibly come along in the middle of this series of economic nightmares to make things even worse? How about a total depletion of local government finances that pay for the things that make up the very fabric of American society? Imagine that rippling across the rest of the world, reducing public services to skeleton operations." Such ramifications are further explored by fiscal analyst Sujit Canagaretna:

> What is most disconcerting about the way this turmoil is panning out is that most state governments were already in a terrible state. But now things have worsened considerably and the credit markets have a real choke hold on almost all state treasuries. It is so bad that economic activity in most states has all but ground to a halt.[24]

The second argument for local currencies is that some diversity in experimenting with a new strategy can only be beneficial to all concerned. If specific issues are considered a political priority, other types of complementary currencies than the B2B ones described above could be considered. For instance, if carbon reduction is considered an important priority, a carbon reduction currency program could be launched and accepted in partial payment in taxes. Some applications of the eco-money programs in Japan are relevant precedents in this domain.

Similarly, local or regional taxes could be paid partially in conventional money, and partially in regional currencies. In short, a whole new set of tools to create incentives for specific behavior patterns, either corporate or individual, is now available, tools that in most cases have already been tested somewhere in the world.

Obviously, implementing a strategy of this nature should be done in careful steps, starting with pilot application on a limited scale. A European-wide project, for instance, should be started with a cooperative venture on a smaller scale.

ANSWERING SOME OBJECTIONS

The first objection will obviously arise from the banking system, which would prefer to keep the status quo. However, banks are going to be disintermediated by a broader use of B2B currencies only if they themselves remain aloof.

The second objection that is quite predictable will come from traditional economic thinking: using multiple currencies within a national economy reduces the efficacy of the price formation process and of the exchanges among economic agents. While this argument is valid, we know now that this overarching emphasis on efficacy is precisely what has reduced the resilience of the system, and made it so brittle.

SOME ADVANTAGES OF THE PROPOSED APPROACH

Our proposal, therefore, provides a systemic solution to the instability of the monetary system, something that the current approaches are not even trying to achieve. Systemic solutions are the only ones that will avoid repeatedly having to go through the same type of problem in the future. For example, as the WIR example demonstrates, complementary currency systems have proven to be a key factor in fostering counter-cyclical stability.

A multiscale multistakeholder strategy has a number of advantages for the different parties involved, particularly during the transition period that we now have entered. Leadership will be required at all levels—public and private, local and national—to guide ourselves out of this crisis.

- This approach will avoid or reduce the strangulation of the real economy by the banking credit contraction that unquestionably is going to continue for a while.
- The decision that governments should reach—accepting payment of taxes in money other than exclusively bank-debt money—rests completely within their own political decision power. This strategy is also very flexible: a government can decide to accept payment of certain taxes only, only for a given percentage, for specific types of complementary currencies chosen for their robustness and have other positive effects, and/or only for specific fiscal years.
- Until now, taxes have been payable only in "legal tender," which means conventional bank-debt money. Any currency is an incentive scheme, and our current way of dealing with taxes and subsidies is limited to that single instrument, which needs to be scarcer than its usefulness to keep its value. With complementary currencies, a whole additional array of options become available, which can focus on—and fine-tune precisely—the objectives that one wants to reach. We can, therefore, tailor the complementary currencies accepted for payments of taxes to the massive challenges currently faced around the world.

- Complementary currencies have proven a useful tool for enabling the design of incentive schemes in a wide variety of domains, regardless of whether a crisis is at hand. The evidence for this can be found in a number of publications.
- Perhaps most importantly: This strategy will avoid repeating the worst part of the 1930s scenario where economic strangulation was left to play out fully, which resulted in massive bankruptcies in the productive economy, intolerably high unemployment and untold suffering, and a toxic political fallout that has proven a dangerous mess to disentangle once started. Hjalmar Schacht, Hitler's central banker, pointed out correctly that the electoral popularity of Nazism was directly due to mass "despair and unemployment."

10

POVERTY (UN)CONSCIOUSNESS

ANTONIO LOPEZ

If you want an image of post–American Empire collapse, there is at least one contemporary portrait to draw upon. It looks a bit like a nuclear war circa 1958, which is akin to what I witnessed in Havana after the collapse of the Soviet Union and the subsequent "special period" that followed. By the mid-'90s Havana's massive deep port harbor was empty and there was little gas to drive the scant, duct-taped cars that still existed there, yet it amazed me how music and culture remained such a resilient tool of empowerment and happiness. People still played baseball, made love, wrote books, painted paintings, and jammed. In fact, in a postfinancial world, jamming might be a good skill to cultivate. Improvisation requires openness, creativity, and ingenuity, which certainly are the hallmarks of survival and evolution (both cultural and natural)—which helps explain why during this period Cuba emerged as a world innovator in organic agriculture. No doubt, it was also hard to walk down Havana's streets without being solicited by prostitutes and drug dealers, but when I visited there over a dozen years ago it was a veritable hub of African and Caribbean students who were there to take advantage of an innovative educational system focused on provisioning without industrial resources. And unlike the polluted and dangerous streets of modern capitalist cities, Havana's avenues were quiet, with the exception of the clanging bells of Chinese bicycles and the breezy music wafting through the air.

What is amazing about culture is how it persists in the face of cataclysmic adversity. Consider jazz, flamenco, reggae, and hip-hop as examples of high art forms that have absorbed and digested the oppression and destruction of so many lost lives. In the case of the Mexica (the tribal name for the Aztecs), their culture transcended the "conquest" because of an underlying philosophy, *flor y canto*— "flower and song." I put *conquest* in quotation marks because many of my Native American friends remind me that it's a transient state; consider the fate of Spain in the Americas. After five hundred years, who remains standing? Even in California, as urban historian Mike Davis argues, "USA" is a temporary identity. In the surviving poetry of preconquest culture, Mexica verse speaks of life's temporality, and how each of us is on loan to each other during our short lives on earth. Mexica poets were wise to know that empires come and go, but flower and song remain. Thus, an open, compassionate cultural architecture, though rare, is absolutely necessary. As the Dalai Lama has warned regarding the Chinese occupation of Tibet, to commit to violence in response to history is to go to war with oneself, because the heart and mind can never be united in such a quest. Flower and song will die, however, if we let civilization destroy our spirit.

In contrast to the survivors of Tibetan occupation or the Spanish invasion of the Americas, affluent Americans should count their blessings. Life has been prosperous and relatively safe by comparison to what so many have endured; we have benefited greatly by other people's misery, as the Situationists once pontificated. The world's "social majorities," whom our system has condemned mostly to death, war, exploitation, and malnutrition, may end up being our biggest teachers. Let us listen with open hearts to what they can teach us about survival in harsh economic times. One such teacher is the only artist I have heard everywhere I have traveled in the world: Bob Marley. That kind of wisdom doesn't come easily.

As it stands we will need lots of new allies. Due to the unfolding financial crisis, we Americans are likely on our way to joining the majority of the world in terms of economic resources, or the lack thereof. With deindustrialization, decapitalization, deconsumerism and all the other *d*'s that accompany Depression, this is a good wake-up call for a minority of the world's population with the highest per capita ecological footprint. Still, it goes without saying that economic decline is not happening without considerable pain and difficulty for many people. I don't mean to trivialize suffering, but we can survive. Ask an Aztec. Reflect on how the majority of the world manages while living with considerably less; in many cases the "poor" are significantly happier than rich Americans who consistently rank lowest in the world's happiness index (Indonesians, for example, are ranked as the happiest people in the world, despite their considerably lower standard of living than Europeans or Americans). We all know by this point that consumer goods don't equate with contentment. Having a refrigerator and dishwasher make life simpler, so we're told; yet when the final bill comes due, maybe that perceived comfort comes at a terrible cost of unmanageable economic and ecological complexity.

Oikos, the Greek root for ecology and economics, means "household." Like in Cuba, our financial home environment can be "disturbed," to borrow a term from ecology, but our reaction depends on the level of diversity maintained in our state of being. The lesson from ecology is that disturbances have less impact when there is greater biodiversity to absorb the change in an ecological system. Just like the tightrope walker's balance pole, the shorter it is, the less ability to absorb shock to the system. Like the Buddha said, add a touch of salt to a glass of water, and it will taste salty. But throw the same amount of salt into a lake, and you won't taste the difference.

Consider, then, that your attitude is potentially the most diverse asset at your disposal, because it is the one thing you have control over (that is, unless you let it control you, as is the case with most unconscious beings). We suffer from mechanistic interpretations of the world and act out of addictive behavior. It's not just about the collapse of the petroleum economy or the disintegration of the finance pyramid, but the implosion of the guiding paradigm of Western civilization. If you think the global elites have a grip on the situation, you are very wrong, because grip is the opposite of what we need. We are badly in need of an expansion of consciousness, and again, it is something you have access to: given an average baseline mental state, no amount of economic despair will prevent your mind from functioning as evolution intended.

Still, Marx was right when he argued that material conditions produce consciousness (we make history but not in the environment of our choosing). Let's not lose site of the fact that hunger and withdrawal can lead to desperation and confusion, while at the same time acknowledging that if you do have food in your stomach and a roof over your head, be thankful and continue to work on the big picture in little ways, both internally and externally.

George Bush Sr. once said that the American way of life is not negotiable. This kind of mentality will not handle the disturbance of crashing markets very well. That's why Americans, who are accustomed to a certain lifestyle, should reconsider what it means to be "wealthy." Lynne Twist, author of *The Soul of Money,* argues that "abundance" is the wrong material goal, both personally and socially. She says it's better to be "sufficient." I find this an aspiration that is in keeping with the justice and equity equation of ecological sustainability. It's in line with Gandhi's notion that the world has enough for our needs, but not for our greed. Sufficiency suggests that we live within our means, that we only consume that which is available in real time. The ecologically disembedded financial system has brought the world economy to its knees, reminding us that we have to stop borrowing against the planet's resource bank through our extraction of ancient solar energy, and return to using the solar energy that is available to us on a daily basis, such as from local agriculture and our labor. This is how our ancestors lived, and this is how the surviving humans of this age will carry on. Labor, especially with our hands, has been a dirty word since antiquity. It's time to reintroduce craft (work with our hands) as an asset and value. As such, DIY may be one of the best cultural attributes that Americans have for surviving this phase. But let's unify the "handiness" of DIY with spirituality as well. To paraphrase a Sufi saying, talk to God but tether your camel.

Sufficiency is a spiritual issue; a sufficient consciousness is in a state of gratitude. Many of us are blaming the capitalist bankers and system for the demise of our society, but haven't we as consumers also collectively bought into the hallucinatory orgy of the market? How many of us have harbored secret fantasies to be like the crazy guy in the infomercials with his yachts, beautiful women, and real estate Ponzi schemes? How many of my deepest spiritual allies have bought into those sleazy pyramid schemes or network marketing plots to sell new age happiness that turn friendships into marketing opportunities? Like the ideology of the capitalist system, are we always aspiring to a better, utopian future rather than being grateful for what we have?

I once participated in a "prosperity group," which was a weekly gathering of friends (mostly folks from my yoga class) who wanted to read a "channeled" book, *Creating Money,* and to do the chapter exercises together (it's a great book, by the way). I realized rather quickly that most people in the group would never transcend their state of "poverty," because they were mentally impoverished. That is, they believed that their lives lacked sufficient resources in that moment; they would always be trapped on the treadmill of negative thinking about their present state of being, postponing happiness to the future. I don't mean this in *The Secret* kind of way, in which positive thinking is the panacea for all of life's inner conflicts, but in the sense that we are constantly projecting into the world like a waking dream the innermost challenges at the core of our being. We relentlessly seek healing, and oftentimes we externalize from our inner depths that which cannot be articulated by the egocentric (and protective) mind. Consider how we attract substitutes for our parental figures in both our work and romantic relationships. Is money any different? Maybe some would consider *Secrets of the Millionaire Mind* a silly and exploitative airport self-help book, but I believe T. Harv Eker is onto something when he can detect whether or not someone has the capacity for "wealth." "We've confused attention with love," he argues. Joseph Jaworski in *Synchronicity* puts the problem this way: we mistake "having" with "being." Are we always putting the cart before the horse?

Again, returning to the metaphor of the glass of water with salt, can we really contain our true desires, or more to the point, our self-destructive thoughts? It's important to distinguish desire—something Buddhists say inevitably leads to suffering—from nourishment. Along these lines, after closely reading *Creating Money* I discovered something quite useful. The book asks us to imagine what our life would be like if we suddenly received a million dollars (or any large lump sum)—not to visualize the material goods we would accumulate, but to focus on the feeling. What emotion or sensation would it be? What state of consciousness am I aspiring to? At the time I was a struggling freelance writer, so my simple goal was that I wanted to be able to write without the stress of having to query editors and to pen BS articles to pay the rent. The exercise forced me to deconstruct my yearning and to discover why I wanted to write in the first place. I realized that it was because it allowed me to connect with a higher, creative force than what I normally experience in the routines of daily life; that I like to solve puzzles and explore ideas; and that I love to lose myself in the process of discovery. To put it in more intangible, esoteric terms, writing allows me to connect with the cosmos, which is this expansive architecture of creativity I keep alluding to. By the end of *Creating Money*'s visualization I learned something very important: I didn't need a million dollars to achieve my wish. All I had to do was to sit down and write. Problem solved.

The money would come later. Or not. But at least I would be happy doing what I love.

In retrospect, I was probably also grasping for something precious that we adults tend to lose when we "grow up." For a countercultural type like myself it will probably sound funny to say that my most precious moments in childhood involved building model airplanes and listening to Dodgers baseball games on the radio. In many ways we have not integrated these childhood experiences of exploration into our adult lives because we suffer from so much pressure, either from the material economy itself (let us remember that the recent stock market and financial crisis was not news to most of us who have been two paychecks from homelessness most of our lives), or from our wounded psyches still trying to prove our worth to disapproving parents. When I write, I feel like that kid solving problems while roaming a dream world.

All of this has to be put into some context. I'm well aware that everything I believe and say is benefited by my "cultural capital." That is, I'm the product of an investment of both my family and society in terms of education and opportunity. I'm self-conscious that what I say reeks of privilege. I have lived in a relatively affluent capitalist setting in which these experiences of inner exploration are permitted and encouraged. Still, I think it's OK to talk about achieving happiness within the realm of my given reality, even though I empathize with the person running from rockets and take a certain responsibility for being part of the problem (as my taxes paid for the missiles being fired at innocent civilians who live in the periphery of our walled electronic castle). In my world travels, I've been lucky to do so from the vantage of exploration and personal growth rather than as a migrant worker. But in the process I have encountered economically disadvantaged people who still maintain positive feelings about their reality because they have strong relationships with their community, family, and nature. Many have not been spiritually colonized by Western ideology. For example,

I recall a story I heard while living with a Hopi family. They reminisced about a time when government officials had come to tell them they were poor and that they needed help. In recalling the story, they laughed about the reaction of government agents when they said no thanks. To this day there is a brand new tractor sitting in the yard that was given to the family by well-meaning German philanthropists. It remains unused, and will do little good when the oil dries up, anyway. Many Hopi still plant corn with a stick and finger, and can harvest with the desert's morning dew. There is something highly advanced about that kind of simplicity.

The truth is that we all operate from the means that are available us. I just want to give thanks that I have lived a "sufficient" life and I hope that I can share whatever wisdom this life has afforded me. As it stands, by blogging I write for fun and generosity. I am fulfilled by the reciprocal relationship that media and communications of the Web 2.0 offer. Meanwhile, I can make money for my "services," which is teaching. For those of us with the means, the internet uniquely positions us to engage in service leadership, which means we help solve each other's problems. After all, we are just on loan to each other. In the midst of this richly unfolding economic crisis we can discover how the power of flower and song will sustain anyone with an alternate vision of our place in the world.

11

TIME BANKING IN SANTA FE

STELLA OSOROJOS

In January 2010, a group of Santa Fe volunteers excited about the opportunity to help their city transition through the economic shift and reweave community in the process launched a Time Bank. In a town known for its *mañana* attitude, the response has been phenomenal. Could this be the beginning of a new way of life?

Time Banks are the brainchild of Edgar Cahn, a Yale-trained lawyer who cofounded the National Legal Services Program and founded the Antioch School of Law. In 1980, while recuperating from a heart attack, Cahn thought up the concept of Time Dollars as a way to redress the chronic lack of funds available to solve important social problems. If money was getting in the way of fulfilling needs, he reasoned, why not just make up a new currency?

Time Dollars are based on the idea that everybody's hour is equal. When I do one hour's worth of work for Joy, I earn one Time Dollar to spend with Bob or Adrienne or Genevieve. What can be exchanged within a Time Bank is only limited by the services its members offer. It's similar to barter, except that I don't have to find an immediate match for my exchange. (Time Dollars are held in trust by the software that engines the whole thing.) And it's different from barter in that it's based on time and not cash value, which is why the IRS doesn't tax Time Bank exchanges. Additionally, Time Banks can be broad or narrow in their scope. There are examples of Time Banks that service specific populations, like people with disabilities, as well as specific missions, like church groups.

As we help people learn about Time Banking, the idea that seems to trip them up the most is that everybody's hour is equal. I can't tell you how many times people have asked me how many Time Dollars they should "charge" for their service, even when they understand the simple agreement that one hour equals one time dollar. Sometimes that equation doesn't feel like enough, especially if they have a clear understanding of what their service could earn within the cash economy. It's not a problem if a plumber or dentist or accountant doesn't feel comfortable offering their particularly valuable job skill on the Time Bank; we simply encourage them to offer different services.

Equally often, many people's instinct is to undervalue their work. In one case, a woman was asked to make a prom dress and determined that it would take forty hours to do so, but felt uncomfortable with what seemed to her to be such a "high price." It could be that she had an underlying inferiority complex that disallowed her from equating her time and talents with another person's, but I'm sure there were other forces at work as well, not least of which is the way that we value goods and services in this country. In an economy flush with cheap labor from oversees, the prices of prom dresses, out-of-season strawberries, etc., are kept artificially low. We simply don't understand the real value of things anymore. Time Banking helps remind us of what our goods and services costs us in human terms.

Time Banks also do a good job of reweaving community ties. Because our Time Bank exists alongside a cash economy, where we pay money for our plumbers, dentists, and accountants, people turn to the Time Bank for the smaller interactions that make us neighbors, friends, and ultimately communities—things like picking up the mail, walking the dog, showing up with a pot of chicken soup when someone's sick. These types of trades used to happen all the time and they forged bonds that were valuable because they were necessary to get along. Nowadays, when Whole Foods does our cooking, canine day care operations take over pet exercising, and the internet solves the rest, we're hard-pressed to find time to introduce ourselves to the neighbors, let alone exchange anything with them. Time Banking becomes a set of training wheels that helps to reknit cohesive communities.

In *The Ascent of Humanity,* Charles Eisenstein talks about how our ideas about separation have contributed to this culture of isolation as well as how to heal it. He argues that we remember and embrace a "gift culture," in which our personal gifts are expressed and shared freely. Basically, gift culture says that if we do what our hearts long to do and everybody else does too, the rest will take care of itself. Reciprocity is ensured by our trust in the inherently generous nature of the universe. While I subscribe to this idea, I think that Time Banks and organizations like it help people transition to that level of trust.

Why might it be hard to trust in the generous nature of the universe? Another way to say that a culture is organized around separation to say that it is traumatized. According to trauma author Peter Levine, of *Waking the Tiger* fame, one of trauma's major characteristics is freezing, or immobility and numbness. It's not that much of a stretch to view the typical suburban American household in this way, where each family is sequestered in their own locked house, afraid to let their children go outside to play or to interact with their neighbors. Breaking trauma patterns isn't easy, but organizations that provide relatively safe arenas for interaction can surely help.

Of course, Time Banks can also serve economic functions, especially in times of crisis. By reducing the need to pay for every little service we need, money is freed up for things that operate exclusively within the cash economy. In Santa Fe, New Mexico, we're also hoping to enroll businesses in the Time Bank. We're not there yet, but we envision member restaurants offering a percentage off of their prices for Time Bankers in exchange for helping with inventory or whatever else they might need. The same goes for beloved venues like the Lensic Performing Arts Center, the Santa Fe Opera, and any other business that might like to lower its own costs and participate more closely with its community.

In Portland, Maine, where the Portland Hour Exchange (PHE) is fifteen years old and six hundred plus members strong, health care is the most utilized service, presumably helping to make up at least some of the insurance gap. They've also embraced their role as an incubator for small businesses, providing the introductions for scores of massage therapists, interior decorators, handymen, etc., to develop crucial client lists as they first start out. We see these models as being a great fit for Santa Fe or any town where the entrepreneurial spirit is strong.

In one fascinating case study, the PHE received a grant to weatherize one home. Thinking ahead, they used the opportunity to train a coordinator in weatherization instead, who then trained a weatherization team, which then began to offer weatherization services for Hour Exchangers. Members have to pay for materials, but may use Hours for the rest. At least one team member has gone on to be hired as skilled labor by an outside weatherization business. It's a great example of how Time Banking can help cushion the fall during bleaker economic times and grease the wheels of change in the meanwhile.

In less than a year, Santa Fe's Time Bank has since grown to have over one hundred members—and more sign up every week. People's eyes simply light up when they hear about Time Banking—and I know why. The truth is, we're hungry for new ways of living and relating to each other. We want to know each other and share in each other's lives. We feel our interconnectedness. And the organizations that help us to realize it are welcome.

12

YOGA AND MONEY

SHARON GANNON

What would it take to be wild, free, and independently wealthy?

I'm sitting in a small, dirt-floor restaurant in Bombay just finishing a meal of yellow dhal, chapatti, mango pickle, and a bottle of Duke club soda. I get up from the wooden bench to walk over and pay my bill. On the brightly painted, plastered, turquoise-blue wall, above the man with the cash box waiting to take my rupees, is an elaborately framed poster of a young woman. Around the picture are small flashing Christmas lights. Draped across the glass are strands of pearls. Like Botticelli's Venus, this alluringly divine being comes into view emerging from the water, her body gracefully curvaceous, her hair and clothes flowing unrestrictedly around her like intoxicated devotees imbibing nectar wafting from the scent of her skin. She stands upon the water perfectly balanced, floating in an open pink lotus flower "boat" with outstretched arms, gesturing toward me. From the palms of her delicate hands flow masses of tinkling golden coins. It all looks surreal as I stand here in this dirt-floor restaurant, flies buzzing around us all. With a huge smile and enraptured eyes, the man enthusiastically tells me, "She is my Ishtadevita—Lakshmi—the goddess who is making the money for us!"

This was my first introduction to the Hindu goddess of wealth. After that, throughout my travels in India, I began to notice many similar posters of Lakshmi (pronounced "lukshmee"), mostly in restaurants and shops; in fact, wherever business was being conducted you would likely find Lakshmi with her generous hands lavishly pouring money upon her devotees. I was never sure if the message of the goddess was supposed to inspire the customers to be more generous, or if the shopkeepers hoped that Lakshmi herself would be generous to them and bestow them with wealth, or if they keep her picture to remind them to be generous to their customers and others and not to steal or cheat.

The Indian sages tell us that we become whom we worship. So if to become rich is your ambition, then to be more like Lakshmi—generous to others—would help you realize your goal. Central to the teachings of yoga is the concept that in essence our true identity is divine. To be divine is to be whole, to be holy—not separate from reality. My teacher, Shri Brahmananda Sarasvati, described yoga as that state where you are missing nothing—you know yourself as holy, as whole and complete, connected to all that is.

> Whatever joy there is in this world all comes from desiring others to be happy, and whatever suffering there is in this world all comes from desiring myself to be happy at the expense of others.
> —Shantideva, *A Guide to the Bodhisattva Way of Life*

We live in a slave culture. Our present economy is based on the domestication and exploitation of animals and nature. We perceive all animals, as well as land and water, in terms of usefulness to us, as slaves or potential slaves—property to be owned. Our money comes to us as stolen wealth from the lives of the animals we buy and sell and from the natural resources we are exhausting. Without so much as a thank you we have come to feel entitled to use the earth and all living beings as if they had no purpose other than to be used by us. We are quickly removing all traces of wildness from the planet as we gun down mustangs from helicopters and dam "wild" rivers. If our culture had a mission statement, it might very well read, "The Earth Belongs to Us."

We operate from a self-centered, hierarchal, dominionist world-view, which places human beings above all other life forms—above the world of nature. With this placement we assume ownership of the earth; in fact, those of us who have enough money to buy a piece of what is real—real estate—actually take legal ownership of a piece of the earth. Ownership implies complete authority, allowing the owners to do whatever they want with whomever or whatever they own. In other words, we are operating from a master/slave mentality. Our whole way of life, and certainly our economy, which supports that way of life, would collapse if we didn't have slaves to lord over. Wealth yields power, and power is essential to the maintenance of an exploitable relationship with others. Power that is derived from force is insatiable as well as unstable and must be constantly maintained through aggression, and that means war.

We have been at war with nature for the past ten thousand years, ever since we began to move from living *with* nature to conquering and exploiting her, and this war has been escalating—all other wars stem from this one. The first wars in our culture's history were fought over disputes about animal ownership and the land needed to confine, graze, and provide food for those animals. The word for war used by the ancient Aryans, *gavya,* literally means "the desire to fight for more cattle," and *gavisthi* means "to be desirous of a fight." Both words come from the root *gav* or *go,* which means "cow." The domestication (enslaving) of cattle led to war. It may be interesting to note that today in the Middle East we are fighting a war for oil, and the second biggest consumers of oil in the world, second only to the military, are the meat and dairy industries.

When human beings started to move away from the natural orderliness of wildness and toward the imposed order of civilization, we became herders of animals, enslaving them and exploiting them primarily for the four *m*'s they could provide: **m**eat, **m**ilk, **m**anure and of course **m**oney. Animals also provide a continued source of renewable income, because they can produce offspring—born to be used. To exploit is to steal. In war it is expected that the losers lose what was once considered their own: their lives, their dignity, their freedom, their home, their children, etc. The word *exploitation* means "to treat with little regard for the welfare, benefit or happiness of the other." To be able to successfully exploit another, it is essential that you don't see the other as part of yourself. Nature becomes your enemy in the quest for control and commodification of the things of the world. So we have separated ourselves from the natural world by first separating ourselves from the other animals, and with this separation came a denial that we are also animals and that we are also part of the natural world. To exploit a person you must see them as a thing, devoid of the same kinds of feelings and yearnings as you know yourself to have, so we don't relate to cows and pigs as people, because then it would be difficult to enslave, slaughter, and exploit them for monetary gain. In a similar way we have had to deny that trees and other forms of life are people, because if we saw them as persons it would be more difficult to clear cut a whole forest in order to plant crops or build a shopping mall.

History shows us that the enslavement of animals served as the model for the exploitation of the natural world as well as for human slavery. Domesticated animals were the first form of money, of measurable wealth exchange, which continues today in the form of our stock market or stock exchange—a reference to livestock market or livestock exchange. The word *live* has been dropped, because most of the money is made in dealing dead animals. The Latin root word for capital is *capita*, which means the head of a cow, goat, or sheep—the first animals to be domesticated. In ancient times, the head count of the animals that a man owned determined his wealth. The roots of modern capitalism are in those ancient enslavers, herders, and exploiters of animals. Today, no matter how far away from the open range or from farm life we may feel ourselves to be, we are still part of this system that was put into place thousands of years ago.

But around the same time a smaller number of our ancestors did not go along with this plan and felt that happiness and success could be attained not by dominating nature but by continuing to live in harmony with nature. Those people were the first yogis. Alain Daniélou writes in his book *Gods of Love and Ecstasy: The Traditions of Shiva and Dionysus*, "Throughout the course of history, urban and industrial societies—those exploiters and destroyers of the natural world—have been opposed to any ecological or mystical approach to the liberation of man and his happiness." The aim of yoga practice is liberation and happiness.

If we are to survive, then we must change our viewpoint about the natural world and not see it as just existing to provide us with money to buy stuff. If we could allow ourselves to see that the earth is our greater heart—that we do not exist as separate from the rest of nature—we would develop a different relationship with the world. Yoga provides the means to do just that.

Patanjali's *Yoga Sutras*—a two-thousand-year-old scripture—is a manual that gives directions for how to become free, how to become an enlightened being, a being who knows how to live in the present moment, beyond the limits of space and time: a being who is eternally one with all that is—and is also ecstatically happy about it! But in this ancient book there is also advice that can be applied to the present circumstances in the world today, including the global financial crisis.

How one relates to others is a reoccurring theme in the *Yoga Sutras*. When economists talk about global communities, I do not think most of them are actually talking about global communities in the same way that a yogi would. A yogi includes *all* members of the community—not just the human beings but all living beings who may be living in the area. In other words, from a yogic point of view, in a truly sustainable global economy, the animals, plants, and the rest of nature are not seen as mere commodities. In fact, the yogi would extend the concept of community to include the caretakers of nature, referred to in the yogic scriptures as the *devas,* a word meaning "godlike." Devas are subtle spirit forms whose job it is to ensure the prosperity of the natural world. In our "modern" times it is difficult for most human beings to believe in the existence of such beings as angels, elves, and fairies, but to the yogi who is attuned to the workings of the natural world, these beings are as real as your next-door neighbor. We are stealing from nature in a vain attempt to maintain and/or increase prosperity for ourselves. According to the yogic teachings, there is great risk in this type of one-sided, selfish relationship with nature. Verse III.11 in the Bhagavad Gita says that without giving to, honoring, and cooperating with nature, humanity will not be able to exist.

The idea of individual happiness being related to the happiness of the community is not found only in the ancient yogic texts. In fields as diverse as economics, political science, mathematics, sociology, and biology, scholars and scientists have been exploring the decision-making behavior of individuals in groups, and they have seen that in situations where one individual's behavior has an impact on others, the outcome improves when individuals cooperate. This is in stark contrast to the idea put forth by Adam Smith, father of modern economics, which simply stated that individual ambition serves the common good—or in the pursuit of happiness, every man for himself.

But the notion of cooperation is threatening to a culture that is based on defending an individual's right to be selfish. We are taught that in order to create a happy society, each individual in that society should be allowed to pursue happiness for himself or herself.

In the Declaration of Independence, our founding fathers put forth the ideology that we exist so that everyone can be allowed to be free to pursue happiness. If we look at our present society, we can easily conclude that we have not achieved happiness based on this paradigm. Instead, we have reached a tipping point where if we do not find a different way to live with each other, we may all perish.

New approaches based on cooperation among living beings which include all the rest of the natural world offer a radical message: in order to create a happy equilibrium in a society, each individual should only be allowed to pursue happiness to the extent that it does not cause unhappiness to any other member of that society, whether it be fish, bird, cow, dog, tree, river *or* human.

All of the suffering that we experience in life, including the suffering that comes from financial worries about not having enough, comes from being ignorant of who we really are. We act from that ignorance when we think that what we do doesn't matter to the whole. In yoga, the term for that ignorance is *avidya*. But who we really are is not our personality selves encapsulated in a mortal body existing separate from the rest of the natural world. People steal from others because they feel deprived. Our culture teaches us that it is not really stealing if we have the money to pay for it: if we pay for it, we have a right to have it. But who do we think we are when we think that we could really own a thing or another being or a piece of a being or a piece of land or a river?

The practices of yoga are tantric practices, which help us to uncover our true identity and reveal to us our purpose in life— why we were born. The Sanskrit word *tantra* is composed of two syllables: *tan,* which means "to stretch," and *tra,* which means "to cross over." Tantra refers to various techniques or methods used to stretch or expand consciousness, enabling one to cross over avidya, to realize who we are through reuniting with life. The practices allow us to become whole—holy.

One of the primary techniques used in tantra is to relate to everything and everyone that you see as a person. This is done by putting a face on the "other." So trees, birds, cows, sheep, wind, dogs, cats, and rivers, for instance, become identifiable as persons. The whole world becomes alive, no longer composed of two separate camps: you and the human beings that you know and like, your friends and family, on the one side; and strangers, people from other countries or even planets, people of other religions or races, and those who *really don't* look like you and speak foreign languages that you can't understand, like animals, birds, trees, plants, fairies, elemental beings, rivers, lakes, oceans—the huge panoramic world of nature—on the other side.

A yogi wants to be free. *Moksha* means freedom. So from a yogic point of view, if we ourselves want to be free then it would not suit our purpose to deprive others of their freedom by enslaving and exploiting them.

In the second chapter of the *Yoga Sutras*, Patanjali provides practical tips—things you can do in order insure your own freedom, health, happiness, and wealth. In regards to wealth, he suggests that if you want prosperity to appear in your life, then don't steal from others. The actual sutra is: *asteya-pratishthayam sarva-ratnopasthanam* (*YS* II.37). *Asteya* (pronounced "ah-stay-ya") means not to steal, and the whole sutra means, "When one stops stealing from others, prosperity appears." If we do not deny others their prosperity, prosperity will not be denied to us.

The *Yoga Sutras* also has something to say about greed. Success in our culture is measured in capital gain. Our importance as individuals is measured by our wealth, and wealth comes from owning things and controlling others. Greed and hoarding are not only accepted as normal, they are encouraged as an indication of prosperity. To live simply so that others may simply live is a radical concept to embrace; yet in the *Yoga Sutras*, Patanjali tells us that the practice of greedlessness is extremely powerful—so powerful that it can reveal to us the reason we were born, our purpose in life. The actual sutra is: *aparigraha-sthairye janma-kathamta-sambodhah* (*YS*

II.39). The Sanskrit word for this practice is *aparigraha* (pronounced "ah-par-ree-gra-ha"), and it means greedlessness—not taking more than one needs—and the whole sutra means, "When one becomes selfless and ceases to take more than one needs, one obtains knowledge of why one was born." Real needs are not wrong; wants, on the other hand, can become problematic. We are in the midst of a global crisis caused by insatiable human greed. We have consumed far more than we need. The consequences for the survival of many animal species, as well as our own, are dire. There has never been so much poverty in the world. The more we have, the more we want.

Influenced by media imagery and advertising, we have become habituated to look outside ourselves for happiness and in the process have created powerful addictions that drive our choices. Each time we allow an outside stimulus to program our actions, we allow our own inner power of intelligent discrimination to atrophy, leading to further addiction. Many of us have become so out of touch with our innermost selves that we do not know where need ends and want begins.

The directive aparigraha, in contrast, helps one to curb one's actions in accordance with what is beneficial for all. We begin to understand ourselves as beings who thrive as part of a whole organism working together, and we begin to feel our unique contribution to the wholeness of life. In our culture we have been told that we as individuals don't have to take responsibility for our actions, because our individual actions don't matter much to the whole, much less to ourselves. But they do matter; in fact, they are the most important and defining aspect of how our own destiny and future world will be shaped.

But how can we know when we are taking more than we need? How can we know when our needs have become excessive wants, and what is enough? Is greed really that evil? If you look up the word *evil* in the dictionary, you will find that it comes from the Germanic root word *übel,* which means "up" or "over," meaning to go beyond the limits of what is helpful. In other words, that which is excessive *is* evil. According to the UN Food and Agriculture Organization, over fifty-two billion animals are killed by human beings for food worldwide every year. There are only six and a half billion human beings on the planet. Our present exploitation of animals and the natural world is excessive, and by the dictionary definition that means it is also evil. We don't kill animals because we are hungry. We kill them to make money so that we can buy stuff—most of which we don't even need or want. I once read that 85 percent of everything bought in an American shopping mall ends up in a landfill within two weeks after purchase.

How does the yogic practice of greedlessness result in the realization of one's purpose in life? To be greedy and to hoard comes from being afraid of not having enough in the future. We have become bound by linear time. We spend our lives in regretful or longing memories of the past and hope and fears about the future. We have learned to "stock" pile surplus from our ancestors, who taught us to enslave and exploit animals and nature and the commodities we force them to produce. When we let go of the habit of accumulating money and material things, we might have a chance to drop into the present. It is in the present that our true multidimensional self exists, and when we allow ourselves to be present we will find ourselves—our destiny will be revealed. Eternity *is* happening now—now, in the present moment. To drop into the present moment one must allow for a more flexible or open-ended relationship to time as well as to space. By letting go of attachments to material things, this will be more possible. It is the fear of losing and the subsequent habit of hoarding that keeps us bound to linear time and blocks us from entering into the eternal now.

We are on the brink of an apocalypse that some have prophesied will result in a radical shift in how we relate to time. The Greek word *apocalypse* means "to reveal; to uncover; to stand naked, exposed without artifice, clothing or possessions." This present age or time, or yuga, has been spoken of in Hindu scripture as the Kali Yuga. Kali is derived from the Sanskrit word *kala,* meaning "time." Some say that in the year 2012, there will be an end to time as we have been conditioned by our culture to relate to it. Civilized men and women are afraid of the present and instead cling to the past and the future. Nature thrives in the present. Wild beings live in the present moment.

We have robbed domesticated animals of their wildness and made them slaves—victims of our greed-based economic system— and because we are interwoven with the web of life, we ourselves cannot escape from the repercussion of our actions upon others. We have also become domesticated and see ourselves as victims of our own system. Many of us in our culture are so dependent upon "others in high places" to take care of us that when we become afraid of not having enough, we blame our "masters" (parents, landlords, employers, corporations, government—i.e., those with whom we do business), as if we did not know how to take care of our own needs. We too often deny that we ourselves had any hand in our misfortunes. We like to insist it was someone else who caused the trouble in our lives, so we become complainers. We have given away our power, and in exchange we have become powerless, needy and afraid of the future.

We get our food from the supermarket and our money to buy that food from a boss or corporation. We live in fear of being fired or laid off from our jobs. When we are sick we pay a doctor to write a prescription, which we take to a drug store to buy medicine. As we have domesticated animals, we have allowed ourselves to become domesticated, and with that domestication comes a disconnection from intelligence and intuition. We have compromised our natural instincts and senses and become crude, dull, and bored. We need constant entertainment to feel that our lives are worthwhile (or "worthwild"—meaning worth the wild that we have given up). Wild beings know how to take care of themselves. They know how to provide food and medicine for themselves and their children. They are "independently wealthy," as they are dependent inwardly for their knowledge; they look into the depths of their own souls—that unseen place where all of life is joined and time is eternal. A wild being would not cause the mass destruction of others for such silly compensation as a few dollars. The karmic costs are too great, and no amount of money could compensate for being disconnected from the living world, the source of vitality itself. Perhaps wild beings realize more than we do the multidimensional complexities of reality and how what we do to others we do to ourselves, because we are not separate from others. Wild beings live in harmony with the natural world. We could too. We could take our place with nature and become whole. But it would mean that we would have to get a little wild and begin to see ourselves in others—to see so deeply that otherness disappears and we come to know ourselves as holy, as part of the whole—the whole mysterious scheme of life. What a great relief it would be to let go of so much artifice and pretension that we ourselves have allowed to be imposed upon us for so many thousands of years. No need for money. No need to buy things, because we have ceased to see the world as made of things. Instead we have opened our eyes to the wonder of life and see it peopled with a vast diversity of living beings—people like ourselves, not things to service us, or to be used, bought, and sold. Like our animal brethren, we have become independently wealthy.

I would like to conclude with an excerpt from an essay by Andrei Codrescu lamenting the opening of a new Burger King restaurant:

> Someone [said] that the reason we treat animals so badly is because they don't have any money. We treat children badly for the same reason, though we don't eat them. Perhaps the time has come for animals to get paid for what they do. Perhaps the time has come for us to eat our children. Or maybe we should just tear down the Burger Kings.[1]

13

THE INTENTIONAL ECONOMY

DANIEL PINCHBECK

While exploring shamanism and non-ordinary states, I discovered the power of intention. According to the artist Ian Lungold, who lectured brilliantly about the Mayan calendar before his untimely death in 2005, the Maya believe that your intention is as essential to your ability to navigate reality as your position in time and space. If you don't know your intention, or if you are operating with the wrong intentions, you are always lost, and can only get more dissolute.

This idea becomes exquisitely clear during psychedelic journeys, when your state of mind gets intensified and projected kaleidoscopically all around you. As our contemporary world becomes more and more psychedelic, we are receiving harsh lessons in the power of intention on a vast scale. Over the last decades, the international financial elite manipulated the markets to create obscene rewards for themselves at the expense of poor and middle class people across the world. Using devious derivatives, cunning CDOs (collateralized debt obligations), and other trickery, they siphoned off ever-larger portions of the surplus value created by the producers of real goods and services, contriving a debt-based economy that had to fall apart. Their own greed—such a meager, dull intent—has now blown up in their faces, annihilating, in slow motion, the corrupt system built to serve them.

Opportunities such as the current economic meltdown don't come along very often and should be seized once they appear.

When the edifice of mainstream society suddenly collapses, as is happening now, it is a fantastic time for artists, visionaries, mad scientists, and seers to step forward and present a well-defined alternative. What is required, in my opinion, is not some moderate proposal or incremental change, but a complete shift in values and goals, making a polar reversal of our society's basic paradigm. If our consumer-based, materialism-driven model of society is dissolving, what can we offer in its place? Why not begin with the most elevated intentions? Why not offer the most imaginatively fabulous systemic redesign?

The fall of capitalism and the crisis of the biosphere could induce mass despair and misery, or they could impel the creative adaptation and conscious evolution of the human species. We could attain a new level of wisdom and build a compassionate global society in which resources are shared equitably while we devote ourselves to protecting threatened species and repairing damaged ecosystems. Considering the lightning-like pace of global communication and new social technologies, this change could happen with extraordinary speed.

To a very great extent, the possibilities we choose to realize in the future will be a result of our individual and collective intention. For instance, if we maintain a puritanical belief that work is somehow good in and of itself, then we will keep striving to create a society of full employment, even if those jobs become "green collar." A more radical viewpoint perceives most labor as something that could become essentially voluntary in the future. The proper use of technology could allow us to transition to a post-scarcity leisure society, in which the global populace spends its time growing food, building community, making art, making love, learning new skills, and deepening self-development through spiritual disciplines such as yoga, tantra, shamanism, and meditation.

One common perspective is that the West and Islam are engaged in an intractable conflict of civilizations, and the hatred and terrorism can only get worse. Another viewpoint could envision the Judeo-Christian culture of the West finding common ground and reconciling with the esoteric core, the metaphysical purity, of the Islamic faith. It seems—to me anyway—that we could find solutions to all of the seemingly intractable problems of our time once we are ready to apply a different mindset to them. As Einstein and others have noted, we don't solve problems through employing the type of thinking that created them, but rather dissolve them when we reach a different level of consciousness.

We became so mired in our all-too-human world that we lost touch with the other, elder forms of sentience all around us. Along with delegates to the UN, perhaps we could train cadres of diplomats to negotiate with the vegetal, fungal, and microbial entities that sustain life on earth? The mycologist Paul Stamets proposes that we create a symbiosis with mushrooms to detoxify ecosystems and improve human health. The herbalist Morgan Brent believes psychoactive flora like ayahuasca and peyote are "teacher plants," sentient emissaries from super-intelligent nature, trying to help the human species find its niche in the greater community of life. When we pull back to study the hapless and shameful activity of our species across the earth, these ideas do not seem very far-fetched.

In fact, the breakdown of our financial system has not altered the amount of tangible resources available on our planet. Rather than trying to rejigger an unjust debt-based system that artificially maintains inequity and scarcity, we could make a new start. We could develop a different intention for what we are supposed to be doing together on this swiftly tilting planet, and institute new social and economic infrastructure to support that intent.

14

AN ARMY OF JACKS TO FIGHT THE POWER

PETER LAMBORN WILSON

In fairy tales, humans can possess exterior souls, things magically containing or embodying individual life force—stone, egg, ring, bird or animal, etc. If the thing is destroyed, the human dies. But while the thing persists, the human enjoys a kind of immortality or at least invulnerability.

Money can be seen as such an exteriorized soul. Humans created it, in some sense, in order to hide their souls in things that could be locked away (in tower or cave) and hidden so their bodies would acquire magical invulnerability: wealth, health, enjoyment, and power over enemies—even over fate.

But these exterior souls need not be hidden away—they can be divided almost indefinitely and circulated, exchanged for desire, passed on to heirs like an immortal virus—or rather like a dead thing that magically contains life and "begets" itself endlessly in usury. It constitutes humanity's one really totally successful experiment in magic: no one calls the bluff, and after six thousand years, it seems like nature. (In fact, an old Chinese cosmogonic text claimed the two basic principles of the universe are water and money.)

It's worth noting that in märchen, or folktales, the characters with external souls are often the villains. Clearly, the practice must appear uncanny to any normal society, in which magic (call it collective consciousness in active mode) is channeled through ritual and custom to the life of all—not the aggrandizement of one against all (black magic or witchcraft). Yet in the form of money, the exterior soul, shattered into fragments, is put into circulation but also stolen, monopolized, and guarded by dragons—so that some unlucky humans can be stripped of all soul, while others gorge or hoard up soul-bits of ancestors and victims in their ghoulish caves or "banks."

The beloved in the tale may also have an exterior soul. It falls into the grasp of the evil sorcerer or dragon and must be rescued. In other words, desire, which is alienated (reified, fetishized) in the form of a symbolic object, can only be restored to its true fate (love) by reappropriation from the expropriator, stealing it back from the wizard. The task falls to "Jack," the third and youngest, sometimes an orphan or disinherited, possibly a fool, a peasant with more heart than any prince, generous, bold, and lucky.

Exactly the same story can be seen acted out in every honest ethnographic report on the introduction of money into some pre-monetary tribal economy. Even without the usual means of force, terror, oppression, colonialist imperialism, or missionary zeal, money alone destroys every normal culture it touches.

CARGO CULTS AND GHOST DANCES

Interestingly, in nearly every case, some sort of messianic movement, cargo cult, or Ghost Dance–type resistance movement springs up within a generation or two after first alien contact. These cults invariably make appeal to spirits (or even demons when circumstances really begin to deteriorate) for the power to overcome money, to "provide good things" without recourse to the black magic of money and the vampirization of other peoples' external souls—to combat the malignancy of wealth that is not shared.

This is a major trope in all the tales. Jack gives away part of his last loaf precisely to the power-animal or shaman or old lady with the very gift he'll need in his quest, but he gives unwittingly, not in expectation of exchange. Jack always stands for what Karl Polanyi and Marcel Mauss call the economy of the gift.

A great many fairy tales must have originated in "folk memories" of earlier nonhierarchal social structures, embodied in narrative (myth) and ritual, and given focus during the period when this ancient polity was threatened and finally overcome by later or alien systems—particularly by money, by the coins that always appear in these tales.

Pierre-Joseph Proudhon believed that people originally invented money a means to pry loose and force into circulation the hoarded wealth of the "dragon," the oppressor class. This idea has interesting resonances.

It points to the fact that for "the people," money in hand represents not oppression but pleasure, gratified desire. Money may not be the root of all evil, but given the existence of money, "love of money" is quite natural. Alchemy epitomizes this jouissance of money in the fairy tale concept of transmutation, production of gold without labor as a free gift of nature to her lovers: Jove's body as a shower of golden coins.

As a stand-in for "the people," Jack wins the treasure, but in doing so removes its curse, its dragonish malignancy, because in him the treasure finds its rightful end in happiness (i.e., free distribution, the gift). Hence, the great feast that ends so many tales, and the wedding between peasant lad and princess that levels distinctions and restores external souls to their bodies.

But Proudhon's notion is contradicted by myth, which attributes the invention of coins to a king—not Croesus of Lydia, who actually did invent coins (seventh century BC), but Midas, who choked on magical gold, his externalized soul. Dionysus and Silenus gave him his wish and then saved him by revoking it, allowing him to vomit all the gold into the river Pactolus in Phrygia.

The historical Midas lived in the eighth century BC, and Phrygia is not far from Lydia, where rivers also ran with gold and electrum and coins first appeared as temple tokens. Coins may seem to regain their innocence when they are spent rather than hoarded, but in fact just at this moment they betray us by leaving us and never returning. In the end, all coins end up in the usurer's vault. Money is already debt. It says so on the U.S. one-dollar bill, that encyclopedia of hermetic imagery and secret doctrine of money.

JACK NEVER REALLY WINS

Jack's triumph lies not in the "ever after," but only in a moment that is forever remembered and invoked as lost. Obviously Jack never really wins, otherwise we wouldn't call these stories fairy tales and relegate them to the nursery, the savage pre-monetary world of mere childhood. The idea that märchen contain esoteric teachings on economics will probably sound ridiculous, but only to those who've never really read them with Polanyi's or Mauss's economic anthropology in mind.

The old Russian cycle (Jack = Ivan) strikes me as particularly sensitive to this aspect of the material, almost as if socialism had a subconscious pre-echo in the great Russian fairy tale collections of the early 1900s.

Among the uniquely Slavic motifs of this cycle, everyone loves the tales of Baba Yaga, the little house on great chicken legs that walks and moves wherever the wicked witch desires. The image's power involves implications that Baba Yaga functions not only as the witch's house, but also as her external soul. It is both shield and weapon, space and motion, cave and magic carpet. I can't help thinking of it as a symbol of capital itself, especially in its purely magical end phase in the global era. The Baba Yaga might be an offshore bank ready to pull up stakes and flee to some freer market or a shoe factory on its way to Mexico.

Speaking of Mexico reminds me of a story about the Mexican Revolution: around 1910, thousands of North American anarchists,

Wobblies, and adventurers crossed the border under false generic names to join Pancho Villa or the Magonistas and thus came to be called the "Army of Smiths."

Given the proliferation and gigantism of Baba Yaga in our times, perhaps what we need is an Army of Jacks.

15

ONE THOUSAND WORDS ABOUT WHERE FREE MUSIC IS TAKING US

PAUL D. MILLER,
AKA DJ SPOOKY THAT SUBLIMINAL KID

> I can't understand why people are frightened of new ideas.
> I'm frightened of the old ones.
> —John Cage

> In a race, the quickest runner can never overtake the slowest, since the pursuer must first reach the point whence the pursued started, so that the slower must always hold a lead …
> —Aristotle, *Physics*

Warning: This text contains uncredited samples. The smart reader is advised to search online for terms in various sentences to find out the context. Simply type them into a decent search engine, and see what else pops up in the browser.

Begin: These days, at the beginning of the twenty-first century, we're faced with a kind of social entropy. Whenever one is exposed to the financial world there's a kind of surrealism to the situation. Credit default swaps, futures markets, abstract financial instruments: these are terms based on complex, expensive loans that most people don't understand. But what makes all of this converge on the topic I'm writing about—"economics" as it relates to cultural production—is a kind of pro forma switch between artistic practice and how the world is represented. Think of it this way:

economics, the "dismal science," is for most people the "real" of the real, the financial underpinnings of modern life in an information based economy. Let's take a look at the root of *economics:* *eco* is derived from the Greek term *oikonomia* (*oikos*—"house" and *nomos*—"custom"). It's resonant with the later Latin-derived term *credit,* derived from *creder,* which simply means "to believe."

This is exactly what the founder of modern economics, Adam Smith, meant when he said "all money is a matter of belief." Or even more when he said "on the road from the City of Skepticism, I had to pass through the Valley of Ambiguity." What kind of music comes out of these statements?

Let's put it this way: the absolute top-selling album of all time is the blank CD. More than the Beatles, more than Elvis, Bob Marley, or Michael Jackson—I'm talking about the simple utilitarian object of the humble 700 megabyte CD. Why? Here's the basic scenario: when you face the idea that digital reproduction equals infinite abundance, the result is that you have so many options available that the normal business model of scarcity simply no longer applies. And so music should be, could be, and will be free. It's that simple. Infinite amount of copies equals zero value. You resequence, resplice, and redice the materials of your audio or video archive because your individual choice is what gives the situation a robust and deeply personal satisfaction. The consumer is sovereign in this scenario, and the cultural producer becomes content for the palette of the consumer. The abundance of music, its low cost, and its widespread availability contribute to the sense that all music from every part of recorded history is equally available, and can be mixed together into new forms. In a networked economy, the simplest of terms: anything that can be digital, will be. And that scenario, in turn, fosters the end of normal economics in the culture industry—that's the real freakonomics. And no, I don't have any nostalgia for the old music industry model of the album—it was always an artificial construct to boost profits for the major record labels. Music was better when people had to put more creative intent into the single. But I do think that the vinyl LP will outlast CDs precisely because it's got collectors appeal—it's become scarce in a way that fosters real value.

In the twenty-first century we face so many variables about what it means to "believe" in a system: a computer operating system? A church? A "lifestyle?" I love to play with these kinds of conjunctions, because, put simply, that's about all that makes any of this make sense: it's all a kind of theater, a place where we create roles, and read from a script made of numbers that many of us don't understand. Ask your average person on the street—we in the United States face a scenario anticipated by Gordon Gekko in Oliver Stone's 1987 film *Wall Street,* who sneers at the belief of the audience in morality, and simply says, "90 percent of Americans have no net worth." Almost true ...

If we go back a little ways, and think this idea through, we come up with some different issues. What some economists are calling "social capital" comes into play; it gives a sense of dynamism to the way we think about "intangible goods" and comes into direct collision with the norms of a capitalist society based on scarcity. Got it? It's been a while since 1989, when the Berlin Wall fell. If we turn things upside down and think about the "values system" of American capitalism versus, say, what's going on in post-Mao China, we can see things looking like this: In 1989 the claim was made that what had been defeated was not an enemy—the Soviet Union—but rather the entire opposition to capitalism. At the time neoliberal author Francis Fukuyama argued that the world had reached "the end of history," because from that point on there will only be capitalism and continuous growth, unrestrained by annoying things like federal regulation, etc. You can see where that got us. Ask Lehman Brothers, Bernie Madoff, or anyone else involved with the financial fictions of the Bush era.

Recall and rewind: The script of our era is what theorist Arjun

Appadurai likes to call the "social life of things," or what philosopher Alain Badiou has simply called "theory of the subject." We reflect, we generate intangible links and connections between tastes, styles, and above all, the way we combine those tastes and styles. That's the catch with digital media and music; there is no "there"—everything is routed between connections, and end points are material for the scrapheap of postmodernity.

Post-everything music asks this: Why pay for anything? Why not just create the gift economy that we all live in and call it quits? The way the law is written, and the way we live, simply part ways. I tend to think of sampling and uploading files as the same thing, just different formats—to paraphrase John Cage, sound is just information in a different form. The old world production model, scarcity, always seemed annoying and physical. I want to see people's imaginations take flight; they should create their own values, and a soundtrack to go with it, to inspire new forms for new ways of living. To get rid of the twentieth century's old physical forms, and to become an emotive, free space. That's the basic idea for twenty-first-century aesthetics—here and now, as always. Dig?

Finance of fictions. Fictions of finance. How does music factor into this entertainment industry? What's the matter with finance? Start with the fact that the modern financial industry generates huge profits and paychecks, yet delivers few tangible benefits.

Remember when *Wall Street*'s Gordon Gekko declared, "Greed is good"? By today's standards, Gekko was a piker. In the years leading up to the 2008 crisis, the financial industry accounted for a third of total domestic profits—about twice its share two decades earlier.

These profits were justified, we were told, because the industry was doing great things for the economy. It was channeling capital to productive uses; it was spreading risk; it was enhancing financial stability. None of that was true. Capital was channeled not to job-creating innovators, but into an unsustainable housing bubble; risk was concentrated, not spread; and when the housing bubble burst, the supposedly stable financial system imploded, with the worst global slump since the Great Depression as collateral damage.

For most of us these days, the fact is that much of the financial industry has become synonymous with the term *racket*—a game in which a handful of people are lavishly paid to mislead and exploit consumers and investors—but which also comes from a humorously resonant term that simply means "to make a lot of noise." I love to think about credit, finance, and noise as terms that lend themselves to systems of belief—tuning systems, harmony of markets, and utopian derivatives. Stuff like that. And if we don't lower the boom on these practices, the racket will just go on. That is what I mean when I say free music. Bring the noise. NOW.

> If you develop an ear for sounds that are musical it is like developing an ego. You begin to refuse sounds that are not musical and that way cut yourself off from a good deal of experience.
>   —John Cage

16

I AM ... WE ARE ... IT IS[1]

LARRY HARVEY

I usually talk about the flamboyant aspects of Burning Man. These are what attract attention. Black Rock City, as many of you know, is a hyperconnective environment. It's full of interactive art. It's very antic and it's a lot of fun. But I've decided to focus here on economics, the dismal science, because, in the end, doesn't everything come down to economics, of one kind or another? I will begin by quoting an almost forgotten author, Richard Jefferies. His writings belong to a British literary genre called "country writing" that flourished in the nineteenth century. In "Absence of Design in Nature: The Prodigality of Nature and the Niggardliness of Man," Jefferies talks about the law of natural increase, which describes the propensity of living things to reproduce themselves at exponential rates: "There is no 'enough' in nature. It is one vast prodigality. It is a feast. There is no economy: it is all one immense extravagance. It is all giving, giving, giving: no saving, no penury; a golden shower of good things forever descending." Contrast this with the material economy of our world, in which each individual is in order to exist, compelled to labor, save, and compete with other people for control and possession of scarce resources. Such is the iron law of economics in our world: the superabundance of nature and the utter niggardliness of man.

This is the contrast he draws. It is as if we've fallen out of some happy Eden into a world where we must hoard and struggle to wrest what we can from the universe and one another. But I am more hopeful than Jefferies. He was writing about both nature and society in the midst of the first great phase of the Industrial Revolution, a time of massive social dislocation and widespread poverty. Think Dickens. The folkways of rural England and the networks of communal obligation that once sustained it were being brutally uprooted by the marketplace. An anonymous mass society was taking shape, and Jefferies came to feel that the factories and enormous cities of our industrial age represented a principle of evil and selfishness. But I have had the opportunity to observe a very different kind of city with a very different kind of economy, and I've come to see that there is more of nature in the social world of human beings than he or any of us today have yet understood.

I'm thinking, of course, about Burning Man and Black Rock City, the civic entity we annually create in the Black Rock Desert. I would like to start by describing the most radical and under-reported aspect of our city. It is under-reported because it's so very foreign to our current way of life. Reporters simply can't perceive it most of the time, because it just doesn't fit with what we're used to. They see a vitally creative world, filled with a super-abundance of art, animated by an electric spirit, and full of a whole lot of eccentric and entertaining behavior. That's the big story that gets reported.

But if they peel off the onion skin and peer a bit closer, there is another story. They will find that Black Rock City is one of the most public-spirited places on earth. We have, for instance, an incredible rate of volunteerism. We did a poll on the internet recently and the results were astonishing: 84.7 percent of our citizens contribute some form of volunteer service to our city. I challenge anyone to find another city in America that can equal that. We're the seventh-largest city in Nevada for eight days, and our crime rate is negligible. Think what the police blotter in New Orleans during Mardi Gras must look like. And Black Rock City is a party that's certainly equal to that in intensity. We are also committed to a

Leave No Trace effort. We say Burning Man is a disappearing act: we miracle up an entire city, it lasts for one week, and then it absolutely disappears. And I mean everything disappears: every sequin, every boa feather, every cigarette butt, and especially those damn pistachio nutshells. Our cleanup crews work hard, but our organization couldn't possibly cope with this task if it wasn't for the public spirit of our citizens. There are no trash cans in our city, yet our citizens take the responsibility to pack out their own trash. That's almost inconceivable, but that's what happens in Black Rock City.

And that's one of the problems reporters have. Burning Man is this wild and abandoned party on the one hand, and it's the most public-spirited city in America on the other. And this leads to a kind of cognitive dissonance. It doesn't make any sense to them, and that's because they don't understand the *really* big story, the story that lies behind all of this which is the cause of these two things conjoining. And the reason this doesn't get reported is because it's profoundly foreign to our current way of life.

The essential cause of all this is the giving of gifts. We've intentionally designed Black Rock City to foster a gift economy. We allow no vending, no advertising, no buying or selling of anything. We discourage bartering because even bartering is a commodity transaction. Instead, we've originated both an ethos and an economic system devoted to the giving of gifts. This is a radical departure from the marketplace because, of course, the marketplace invades every crack and corner of our lives today. A gift economy is founded on principles that are diametrically opposed to those that dominate our consumer culture.

Let me draw a contrast between the market and a gift economy. The value of a thing in the marketplace is based on its scarcity in relation to demand. And capitalism itself is based on the competition to acquire the scarce resource of money. The great utility of this system is that an organized market serves individual desire.

A simple act of purchase allows me to command the resources of the world. With a single expenditure, the magnesium of South Africa, the oil of Arabia, and the labor of China can be fetched from around the globe and delivered into my hands as if by magic; all that's required of me is a sum of money. There has never been a better method for the productive allocation of wealth and the distribution of goods and services. As a result, we live today in a large-scale global economy that continues to expand into every area of human activity. Adam Smith, many years ago, rightly regarded this as a kind of miracle. The market, mated today with our modern system of mass production and mass distribution, has produced more wealth and distributed it more widely than in all other epochs of human history. This has liberated us from toil, but more importantly, it has freed us to pursue uniquely personal visions of happiness.

At least, this is the version of our modern market that is constantly extolled in our society. But this economic revolution that has occurred so recently in human history has a darker side. The social contract we have signed contains a hidden clause and we have failed to read the fine print. And this is because the very virtues of our system represent its liabilities. The great efficiency of the marketplace depends on the fluidity of value as it flows in one form of commodity to another. If I buy something from you, no relationship and no moral connection is left to relate us to one another. The value of the money I have spent speeds on to take new forms as further goods and services. This is the fuel that powers our economy and produces a flow of never-ending capital around the world.

But what this transaction does not produce is connections between people. It does not produce what Robert Putnam has described as "social capital." Social capital represents the sum of human connection that holds a society together, and it is fostered by networks of personal relationships. In *Bowling Alone,* he objectively charts what all of us intuitively know: the social capital of America has begun to disintegrate.

Putnam talks about two kinds of social capital. First, there is "bonding" social capital. This consists of our intimate ties with our family and friends, communal relationships with that circle of people you know well. It doesn't consist of more than one hundred people because you can't keep up intimate rapport with over one hundred people. And these circles tend to be exclusive. Not intentionally, but when you are huddled with your friends, you turn your back on the world and it's hard to let the stranger in.

Another form of social capital called "bridging" social capital. This refers to looser ties within a broader social circle that encompasses larger networks. It could be people you meet at parties or at work, people you exchange cards with. Here's the difference: if you get sick and you need chicken soup, you'll call someone you are bonded to because they'll care. On the other hand, if you get fired and need a job, you are probably not going to talk to your brother or your close pal. You're going to talk to someone who is part of that bridging network because they are connected to an extended network that moves out into the world. This might be a group of people who get together to play cards or hold softball games. More formally, it might consist of civic organizations or other sorts of clubs. As a rule, these groups are inclusive. Anyone who is interested can gain entry. You don't need an intimate tie with other members. If you're interested in making ships in bottles, anyone is welcome who wants to make ships in bottles.

Putnam found that in America today, bonding social capital is eroding rapidly. The average American household spends seven hours a day watching television. A lot of people just turn the TV on to listen to the laugh track so they feel that they are not alone. The average American household possesses 2.4 television sets. And that means that husbands, wives, teenagers, and toddlers are all watching television independently of one another. If you could take the roof off the average suburban home, you would see each family member in a separate room watching a TV that has a separate set of commercials on it hawking a separate lifestyle. And if you looked more closely, you'd see that they're surrounded, barricaded, by all this stuff they've bought to support these lifestyles that are being sold to them. This is hardly connective: 81 percent of Americans say they spend most evenings watching TV, but only 56 percent report that they talk to family members.

There are more cars in America than there are drivers, and 90 percent of our citizens drive to work alone. In 1992, we each spent nineteen hours per year stuck in traffic jams. We each spent forty hours stuck in traffic in 1997, and I'm sure it's more than that now. So here you have an entire nation on the freeway, trapped in the metal carapace of an automobile, isolated from everybody around them. I think I'm an affable guy. I think I bond with other people. But when I get into a car I become demonic. "You jerk! Cut me off?!?!?" You know what's pathetic? Putnam found that people report they like being in their car during these long commutes because it's a time to *think*. To think, as they sit in these isolation booths cursing their fellow citizens! Here's another statistic: Putnam has found that each additional ten minutes of daily commuting reduces involvement in community affairs by 10 percent.

This leads us to an even darker picture. For when we get to bridging social capital, we find that membership in clubs and civic organizations has fallen by half since 1975. He calls his book *Bowling Alone* because bowling leagues, which are a form of bridging social capital, have declined so precipitously that, if you follow the curve, in another ten years everyone—even though there is a retro fashion in bowling—could be bowling alone. This pattern also applies to more formal organizations: organizations that do good works in the world, like the Lions or the Kiwanis.

At the back of the book he features charts that are really quite fascinating. Chart after chart crests at the height of civic involvement in America in the last century, around 1950, and then starts a decline until it reaches a point about twenty years ago, and then it makes a beeline for the drain. It resembles one of those mass die-offs when asteroids hit the earth, and that is what is happening to the civic tissue of our country.

I think we all know what some of the causes for this are: TV, cars, metropolitan sprawl. In a land of megamalls, cineplexes, gated communities, anonymous fast food outlets, and retail chain stores it's difficult to connect with anyone or anything. I was born in 1948, and I have seen all of these changes over the span of my lifetime.

But I think if we take a larger view and look at the character of modern-day capitalism, we can diagnose an even more essential cause. It is in the nature of our mass marketing to cater to the desires of the individual. Indeed, it's not surprising that the social ills Putnam describes have accelerated during the last twenty years, because it's during this period that capitalism has perfected many marketing techniques isolating us even more radically from one another. Marketers have identified thousands of new market niches allowing manufacturers to gratify each sector of the population. In other words, we have been sorted by age, class, and income much as cattle might be herded into stalls within a feedlot. And the best minds of our generation aren't writing books like Putnam's, they're doing market research and working for ad agencies.

When parents, teenagers, and toddlers are planted in front of different television sets the commercials they watch do not provide them with a way of life. They merely offer commodities that are presented in such a way that they *simulate* states of being, which is the sin of simony: an unhallowed trafficking in sacred things. Whereas the only thing I know that is sacred is the immediate experience of being, of belonging to your self, belonging to others, belonging to the world, belonging to the cosmos. And all this stuff that we acquire stands between us and the world beyond ourselves.

It muffles our being. The spiritual damage caused by living this way has worked the greatest evil in our world.

In a final statistic, Putnam finds that Americans born and raised in the seventies and eighties are three or four times more likely to commit suicide as people of the same age at the middle of the last century. If you are a latchkey kid and you're watching TV in your separate room, and your only way of belonging to other people is through stuff that *simulates* your being, and you're feeling really lonely, you might be willing to kill yourself.

Well, having painted for you a rather dismal picture of what became wrong with our world, let me now return to the gift economy of Burning Man and Black Rock City. Gifts are *very* good conductors of social capital. Let me illustrate. If I give you a gift, this represents a personal gesture. It is a bonding experience, unlike buying something from someone, where the great convenience is that we *aren't* connected. In a market transaction people who are party to it feel no further sense of human obligation. But interactions based on gifting operate quite differently. In the words of Lewis Hyde, who wrote a wonderful book called *The Gift,* "When gifts circulate within a group, their commerce leaves a series of interconnected relationships in its wake, and a kind of decentralized cohesiveness emerges." What he's saying is that in a gift economy everybody begins to feel like they belong to one another. Value passes from person to person, from heart to heart. To put this another way, gifts are bearers of being. Think about a gift that you loved giving. Didn't it feel as though it already belonged to the person you gave it to? Didn't it feel as if it was just flowing through you?

Black Rock City is devoted to the giving of all sorts of things, the sharing of survival resources, interactive artwork, and our public service roles. The whole tissue of our city is one vast gift. If you look at our budget it amounted to five million dollars in 2001. But if you want to understand what makes our city come alive as a civic entity, then look at the gifts that all our people give to us. It would run into the millions. I cannot begin to estimate it. We've actually created much of our civic infrastructure out of gifts. Volunteers greet every person who comes into our city, they police the environment, and they light the lamps that illuminate Black Rock City.

But I particularly want to call attention to a special kind of gift we call a theme camp, because it best illustrates the gift-giving process. This begins with what we call radical self-expression. We ask participants to commune with themselves and to regard their own reality, that essential inner portion of experience *that makes them feel real,* as if it were a vision or a gift, and then project this vision out onto the world. Now artists have been doing that for a long time. And it is an almost irresistible impulse out there in the Black Rock Desert because the environment is a blank slate. You can project your inner vision out onto the world as if you were projecting a movie. That is what makes radical self-expression so radical.

Along with radical self-expression comes radical self-reliance. Most of our citizens pool survival resources—they have to. They must prepare to survive in really drastic wilderness conditions: one-hundred-degree temperatures, hundred-mile-an-hour winds. And what tends to happen is that people respond communally. They form organized groups and someone says you bring the shelter, you bring the food, you bring the boa feathers, and we'll survive together. And we didn't tell them to do this. They realized that they had to form bonding social capital in order to survive. That's how cultures developed originally, you know. They developed an ethos and a sense of belonging because people had to share resources and struggle to survive together in the world not like the economy of convenience that we live in today.

Now we don't dictate the content of radical self-expression in the theme camps, but we create the societal vessel that helps to contain this creative, interactive, utterly uncontrollable process. We've created a few simple rules. We've said a theme camp must function as a public environment that is accessible to other people whom one doesn't know, and that it must result in some kind of social interaction. I don't know if you notice what I'm saying here, but that's bonding social capital turning into bridging social capital.

Before I go further, let me describe a theme camp because it's hard to imagine in the abstract. I think my all-time-favorite theme camp, after all these years, is Camp Fink. I encountered Camp Fink by chance. I walked into a tent that looked like a seedy sportsman's bar. There were crossed tennis racquets on the wall, and it had all these portraits of famous finks: Roy Cohn, Joe McCarthy, and Richard Nixon—because he finked himself out. But here's the interactive part. They had an ancient Corona typewriter out in front with an endless spool of paper, and they invited you to rat out on your friends. And you'd be surprised, it got really interactive, because everyone wanted to read what everybody else was saying!

In recent years, many of these theme camps have become increasingly ambitious—and that's only a natural tendency because in a space with no physical limits your imagination grows larger and larger. A vision is not defined by the context of the world around it, but radiates reality outward: it starts to define the surrounding world. And people get these visions and end up incorporating two or three hundred people. Now all people are collaborating to produce a public service or an expressive theme of some kind. And they form large communal networks in which everyone is cooperating toward a common goal; this is what Putnam called bonding social capital.

But observe what we've done. We've told people: OK, you've got your tight little world of your mates and your friends, don't close the circle. Leave it open so you can bridge out to a larger world, and, indeed, so you can feel the great world has the same sense of inner reality that you feel in yourself. And the shape of the entire city is like that. It's planned as a huge semicircle with the Man at the geographic center and the streets radiating out. One time someone said, "Larry, why don't you just close that circle?" and I said, "Good God, we'd go psychotic. Don't close the circle!"

So, theme camps are essentially collective gifts, and this, in turn, begins to generate gift-giving networks. We've found that when people join together for the purpose of producing a gift whose scope extends beyond the limits of their little bonded world, it produces a kind of social convection current. The hotter the flame, the more oxygen it will suck in. And these networks suck in a whole lot of resources. They begin in simple ways—and no one plans this— let me make that clear. They just happen. For instance, someone in a camp knows someone else—a friend outside the group who possesses some needed resource—and soon this person is drawn into the circle. If he's willing to give to the gift you don't exclude him, you say come on in. That's the principle of radical inclusivity we discovered many years ago.

As the greater gift imagined by the group begins to grow, this process starts to spread out through networks of acquaintance, connections multiply and a new kind of superabundant wealth appears. A metal grate abandoned in a basement becomes a dragon's jaw, some ancient string of Christmas lights forgotten in the attic forms the perfect accent for its tail. Manifold resources stream in. It's precisely the opposite of what happens in a capitalistic society where a struggle for scarce resources produces relentless competition. And this process can actually rival the capabilities of mass production. Social networks tend to grow on an organic principle. They expand exponentially.

Here's an example of how we are growing. A group of New Yorkers, affiliated with the nonprofit organization SEAL, came to our event in 2001. Burning Man occurs over Labor Day, so that, of course means that when this group returned from Black Rock City in they encountered the events of September 11th. For days afterward a pall of dust and smoke drifted over the island of Manhattan as police manned emergency checkpoints all over the city. Now this group had lived communally at Burning Man. They had seen their bonding world become a bridging world and they responded to this public trauma in a unique way. They began to craft burn barrels. These are oil barrels into which we cut designs. These objects are beautiful—they look like jack-o'-lanterns—and serve as fireplaces that protect the desert surface. So this group put the word out to create a network of people to manufacture burn barrels. They donated several of these beautiful pieces to the New York City Police Department; now, emergency workers had a place to warm their hands during the long winter nights. As I say, the rate of return on social capital is a lot better than the rate of return on normal capital investment in the market world.

This is the good news. All over this country, people are starting to organize. They're starting to form networks and we're helping them. We don't dictate the content of radical self-expression. But we help people create the social circumstances that will sustain an ethos of gift giving. And I can tell you what's going to happen next because I have watched Burning Man grow from two thousand to four thousand to eight thousand participants in the span of three years. In fact, it only stopped growing at this rate because we slowed it down. We didn't want it to grow too fast. We took measures so that we could culturally assimilate people, so they wouldn't just come looking for a party, so they'd realize that our ethos was about giving and not about consuming. We knew that they'd destroy us if we didn't slow it down. But what this growth represents is a rate of natural increase; it's how things grow in nature. And the next big story is that networks all over the country are about to rapidly expand in scope. There have now been burns in several states; we have regional contacts in every place except Mississippi. There's even been a burn on a boat in the Baltic Sea and one in Antarctica.

This returns me to Richard Jefferies and his essay on the

prodigality of nature and the niggardliness of man: "There is no 'enough' in nature. It is all one vast prodigality." I believe that human culture—as distinct from the social institutions that surround it—is a pure phenomenon of nature. Social institutions have the power to protect it and sustain it, much as any vessel—a petri dish or ceramic pot—might help or hinder the growth of any living thing. But the innate vitality of culture belongs to the world of nature; it occurs spontaneously, it is without a plan, and when it is allowed to grow it has a power to affect our world in ways that dwarf our normal estimate of our resources.

I think that the essential lesson that we've learned is, in a way, very simple. People don't have to go out into the world and create a great city. We've made our city as large and as civic as it is in order to create a sufficiently persuasive model of the world to show people how things could be. I still want it to grow larger, frankly. I mean it won't be New York, but I want it to feel like a complete model of civilization so that people can go back home with the confidence that they can change the world and they can share that vision with other people and they can attach to it some transcendent principle. That is why the Man stands at the center of our city.

This process begins with radical self-expression: the feeling that your inmost vital self is real. But most people just don't have the confidence anymore because they're too isolated; they're too passive. So it starts with this, I'll call it "I Am." And it proceeds, as in a theme camp, to a feeling that you are united with others, that you are linked in a bonded circle and together you can share the same experience through an act of giving. And I'll call this, "We Are." Finally there is the feeling that somewhere outside this circle there exists some greater gift that everyone is joined together by as they give to *it*, and I'll call this "It Is." And I have come to believe that whenever these feeling states can be strung together like pearls on a string, as if they were parts of one spontaneous gesture, you will then generate an ethos, a culture, that leads, in Jefferies's words, to a "boundless shower of good things forever descending."

Now I've told you things are getting a bit bleak in our world. We're just so accustomed to this state of things that we don't notice. But I don't think I've told you just how bad they can get. So I'm going to tell you a story. It's like *A Christmas Carol.* This is where the ghost says to Scrooge, "This is Christmas future." I'm going to tell you about Christmas future. This is where we're going.

Some time ago, I went to a dinner that was given for an artist friend who was leaving for a journey up a river into the jungle of New Guinea to confer with some tribal sculptors. And it was a lively party. It was a bunch of my more louche bohemian friends, and it was held in an Italian restaurant that I'd never been to. I was just given an address, and when I got there I was astonished, because it was located on the edge of San Francisco' financial district. I mean all these high-rises and condos, and it was very apparent to me that this was a small family enterprise and that it had been there for years, and I wondered how the hell it had survived. There were family pictures on the walls, mementos, and we went downstairs through a narrow corridor to a special room that was obviously precious to them. It was decorated in primary colors and we were taken into the place of honor, and there was a big round table and on that round table was a giant lazy Susan. It felt really communal. It was so cool that everyone could share. And at the center of this thing, at the center of this communal circle, was this transcendent object. It was a bust of the Pope. In fact, they'd surrounded it with a big square Plexiglas cube, so it looked like a miniature Popemobile.

Now this is what I call a sympathetic bistro! The food was robust, the cuisine of southern Italy, and the waiters were to a one all very jolly. I love this kind of restaurant; I love family places. They brought in bottle after bottle of Chianti. And, of course, we were using this lazy Susan, so the bottles went round and round, and pretty soon the room was spinning round and round as we got drunker and drunker. As I say, these were bohemians and never noted for any inhibition, and they became increasingly rambunctious, and at a certain point one of the guests by the name of Kaos Kitty climbed up on the table and proceeded to do things to the head of the Pope that *I really don't want to describe to you*—let's call it radical self-expression.

This is, of course, the kind of scandalous story that's often better in the telling, something you read about in a memoir of the lives of the artists. There was a lot of laughter, shocked looks from people in the adjoining room, and my friends, on the whole, were thrilled by their audacity. But I will confess to you tonight that I was inwardly chagrined. Think about it for a moment. Here we were in the bosom of this family place around the altar of their simply Catholic piety ... desecrating it? And I left the restaurant that night feeling a pang of guilt and a flush of shame on my face, I really did. I thought about apologizing as I went out, but I was too ashamed, and for weeks afterward I was burdened by this feeling of guilt because I'd sat by ... I'd laughed too.

Well, some months later my girlfriend and I were walking through the slushy streets of Minneapolis in the middle of a midwinter thaw. There was fog filling the air and we were looking for some place to eat at a late hour. We went around a corner and across the street I saw this nimbus of neon light in the air. We crossed over and, sure enough, it was a neon sign and, sure enough, it was a sympathetic bistro—on fact it was *the* sympathetic bistro. It was the same place I'd encountered in San Francisco! And I thought, well gee, did a cousin, a nephew branch out to *Minneapolis?*

We went inside and the atmosphere brimmed with familiar sentiment. Family pictures lined the walls, and they'd painted the exposed plumbing ... and then it really dawned on me. This was *not* a sympathetic bistro. What I'm saying is this was not a communal thing, this was not a bonded group. This was not a family restaurant. The pictures and the keepsakes on the walls had been purchased by the lot at auction. And when I looked at the other diners, all of them white, pretty Anglo-Saxon looking and undoubtedly Lutheran, the full implications of this began to sink in. Most of the tables were for large groups. This was the demographic. A waiter came in with a lighted cake, there was a birthday party, and suddenly I understood what this was. It was a RED, an acronym for retail entertainment destination. This is the fastest-growing trend in retail, and it's remaking our world. REDs are the finest flower of our marketing system and they are a commodification of our lives. You see most of our desire and addictions are really projections of our need *to be*. And they've become really good at finding out what our desires are, and they've learned to create stuff—both goods and entertainment—which we then consume as substitutes for being.

In the case of the jolly bistro, some entrepreneur had determined—using demographic studies and psychographic profiles—what WASPs really need in their lives. And I can tell you from personal experience what WASPs really *do* need in their lives. Family members often live in different states, and family dinners and gatherings can be awkward. You don't have anything in common with anyone because bonding social capital has broken down a little. So you go to these gatherings, and you find yourself wistfully and secretly wishing that things were, oh, a little warmer, a little more sympathetic, a little more … well, Mediterranean. *If only we could be Italians!* And this environment, this bistro, was designed to fill this gap. Art blended with science. If people want to feel that they belong to one another, then it's wholly feasible and very profitable to manufacture the illusion of this feeling. I had really enjoyed the food at the original restaurant back home, but sitting there with my girlfriend I picked indifferently at my meatball. I kind of herded it around the plate and, as I did so, I forgave Kaos Kitty for her performance. In fact, on the whole, *it seemed very appropriate.*

Let me give you a little profile of retail entertainment destinations. They're usually located in metropolitan areas, and they're devoted to the proposition long understood by marketers that it's more lucrative to sell a state of being than a product. There's nothing new in this. Sell the sizzle, not the steak. That's what they used to say, but REDs in this late stage of capitalism are based on much shrewder and more sophisticated insights. They're not just selling attractive and desirable sensations; they're selling a lot more than that.

REDs come in different shapes and sizes. I've described the little restaurant, but it works up into larger complexes. These typically combine dining, shopping, and entertainment attractions. In the trade journals this is called the "trinity of synergy." Because they know if you're eating and you're shopping and you're being entertained, you'll spend a lot more money. It grows up into very large-scale complexes, and these are being built at a tremendous rate. You know what I'm talking about: Disneyland, the Strip in Las Vegas, New York's Times Square.

Another feature of these places is an air of amenity and authenticity: monumental architecture, open-air loggias, colonnades, fountains, vaulted ceilings, and decorative plasterwork. It's all part of what's come to be called the "experience economy." These places are designed to appeal to our need for community and identity. At times they almost seem to waft a sense, albeit rather cheapened, of classical civilization. At least it seems so superficially, but when you descend to ground level, to the place where humans interact, the place where culture's roots should grow, it is a very different story.

After my experience with the jolly bistro, I became fascinated with these places. So two years ago at Christmas time I decided to go to Las Vegas. I wanted to see the great mother of them all and learn something from it. Now I'll admit to you that I dislike the yuletide season. This great orgy of spending and consumption and forced giving seems to me like the ultimate perversion of what giving should be. So I engage in whatever activity feels like the *opposite* of Christmas. So it was that in late December of 2000 my girlfriend and I embarked on a holiday and we decided to call it our Viva Las Xmas tour.

At the same time, the Guggenheim announced its plan to open a gallery as a magnet attraction at the Venetian. That's an example of what the trade journals call *edutainment*. And later, on TV, a young woman representing the museum described this venture as a noble form of democratic outreach to the hoi polloi, to the unwashed masses—and, I might add, a very lucrative proposition for its gift shop. And an art critic was featured looking like he'd just downed a snifter of quinine water. He was actually wearing a turtleneck, and he talked about the postmodern implications of this daring move and how it was ironic … and so forth.

You see, in the last twenty years Vegas has reinvented itself as a thoroughgoing RED. It used to be this sleazy place where guys went for action, but ah, not anymore! It's now a center of edutainment, infotainment, eatotainment—every kind of 'tainment you can think of. They've torn down all the old facades and, in their place, they've erected palaces that offer up the holy trinity of market synergy. We wandered through these great complexes. We loitered in the shadow of animatronic sculptures. We witnessed the musical fountains and beheld the pharaonic mysteries of ancient Egypt at the Luxor. At Caesar's Palace I actually bought an ashtray, I admit it. It was irresistible. But my favorite place was the Rio, because there we discovered a riverboat that they'd mounted on the ceiling on a curvilinear track, and it was filled with performers who, like performers on Broadway, were dancing and singing their hearts out. It actually was interactive, and I got kind of excited about that. They kept coming around and they were waving at us and we were waving at them.

In fact, this kind of interactivity is typical of REDs. Here is my favorite quote from a trade. It explains that interactivity is a key component of immersion environments: "Free street performances, another form of ambient entertainment, strive to replicate the spontaneity of the archetypal, if not mythical, marketplace. Yet because they work independently, their performance can be unpredictable making them potentially disruptive to both visitors and tenants. Thus authentic performances are not commonly allowed on the private property of destination complexes." Instead they hire performers and typically these performances are of short duration. They've studied this and found that maximum spending is reckoned to take place during a period of three to four hours. This is the reason for the ersatz interactions, why they hire these performers, and why the performances are so brief.

We did witness the great speaking statue of Neptune at Caesar's Palace. It was set in a courtyard, and, in a weird kind of cartoon way it might have been Florence. It could have been a northern Italian hill town with its a public square, a very civic setting. This robotic Neptune spoke to us for about seven minutes, it attracted a large crowd, and then it stopped and everyone dispersed—and where did they go? Right into all these shops that strategically surrounded it. And every one was a brand name high-end retail outlet selling goods at a 200 percent markup! And I'll make an even more embarrassing confession: I went into one and bought a pair of Gucci's. Even knowing what it was, I was caught up in the trance.

You see, these settings are engineered with the precision of a hermetically sealed engine. Though they may look like urban spaces, you'll find no posters pasted to the lampposts, and you will experience none of the spontaneous encounters that are the lifeblood of culture.

What you will discover is what we discovered: the people chute. In the process of reinventing itself, Vegas has built an elaborate system of pedestrian transportation. They've located large parking complexes on the periphery of the Strip, and they funnel people through casino environments by an integrated system of escalators, bridges, elevators, tramways, and a variety of other mechanical devices. We were never more than ten feet away from an opportunity to buy something. It was virtually impossible to escape this. The space of one casino bled seamlessly into the next.

At the very end of our stay we took the elevator upstairs at the Rio, walked into a restaurant and went out on the terrace, and there, spread out before us, was the Strip: this great evil drive train glittering in the desert night. And I thought to myself, *this is just like Burning Man*! We, too, create a scene, a fantasy environment. Each year we create an annual art theme because we believe that stories and myths are one way that people belong to each other and one way that you can get artists to collaborate. What is more, we fill it with interaction and ambient entertainment. The theme camps and art are magnet attractions. We even have our own Electric Parade every year! Spread out on the desert floor, our glittering city is a capsule world that obliges people to linger and loiter and totally immerse themselves in an environment. The only difference is that you cannot buy or sell anything. The only difference is that you are seldom more than ten feet away from opportunities to interact with art and other human beings. The only difference is that you must give of yourself. The only difference, finally, is that it is *real*.

You see, the great irony of this is that the creators of these REDs have almost inadvertently reinvented a model of classical civilization. Pursuing a path of market research, they've learned that human beings crave something greater than themselves to which they can belong. They've learned that we need myths and stories that can tell us who we are. They've learned that we need a coherent theater in which to act out life's drama.

And yet, marketers also know that in our modern world the public craves variety and choice. The Palladian facades of the

Venetian palaces that they concoct allude to an older order in which traditions shaped and governed everything. But underneath it all, beneath the plaster facades and the faux marbling, they know that in today's consuming world the individual and individual's desires are king. It is, in fact, our desires as individuals disassociated from history, place, and any sense of a surrounding community that drive our economic system. Judged by any civilized standard, the mass culture of an RED is an oxymoron. Yet I think there is much we can learn from it.

And this goes back to where I began. I said the great value of our modern system is that it uniquely caters to the individual. We are in the forefront of this consumer revolution, but all around the globe traditional societies that once housed cultural processes and formed social vessels of belonging are beginning to shatter. We used to call these societies the third world, but now they're called *emerging economies*—but we are now, today in America, the most individualized and the most self-conscious people that have ever existed on the face of the earth. And I don't think we are ready to return to a simpler life or the type of society that once sustained culture.

Demands for self-restraint will not be heard because we demand choice, we demand freedom, and we value our individuality more that anything else. Nor do I think we can reconstruct the kinds of societies that once helped culture to thrive. They depended on the fact that people had to struggle together, that circumstances held people together over long periods of time. We want to change our jobs, we want to move freely through the world, we want to redefine ourselves continually: we have exploded that ancient world of tradition.

I've discussed a continuum of being: an *I am*, a *We are*, and an *It is*. But if you look at all previous ages of human culture, the order of this continuum started with *It is*, with gods and myths of supernatural origin, sustained by traditions among people who struggled to survive in a challenging world. And it ended somewhat tenuously with the experience of the individual. Today this sequence works and must work *in reverse*. It must necessarily begin with *I am,* at the level of each individual's experience.

So let me return to my comparison of Burning Man with retail entertainment destinations. The essential appeal of Burning Man is to the individual. We've achieved an ethos, and we have a few basic rules. But no one is required to subordinate himself or herself. Instead, all are invited to expand themselves. Burning Man is available on *their* terms: anyone can engage in radical self-expression. Everyone is free to do and be. The great difference between us and the consumer marketplace, however, is that we have inverted the essential nature of the capitalist system. We are like Disneyland *turned inside out*. Because at the heart and center of this thing you will find a gift and, in so doing, you yourself, your unique spirit will itself become a gift and be consumed like fire in its passage to the sky.

Seventeen years ago, I started Burning Man on a beach in San Francisco. This is frequently the first thing that people ask me about. They want a myth, and I was once incautious enough to tell a reporter that it corresponded to the anniversary of a lost love affair. That story has now circled the globe, and it's been interpreted and reinterpreted as myths often are. I've been told that I was burning myself, that I was burning my ex-girlfriend, that I was burning my ex-girlfriend's new boyfriend, but none of these stories are true. They're factoids. They're myths in the modern sense of the word: distortions of the truth. And yet people keep asking me this question, and I think it's because they're looking for a myth in the older and more profound sense of the term. But myths are not about chains of causation or rational reasoning. They tell us that the essence of things is contained in first causes, and that everything, as in any vision, emanates radically out of this. That's what people are asking me to tell them. That's the nature of the story that they *need* to hear. So I will tell you *that* story.

One day in 1986 I called a friend and said, let's build a man and burn him on the beach. I did this on impulse. There was really nothing on my mind. I've thought about it over the years, and the best I can say is that some passionate prompting, some immediate vision just had to be embodied in the world. Call it radical self-expression … *I Am*. We built our man from scraps of wood, then called some friends and took it to the beach. We saturated it with gasoline and put a match to it, and within minutes our numbers doubled. That's actually when Burning Man began as an institution, you know. We were so moved by that we knew we had to do it again. If we'd done it as a private and personal thing, I'm sure we wouldn't have repeated it. And I remember holding my son in my arms, and I looked at each face illuminated in the firelight. They had formed a semicircle about it, and I was so moved—*We Are*. They'd all come to see this gift. A woman ran over and held its hand. I didn't know who she was. The wind was shunting the flames to one side, and someone took a picture of it—it's the only recorded instant. She just had to touch it. She wanted to belong to it. And then, of course, there was the Man himself. Standing there against the limitless horizon of the broad Pacific, it seemed to belong to the ocean, to belong to the sky—to exist in some realm immeasurably beyond us. It formed a fireball, a second sun brought down to earth, a sudden, uncontrollable and completely spontaneous emission of energy. *It Is*. And when I look at Black Rock City today, I notice that its curving streets are like that semicircle of people so many years ago on Baker Beach. Our city seems to reach out to the Man as if it could capture him, but can never quite possess this gift at its center. *I Am … We Are … It Is*. What more is there to say, except that I believe there is a way that all of us can *be* together.

17

A FAREWELL TO ADVERTISING

KEN JORDAN

I get great pleasure from imagining a world with no advertising. Sure, there's the occasional commercial that gets me to smile, but most ads make me feel like I'm being talked down to; instead of addressing me in an honest, straightforward way, they try to draw my attention to whatever they're hawking through gimmicky manipulations—for instance, paying a celebrity to announce how dearly he adores a certain car insurance, gas-guzzling SUV, or cat litter. Other ads try to freak me out because my breath smells, my armpits reek, and my hair isn't glossy enough to earn me a kiss. No need to list the other approaches ad agencies employ; we've all internalized the myriad strategies used to subliminally coerce us into buying stuff we don't need or want.

The sense I get from advertising is that I'm continually being lied to, everywhere I turn. But more disturbing still is that the picture of the world offered by advertising is of a throw-away consumer culture based on instant gratification, presented as a kind of heavenly paradise. We are in the midst of the Sixth Great Extinction, our country is perpetually at war, Wall Street's investment culture has revealed itself to be irredeemably morally bankrupt, and through it all, we are bathed by a perpetual stream of consumerist messaging that proclaims we live in a material paradise. All you have to do is buy the right beer, and babelicious models climb out of your fridge. Shopping sets you free.

But despite the relentless propaganda, at this point most Americans accept that our version of consumer culture is unsustainable. Not everyone sees this, certainly, but for decades the number has been growing, and some demographers think this long-time minority perspective became the majority in 2008, the year of the Obama election, which is a convenient marker for the shift. And yet, we are assaulted by more ads than ever. They appear on eggs and apples at the store, arrive as cell phone spam, sneak up as product placement in the movies—some sources say that the average American is exposed to as many as three thousand ad messages a day. They blare at us from every conceivable angle: the sides of buildings, the floors of subway platforms, the back doors of public bathroom stalls. They shake, flash, and squeal in mock delight, aching to convince us that our deepest needs can be satisfied on the supermarket shelf. We're only one kitchen cleanser away from having the time of our lives.

The cumulative effect of this non-stop assault, which begins at birth and continues through our final moments, is to make us numb. We know we can't trust ads, but we get suckered in by them; ultimately, they achieve what they are designed to do, which is to sell product. Our understandable response is to develop a thick wall of defense against their come-ons. We become sophisticated critics, armed with irony and a knee-jerk cynicism, knowing better than to accept an ad at face value. At the same time, we can't imagine an alternative to the consumerism they promote, and so fall prey to their manipulations again and again. As good cynics, we realize that any effort to remake society is bound to fail, so we might as well stock up on the latest disposable pleasure and make sure to get our money's worth. But seeds have been planted for an alternative worth considering.

Today, thanks to the internet, once I know what I want, I can usually find it pretty quickly. For instance, it took me about ninety seconds to discover that Americans are exposed to three thousand ads a day, and I was then able to compare that number to estimates from other sources. Search engines have become extremely effective at connecting people to what they're looking for. Recommendation engines, like the kind on Amazon.com that suggests books you might be interested in, based on your previous purchases, have steadily improved, linking you to music and books you probably will like, people you could date, schools to attend, cars to buy. These matchmaking technologies might not be able to look into your soul and surprise you with an offer out of left field, but once you express, for example, an interest in permaculture, automated systems are now quite good at letting you know about new permaculture books and DVDs, and (in theory) permaculture courses, groups, gardening supplies—whatever a budding permaculturist could want.

Matchmaking systems of this kind are popping up everywhere online. Unfortunately, they are guided by the same manipulative practices and questionable ethics endemic to the advertising industry. Companies engaged in digital advertising, like Google, Microsoft, and Facebook, do their best to surreptitiously track the online behavior of whoever they can, creating detailed profiles of each of us that will help them capture our interests and predict our future purchases. Beacon and cookie technology installed by third parties stalks us as we go from website to website, following where we go and watching what we click on. So if I spend a lot of time on car websites, I might notice that while visiting CNN.com, MSNBC .com, or YouTube, suddenly a legion of car ads appear. Marketers will spend extra for these targeted ads, because it helps them narrow in on likely customers, making the ad-buying process less like firing buckshot. And if you do want to buy a new car, all the car ads suddenly flooding your screen might be useful.

But these matchmaking systems, as they currently exist, have serious drawbacks. For a start, you have no idea what these profiles say about you, or what is being done with them. The data collected about you, usually without your knowledge, is owned by the company that collects it, which can do whatever it pleases with that information, including sell it to whoever pays. The lawyers at the Electronic Frontiers Foundation (EFF), the Electronic Privacy Information Center (EPIC), and other privacy advocates are rightly outraged by how little control we have over the data about us that streams across the internet. They are also frustrated by how little the public seems to care about it. People tend to prioritize convenience over privacy, and they don't expect that the owners of these profiles will abuse them, or at least not so badly that a real crisis results.

At the same time, it is also true that mainstream media has barely touched this story, aside from the occasional article in the *Wall Street Journal* or *New York Times,* so who knows how widely understood the situation actually is. Certainly, it is in the interest of media companies to keep concern low, since targeted ads bring them higher rates at a time when their traditional business model is melting down. But it is sadly predictable that abuses will occur without appropriate oversight, just as they did recently in the housing market and on Wall Street, to disastrous effect.

You can expect that soon profiles about you will be compiled with an expansiveness and efficiency that would have made the East German secret service green with envy. How will that information be used? Will that profile be reviewed by an employer to discover if you take part in "questionable" behavior, or will a landlord check into your "desirability" before you sign a new lease? If they can, while reducing financial risk and reassuring investors, it's hard to believe they would resist.

Meanwhile, the ads that get pumped out through this targeting system are unchanged, as annoying and manipulative as ever. And as the number of ad messages we receive grows, the attention that any one attracts drops. Madison Avenue has been complaining for years about how hard it is to cut through the clutter in this crowded environment, that it forces them to push out more and more ads if they hope to have an impact and get precious clicks. But why should you click? Ads swarm around us like gnats, asking to be swatted away. Your first impulse is to not click, because you know ads can't be trusted. The average click-through rate for an online ad is a fraction of 1 percent; a response by more than 2 percent is considered a phenomenal success. Think about it: over 98 percent of viewers prefer to not respond to the interactive ads they see.

But instead of bending matchmaking technology to the purposes of the old marketing paradigm, emerging technologies could support a different model, one that respects our privacy, acknowledges our intelligence, and responds to actual needs, not manufactured desires. Imagine how different things would be if marketing messages had integrity, if their claims were vetted by trusted sources, and if they informed you about things you really want, so you could evaluate whether a product is right for you. Instead of being on the receiving end of an endless stream of crafty seductions that hope to trigger a purchase, you would be exposed to just a few that are clear and informative, and only for products that you deliberately express an interest in. An ad's claims would be validated by independent third parties, like Consumer Reports, and these ratings would be easy to find, even if they are less than favorable.

You're probably thinking: forget it, that's impossible. And, of course, you're probably right. But before you dismiss this prospect entirely, please join me for a thought experiment. Suppose that:

- Instead of an anonymous corporation owning your personal data, and deciding what to do with it without your permission, *you* control the data in your digital profile. You choose to "track yourself" as you go from place to place online, collecting the geologs from your mobile phone, your social network links, your current address and other relevant data in your profile. With this control, you get to decide what information is in your digital profile, what information can be shared with whom and under what conditions. This is not a pipe dream; companies are appearing that can provide these services. For instance, as this book goes to press, a new class of services is emerging that offers data banking to consumers; just as your money is not made invalid when you move it from one bank to another, your data can be portable in the same way between service providers. Companies such as Mydex, Azigo, Personal.com and Singly are offering the first wave of digital data banking services of this kind, and are an encouraging sign of things to come.

- Instead of being on the receiving end of a relentless stream of unwelcome ads, you use your digital profile to express interests and needs, soliciting information about the product categories that matter to you. Rather than being solicited by marketing companies who push out ads based on their best guesses about what you might respond to, you only view the marketing messages you request. It is well known that pursuing "qualified leads" of this kind is a far more effective way to reach a customer than today's buckshot model.

- Instead of producing ads that compete for your attention by making cheesy come-ons or questionable claims—while communicating next to nothing that can be trusted—advertisers agree to follow a code of conduct. Promotional claims are validated by independent third parties. Today, there are scores of certification systems that evaluate claims about product safety, greenness, organic materials, localism, and fair labor practices. Twenty-first-century Green Seal stamps would be printed on every package and be a click away from any ad banner. Product information becomes easily available and transparent—not because the government compels it, but because the absence of third-party certification signals consumers not to buy a product.

- Instead of staring blankly at a new product, unable to learn whether friends and others you trust have tried and liked it, you have access to a list of people you know that says whether they give the product a "thumbs up" or "thumbs down." Every product, of course, has mixed reviews. But you can easily find the percentage of people whose shopping prowess you trust that have endorsed a particular product—not because they get paid for it, but because they want you to support the best green cleanser, the best locally built furniture, the most effective water-saving washing machine. Again, this information is managed through your user-centric digital profile.

- Instead of pushing sales messages onto an unsuspecting public, marketing companies act as brokers that work on behalf of both the producer and the consumer, bringing the two into contact. If you are in the market for a new rug, for instance, your interest is broadcast to floor cover marketing companies, which respond with information about their clients. Based on your desired price point, material of choice, and design type, the marketers target the messages they send to you. Because they have agreed to follow a code of conduct, the ads are substantive instead of gimmicky. Clicking on the banner brings you to a web page that conveys what you need to know about the product, along with a video and a list of stores near you that stock it. The best marketers are known for the effectiveness of their matchmaking capabilities in a trusted environment.

This approach would fundamentally alter the way we shop. The difference was made clear to me by Kaliya Hamlin, organizer of the semi-annual Internet Identity Workshop conferences in the Bay

Area, and one of the leading analysts of digital identity trends. The current model, she explained, can be shown in a simple diagram with three nodes (see figure 1): the buyer, the producer, and the marketer—which is the sole intermediary between the other two, sending messages to potential buyers with little to no idea who the buyers are, hoping to convert a sale. Note that the communication from the marketer to the buyer is in one direction, with the buyer at the receiving end, unable to respond or participate in any kind of dialogue. In many instances, the marketer is supported by services that provide digital dossiers on millions of people that help them to target customers. For instance, Experian proudly boasts that it has detailed profiles of 2.1 billion people which it offers for sale to support targeted web advertising.

Figure 1.

The alternative model, made possible by digital identity technology, introduces two new intermediaries between the buyer and the producer (see figure 2). One is the buyer's agent, which represents the interest of the buyer and broadcasts the message that the buyer is looking for a particular product—such as a dark blue organic wool rug that is six by nine feet. This agent is the trusted broker of the buyer's personal data (its "data banker"), and it only shares this information under the buyer's direction. The second new intermediary is the producer's agent, which broadcasts information about the producer's products to buyers' agents across the internet, looking for matches. This product information would be detailed and vetted by third parties, and should include the product's environmental impact, labor conditions, consumer evaluations, and more. So before the buyer makes a decision about whether or not to purchase that rug, she knows how it was manufactured, the materials that went into it, and what other people think about it. The key to this model is that the buyer's agent is aware of the buyer's personal data, and the producer's agent is not. A fully functioning market like this eliminates the need for services that sell digital dossiers to marketers, such as Experian. The transactions could take place online, but just as likely, the producer's agent could draw potential buyers to come by brick-and-mortar retail outlets to experience the products in person.

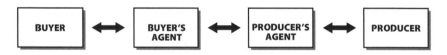

Figure 2.

You can see how a system like this could grow to include all of the essential products you use, from toilet paper and face cream to clothing and hardware. The technology exists today to turn our marketing paradigm upside down—or, perhaps more accurately, right side up. The key innovation is for digital profile data to move easily from place to place online, *under the control and ownership of the person it is about.* Over the past few years, a number of components of this potential new systems have emerged from forums like the Internet Identity Workshop, OASIS, W3C and the World Economic Forum Rethinking Personal Data project. The core of these systems are built by privacy activists to keep governments and corporations from holding information about you without permission. The challenge to this twenty-first-century marketing paradigm is not technical. Rather, it is social. As a society, are we ready to apply existing technology to transform how we exchange goods?

Once products are connected to people's actual needs, the entire thrust of messages that marketers send would change. No more need for misleading claims. The tenor of advertising would shift to propositions coming from a place of integrity. At the same time, the rationale for wasteful, flashy packaging is eliminated. (You bought a computer to send email, not to revel in the layers of perfectly sculpted plastic shards that you had to tear out of the box to get at it.) One possible by-product of such a system could be that, without society's relentless call to consume, people might realize that they would be happier with less than they currently possess. Why burden yourself with your own vacuum cleaner, lawn mower, coffee grinder, crock pot, electric heating pad, washing machine, or any of the other myriad contraptions that clutter up the average middle-class American apartment? All it takes is a moment of reflection to realize that each is used for an hour or two a week, if that. Why not pool resources with your neighbors, put the best appliances in a hall closet, give the extras away, and replace the broken ones (they always break) with really good ones meant to last, which are worth repairing and which you would be stretched to buy on your own? At the same time, you get to know your neighbors. Less *is* more.

We know that America's relationship to stuff has to change, and digital tools give us the opportunity to design the kind of marketplace we want to live with. In the process of constructing it, we transform our communities and ourselves. We heal our hearts, pursuing the path of a more transparent, less materialist society. The earth is calling us to embrace a new politics of the sacred, one which will expand the safe space where the heart can be revealed, available for connection. As hard as it might be to believe such a transformation is possible, in fact, a profound change might be closer than anyone might think, ready to be expressed in how we live our daily lives. Along the fringes, far from the shopping mall, a yearning can be felt for a different kind of commerce.

Thanks to Kaliya Hamlin for reading a draft of this article and offering extremely helpful comments and suggested revisions.

18

THE BNOTE: LOCAL CURRENCY FOR BALTIMORE

JEFF DICKEN AND MICHAEL TEW

Even before printing a single note, everywhere we go in Baltimore people have already heard of the BNote, and businesses are signing on to accept them when we launch in spring 2011. We are finding that people support the idea of pioneering an alternative economic system, one that benefits people instead of corporations. Google searches now show websites referencing Baltimore's new local currency, and the local press radio is starting to cover us. Our currency design contest went global when blogs picked up the announcement. When the BNote arrives in Baltimore, only the birds will be surprised. In less than a year, we have grown from a bright idea into an organization on track to establish a local currency with broad community participation.

Much of this progress is due to the diversity and positive vision that the Evolver Social Movement has fostered among its local groups. Each local Evolver group puts on a monthly event, called a Spore, about topics relevant to the transformation. A Baltimore Spore on local currencies took place in the summer of 2009. Damien Nichols, who attended, asked his friend Michael Tew to join him at the next Spore to meet the people who seemed to share his activist vision. Michael's background is in both microfinance and legislative lobbying, and he had been looking for an opportunity to advance alternative economic systems on a community level. At the Spore, Michael participated in the discussion that followed the panel, and was invited to make a short presentation at the following Spore on the subject of microfinance. There, he put forth the possibility that, by the end of 2012, a microfinance-based economy could become the dominant form of economic organization for most people on the planet. Moreover, he proposed that Baltimore could be a good place to bring together microfinance with a local currency.

After his presentation, Michael met Jeff Dicken, a long-time supporter of microfinance efforts who has a background in information technology and the arts. During this and subsequent conversations, the importance of a local currency to a resilient community in face of economic meltdown became increasingly clear. Soon after, Jill Harrison, a social activist with experience in nonprofits, joined the team, and when Michael moved to Baltimore in March 2010, they began to have regular meetings. As word spread among Evolvers about the effort, more people expressed a willingness to help. By the end of June an effective and growing team of enthusiastic volunteers was gathering.

The next step was to address some basic questions: Should the currency system use a debit system or paper money? What organizational form should the governing body adopt? If we went with paper, how should we design and print the currency? How to attract community participation? We distributed the notes from each meeting to the group, including web links to resources, so everyone stayed informed and involved; we also discussed many of the system's features informally by email between meetings so that face-to-face conversations could be more productive. We decided to issue only one- and five-dollar value notes in the first year, and to call the currency the BNote.

The UK–based Lewes Pound website's guide to starting a currency and Peter North's *Local Money* provided invaluable guidance as we put together the strongest features of other currencies already in existence.

Our currency would be convertible to and from U.S. dollars, and we chose to restrict the pilot launch to a specific, easily identifiable neighborhood. The Hampden community turned out to have many of the features important to the adoption of a local currency:

- **Small-business support.** The Hampden Merchant's Association lists 162 independent businesses as members. There are few chain stores, and Hampden residents tend to do most shopping locally.
- **Defined geographic area.** Hampden is in the heart of Baltimore, bounded by the Jones Falls waterway on the west and Hopkins University to the east, with clear boundaries to the north and south as well.
- **Community.** Historically, the area was populated by immigrant mill workers. While recent years have seen much gentrification, a strong sense of community identity still exists, and there are many longstanding community organizations. At the same time, a wave of young, progressive Baltimoreans have moved into the neighborhood, opening businesses and providing new energy.

To encourage residents to think about the nature of money, and to inspire a continuing dialogue that will help shape the details of the system we establish, we have had a series of community meetings. These start with videos about currency or economic subjects, followed by a discussion about the BNote. We encourage people to get our monthly email newsletter, the *BNote Buzz,* and borrow materials from our small circulating library of books, articles, and DVDs. In addition, we've made some videos and animations that present our vision to stimulate interest in the project.

To encourage community participation, we launched a currency design contest at the annual HampdenFest in September 2010, where volunteers staffed a booth and connected with people from the neighborhood.

U.S. dollars will be convertible into BNotes at a 10 percent discount; ten dollars will buy eleven BNotes, each of which circulates at a value equivalent to one dollar. In this way, people get an immediate benefit from adopting the currency, and merchants who are able to spend their BNotes with other businesses or residents in the system do not see any negative financial impact.

Merchants can use the BNotes they accept in a number of ways. They can use them to buy stock or services for their business from others in the network. They can pay themselves and/or their employees partially in BNotes. They can give them as change, to encourage circulation. They can use them for their own purchases. And if for some reason they choose to exchange some back for dollars, BNotes may be redeemed at the same rate: eleven BNotes for ten dollars. There is a clear financial benefit to using the notes, and this speeds up the circulation.

The more extensive the network of storefront businesses, independent service providers, artisans, and residents who accept BNotes, the longer the notes will circulate (of course, the ideal is them to circulate indefinitely), and the stronger the system will be.

With no spread between the purchase and redemption rates to benefit the governing body, we will rely on other sources of income to fund the system's administration. While we expect to rely on contributions and grants to cover initial expenses, we should also be able to help support our organization through local currency "leakage," which occurs when a currency is bought and then withdrawn from circulation by collectors and souvenir hunters. This will include sales of mint and withdrawn notes to collectors through an organized marketing campaign. Another source of revenue will come from sales of artwork based on the BNote, such as postcards, T-shirts, and posters, and from commissions on sales of original local artwork through our website. In addition, the money on deposit to back the notes in circulation, amounting to 90 percent of the face value of the circulating BNotes, will generate a small amount of interest and will act as a microloan fund secured against cash flow, enabling us to make hybrid microloans.

A key part of our plan includes a microfinance program. We will use the capital gained from currency conversion to offer loans to local microbusinesses. In our view, this can be accomplished best if the microentrepreneurs are among the poorest, most disadvantaged members of the community. Traditional charities rarely reach this sector because it is difficult and time consuming, and so is not a high priority for them, while banks tend to avoid poor people like the plague.

A secondary, but important feature of this process is the filling in of supply and service chains, which enable merchants to use the currency rather than cash it in. This, in turn, will build a stronger currency, enabling the bills to stay in circulation, and also reduce the need for goods to be brought in from longer distances, reducing the area's carbon footprint—another contribution to sustainability.

We have accomplished a lot in just a few months, but much remains to be done. We are in the process of writing a formal mission statement and incorporating. We will also set up an advisory board of Hampden community leaders, as well as experts in currency, microfinance, and social business. And we will continue to enlist businesses to participate in the mid-2011 rollout.

Our discussions with other east coast currency programs have been very helpful, and we continue to reach out to volunteers, both inside and outside of the Evolver Social Movement, who share our vision. As our effort grows in experience, moving forward step by step, we are excited to contribute to a growing national movement that is spreading community currencies across the country, enabling localization projects and helping our economies to become more socially conscious and sustainable.

19

IS GOD EXPENSIVE?

ELIEZER SOBEL

In my early thirties, my favorite uncle, Norbert, recognized that I was on a spiritual path, and in a moment of candor, confessed that when he was around nineteen he used to hang out at the Ramakrishna Foundation, and later became deeply interested in the works of author Paul Brunton, whom he had had the privilege of meeting. Brunton was a well-known disciple of Ramana Maharshi's, and my uncle had a full collection of Brunton's books. Even after Alzheimer's had begun its assault on Norbert's cognitive skills, he was often pulling Brunton books off the shelf to read aloud quotations about the mystery of the inner self. His affinity for these matters was for a long time unknown to everyone in the family apart from his wife, my Aunt Karin, and was a real revelation to me, for even as a child, on some level I had recognized Norbert as a kindred spirit. Or more accurately, I could feel somehow that he had recognized me as a kindred spirit!

The only spiritual advice Norbert ever offered me over the years was surrounding the issue of money. A purist from the old school, he insisted that if anyone ever charged any money at all in exchange for spiritual teachings, I should run the other away as fast as possible. Thankfully my two earliest teachers, Ram Dass and Hilda Charlton, never charged. But as for the rest of my career as a seeker … let's just say I've paid through the nose. Uncle Norbert was not familiar with the sheer magnitude of commerce connected with contemporary spiritual pursuits, and I was reluctant to fill him in on all the teachers I had paid over the years, for surely he would have cast a leery and suspicious eye on all of them and doubted their motivations as well as my acumen.

Nor had Norbert heard one of the popular, prevailing ideas of those times: money is simply "green energy," and like all energy, can be used for good or ill. And who better to use lots of money for good than one's revered spiritual teacher? The problem, of course, was that somehow that approach to spirituality and money matters also often involved Swiss bank accounts, offshore trusts, and ridiculously lavish lifestyles, perhaps symbolized most blatantly by former televangelist Jim Bakker's famous gold-plated toilet seat. Or by Osho's (Bhagwan Shree Rajneesh's) ninety-nine Rolls Royces. (In Osho's defense, one of my heroes, Tom Robbins, insists that the cars were performance art, and that Bhagwan was merely offering a mirror to and making a mockery of our extremely materialistic culture. One does have to wonder, though, why he stopped at ninety-nine.)

One evening in the late '70s I attended an evening talk with Leonard Orr, the founder of Rebirthing. The price of admission was fifty dollars, but in return Leonard was promising to give people an idea that was worth many times that amount, an idea that could easily produce great riches. I revealed the idea in my book, *The 99th Monkey,* which costs $16.95, representing a savings of over 60 percent. And now in this anthology, I'm giving it away for a fraction of that cost!

Here is Leonard's idea. "My personal connection to Infinite Intelligence is sufficient to yield me a huge, personal fortune." The funny thing is, I don't doubt the truth of that at all. Of course, if you speak to Job about it, he might further clarify that "Your personal connection to Infinite Intelligence is also sufficient to bring you to the absolute brink of ruin." Infinite Intelligence is very moody; it can go either way. But in the meantime, perhaps a reader can sell Leonard's affirmation on eBay: "Invaluable Idea, Like New, Barely Used."

My friend Randy simply can't believe the kinds of things people will pay for, and keeps insisting that the two of us could easily create a religion with him as the charismatic leader and make a ton of money. He has already begun working on his fundamental teaching concerning the distinction between what he is calling "The Vertical Path" and "The Path Upward," and which one will cost more. I actually recognized the commercial possibilities of spiritual teachings one morning in the hot tubs at Esalen Institute in Big Sur, California, where I was a group leader. I was commenting to my friend Daniel, a therapist, about how cooperative everyone was in Esalen workshops; as a leader, I could ask my groups to do virtually anything and they would jump right in and try it. On a lark, Daniel and I discussed creating a new therapy, in which participants would be instructed in squawking like a chicken. Students would also learn the theoretical basis behind the technique: how the flapping of the arms stimulates certain acupuncture meridians, and the contraction of the vocal chords while squawking clears out the fifth chakra. As we practiced a few times, within minutes several people from an adjoining tub approached us and asked us which workshop we were in, because they wanted to sign up. We had our first converts!

Last August, I walked into a bar at Burning Man, and in order to receive a drink, patrons were asked to roll a pair of dice, and the bartender would tell you what you had to do. The challenge assigned to me was, "Walk around the room squawking like a chicken." *Ha!* I thought, *they don't know who they're dealing with, the one guy in the room who not only has actually been squawking since way back, but has actually taught it!* (The girl next to me rolled a lucky seven, and she got to be publicly spanked at the bar.)

But apart from obvious and extreme forms of financial exploitation and indulgence, most of us these days don't think twice about the idea of paying a reasonable fee to someone for their time and services, spiritual teachers as well, perhaps even more so.

On my recent book tour a single question kept repeatedly popping up in different cities, and always in response to my rattling
off a humorous and unimaginably long list of the many different
teachers, retreats, workshops, seminars, gurus, ashrams, and techniques I've experienced over the last thirty plus years. The question
was, "How were you able to afford to do all that?" And underlying
the question was the implication, "If I could afford to do all that,
I'd probably be enlightened by now."

My first answer was to remind the questioner of my Uncle Norbert's primary teaching: that God is free. Enlightenment is not for
sale, spiritual truths are not a commodity, and awakening to one's
true nature is not a buyer's market. In this spirit, many teachers
in the contemporary American Buddhist world do their work for
dana, which is the Pali word for generosity. Their teachings are
offered freely, and people may choose to contribute to their support according to their own measure, for what is generous to some
would be impossible to another.

My old friend Michael Freeman, founder and resident dharma
instructor at Southwest Sangha near Silver City, New Mexico, has
been a dana purist for well over twenty years, supporting himself
entirely through voluntary contributions, whether it be for meditation instruction or a carpentry job. His insistence on this practice
once caused a major anxiety attack in an intimate partner when
she realized that not only did her man not have a regular paycheck
coming in, but he sometimes received dana contributions in the
form of a pair of handmade socks or homemade carrot cake. Both
are lovely, heartfelt expressions of gratitude; neither can be applied
toward rent and groceries.

To live one's life that way requires developing a deep trust in
life itself, a knowing that one will be taken care of. Those of us
who never step off that ledge will never find out if it's true or not,
whether life will indeed support us. Indiana Jones illustrated this
leap of faith perfectly in *Indiana Jones and the Last Crusade* when he

had to step out over an abyss, and it was only in stepping off the spot he was standing on that he released the latch on a platform that swung up to meet his next step.

I unwittingly happened upon this idea while hitchhiking across the UK in my early twenties. One Friday afternoon it dawned on me that I had run out of cash and the banks would be closed until the following Monday morning. I had already had enough remarkably generous hitchhiking experiences in the preceding days that I had developed an unshakeable trust, and rather than panicking, I realized that things would work out and I'd find a bed to sleep in and a way to eat. Minutes later, a casual chat with a family on a beach led to my being invited to join them on their weekend holiday, all expenses covered. It felt like grace.

In the last number of years, Rabbi David and Shoshana Cooper and I have experimented with bringing the spirit of dana to a Jewish context, for surely the idea of *tzedakah*, or charity, figures strongly in the Judeo-Christian culture as well. We began offering our twice-yearly seven-day silent Jewish meditation retreats for dana, and discovered that we would receive as much and usually more than had we charged the usual per-head tuition. There was a great difference in feeling, though, in that each envelope we received felt like a gift, and in addition, the process enabled those with limited funds to attend the retreat who would otherwise not be able to. My Uncle Norbert would like the idea.

When the people on my book tour asked me how I had been able to afford my extravagant spiritual seeker's lifestyle for so many years, I explained that I was fortunate enough to have been born into a situation where just enough money had been freely given to me so that I always enjoyed the luxury of living a rather frugal and modest hippie lifestyle while pretty much doing whatever I wanted. And as members of the Doughnuts will attest—the Doughnuts being a philanthropic group composed of those suffering with the burden of great wealth thrust upon them, and all the mixed emotions, difficulties, and strings that come with it—I always found my financial freedom either a blessing or a curse, depending on how well I was using it. I have always felt extremely driven to somehow justify my very existence through using what was gifted to me wisely and productively, something I didn't always succeed at doing, which would plunge me into states of great despair.

I once asked dharma teacher Christopher Titmuss about it, and he said, "When you can relate to the money in the same way that you relate to your hand, you will be free." Meaning, my hand was given to me this time around, and I don't have a problem with it, not a lot of guilt, shame, or issues around having a hand. It was given to me, and I simply use it. May God bless the work of my hands, and may that work be offered freely.

20

LOCAL CONTROL OF CREDIT: THE FOUNDATION OF ECONOMIC DEMOCRACY

THOMAS H. GRECO

Throughout the world today, local communities are struggling to maintain their economic vitality and quality of life. The reasons for this are both economic and political, and are largely the result of external forces that are driven by outside agencies like central governments, central banks, and large transnational corporations. In brief, decisions made by others outside of the community are having enormous impacts on life within the community. Be that as it may, it is possible for communities to regain a large measure of control over their own welfare and to ameliorate the effects of those external forces by employing peaceful approaches that encourage human solidarity and are based on private, voluntary initiative and creativity.

I often use the analogy of the small boat harbor to convey the general idea of how local communities can protect their small enterprises while remaining open to the global economy. The process of globalization, while having many positive aspects, has thus far been carried out in such a way as to be destructive to small businesses, local economies, and democratic governance. It is as if there were a policy to remove the breakwaters from every small boat harbor in the world, the effect of which is to expose small boats to the turbulence of the open sea. As I put it in one of my lecture presentations—a rising tide may lift all boats, but the tidal wave of globalization smashes all but the biggest.

But a healthy global economy and a peaceful world require healthy communities. Is there still a place for small businesses? Must every advantage be given to the corporate megaliths at the expense of small enterprises? The ancient economic debate that poses "free trade" against "protection" is too limiting and out-moded. Healthy economies require both free trade *and* protection, each confined within its appropriate bounds. Communities must create the equivalent of breakwaters to protect their small enterprises and workers, while at the same time remaining open to the national and world economies.

It is encouraging to note that there has been a recent major awakening about the megacrisis that is developing worldwide, and a plethora of creative responses to it. *Sustainability, relocalization, human scale,* and the *devolution of power* are the current buzz. The big question, of course, is how are they to be achieved in the face of the tremendous forces that are driving us toward the precipice?

APPROACHES TO COMMUNITY ECONOMIC DEVELOPMENT

Sadly, the orthodox approach to community economic development over the past several decades has centered upon efforts to recruit some large corporation to come and set up operations in the local region—with the expectation that they will provide additional jobs for local people, stimulate business for peripheral industries and the service sector, and ultimately add to local tax revenues. The consequent competition among cities and states in pursuing that strategy has resulted in corporations wresting enormous concessions from host communities in such forms as tax abatements and infrastructure provided at taxpayer expense. But capital is notoriously fickle and recent developments have given it unprecedented mobility. Quite often the experience has been for companies to leave town as soon as the free lunch has expired, only to play the same game again somewhere else.

It is widely acknowledged that, in comparison to large corporations, small and medium enterprises (SMEs) contribute proportionately more to the economy in jobs, productivity, and innovation. According to the Organization for Economic Cooperation and Development (OECD), "SMEs play a major role in economic growth in the OECD area, providing the source for most new jobs. Over 95 percent of OECD enterprises are SMEs, which account for 60–70 percent of employment in most countries. As larger firms downsize and outsource more functions, the weight of SMEs in the economy is increasing. In addition, productivity growth—and consequently economic growth—is strongly influenced by the competition inherent in the birth and death, entry and exit of smaller firms." The same pattern would seem to hold in other parts of the world, including America.

Doesn't it therefore make more sense to nurture the businesses that are already part of the local economy? Doesn't it make sense to support those companies that are locally owned or managed and have a stake in the prosperity and quality of life in their home communities? Communities that have a high quality of life, an able workforce, and a clean and pleasant environment do not need to offer bribes to outsiders. Relocalization efforts cannot get very far without the creation of metasystems that support buying locally, selling locally, investing locally, and saving locally. Conventional political forms of money, and huge banking companies that are owned and managed by remote entities, by their very nature militate against relocalization. There is no need for antagonistic opposition to those entities; they can be made less relevant and less destructive by implementing creative methods that localize control over both exchange and finance.

I propose that groups and organizations that seek to promote healthy, sustainable local economies should make it a priority to organize regional mutual credit clearing associations as the centerpiece of a comprehensive program. As these associations develop and grow, they will provide their regions with an increasing measure of independence from the outside forces that control conventional money and banking, enabling communities to rise above "the race to the bottom" that has resulted from the kind of globalization that has been erected and forced upon the world by the World Trade Organization, the International Monetary Fund, and the World Bank. The credit clearing exchange is the key element that enables a community to develop a sustainable economy under local control and to maintain a high standard of living and quality of life.

The possibilities inherent in such a plan should not be judged by past experience with local currencies and other exchange alternatives. Just as a modern jet aircraft bears little resemblance to the Wright brothers' first airplane, so too are the more optimized exchange structures I propose unlike any community currency, LETS, or commercial "barter" exchange with which people might be familiar. Based on the principles we have outlined, it is now possible to engineer and build exchange systems to carry heavy economic loads within local bioregions and to operate them according to sound business principles. This is a multistage project that will proceed in the following sequence:

1. Institute measures that promote import substitution.
2. Provide an alternative payment medium, independent of any political currency and banking establishment.
3. Issue a supplemental regional currency.
4. Develop basic support structures that strengthen the local economy and enhance the community's quality of life.
5. Develop an independent value standard and unit of account.

STAGE I: MAPPING THE TERRITORY
& IMPORT SUBSTITUTION

Jane Jacobs has argued that cities, not nation states, are the salient economic entities, and that city and regional economies develop through a process of import substitution. That being the case, it would seem reasonable that a regional economic development program should begin with actions that support that process.

The first stage of the development program might look rather conventional and similar to some buy local programs of the past, but it will be more comprehensive in its social, economic, and political aspects. It begins by organizing solidarity groups that include *all* sectors of the constituent communities—particularly the locally owned and controlled businesses, municipal governments, the nonprofit sector, social entrepreneurs, and activists. By building bridges between these groups and identifying common objectives, it should be possible to achieve the commitment to do the hard work necessary to move together toward greater regional economic self-sufficiency.

The first major task is to launch a buy local campaign in which the economic resources and business relationships within the region are clearly mapped. That database can then be used to assist businesses in finding local sources for the things they buy and local customers for the things they sell. The services of brokers can be employed to help match up supplies with wants and needs. Critical gaps are identified and local entrepreneurs can be encouraged to find ways to fill them, perhaps with support from a local microlending agency. As this process proceeds, the community becomes less dependent upon outside entities and more resilient and self-determining.

These measures alone, however, are far from sufficient. Given the fact that conventional money and banking are themselves externally controlled and act in ways that are parasitic upon the local economy, some way must be found to reclaim at least a portion of the "credit commons" and bring it under local control. So unlike conventional buy local initiatives, this project moves quickly to implement the second stage.

STAGE II: MUTUAL CREDIT CLEARING PROVIDES AN ALTERNATIVE MEANS OF PAYMENT

The second stage is the most important and unique stage of the project. It provides an alternative means of payment based on the community's own credit through the process of direct credit clearing.

Working capital in the form of conventional money is always scarce and expensive for most businesses. Mutual credit clearing is an extension of the common business practice of selling on "open account," but it is done on a more organized multilateral basis, which has the effect of sharing the risks and enabling a participant's sales to pay for purchases without the use of any third-party credit instrument such as conventional money. As a member of a mutual credit clearing exchange, a business can have an interest-free line of credit, it will be able to acquire the things it needs without the use of cash, and (because it accepts payment in the form of exchange credit) will be a preferred source of supply for others who are members of the exchange.

The allocation of credit in a clearing exchange involves the granting of an "overdraft privilege," which means that a member's account may have a negative balance up to some specified limit. In allocating lines of credit, it is important (especially in the beginning) to allocate the greatest share of credit to "trusted issuers"— i.e., those that are well established, financially sound, and whose products and services are in greatest demand within the local region. This is the key to maintaining a rapid circulation of credits through the system, avoiding defaults, and preventing the excessive accumulation of credits in the hands of businesses that cannot easily spend them. In brief, the businesses that you wish to have accept community credits in payment are the ones that should be issuing them in the first place. By beginning with trusted issuers, the value and usefulness of the community credits is quickly demonstrated beyond any doubt. As the process gains credibility and general acceptance in the community, more businesses and individuals will want to join the credit clearing exchange and as each member develops a trading history they too can earn an overdraft privilege commensurate with their volume of sales within the system.

Like any network, a credit clearing system becomes more valuable and useful as it continues to expand and a greater variety of goods and services become available within the network. By way of example one may note that the first fax machine was very expensive—but useless. As more fax machines were deployed and connected in an expanding network, the fax became more valuable to *all* users—even as prices plummeted and quality improved. The same will happen with clearing networks, but it is essential that the network and each node in it be properly designed and operated from the very start.

STAGE III: THE CREDIT OF TRUSTED ISSUERS PROVIDES AN ALTERNATIVE CURRENCY FOR REGIONAL CIRCULATION

The third stage of the program will be the joint issuance of credits into the general community by the members of the clearing association. This is accomplished by the association members buying goods and services from nonmembers who are outside the credit-clearing circle. They make these purchases by using some form of uniform credit instrument, like a voucher or certificate, which all association members are obliged to redeem—not for cash, but for the goods and services that are their normal stock in trade. That provides a sound regional currency based on the productive capacity of the region's leading enterprises, a currency that can circulate among any and all as a supplemental medium of exchange. The availability of such a currency to supplement the flow of official money *insulates* but does not *isolate* the local economy. Just as a breakwater protects a small boat harbor from the turbulence of the open sea, a sound regional currency provides a measure of protection from the turbulence of the global economy and centralized banking and finance.

This externalization of credits from the clearing association into the general community can be achieved using any of several available forms and devices. Credits may take the form of paper notes, coupons, vouchers, or certificates; they might be placed on stored value cards like the gift cards that are commonly issued by major retailers and are so popular these days with consumers; or they could manifest as credits in accounts that reside on a central server that can be accessed by use of a debit card and point-of-sale card reader.

STAGE IV: SUPPORT STRUCTURES FOR LOCALIZATION—SAVING, INVESTMENT, FINANCE, AND EDUCATION

While the most fundamental need is for mechanisms that enable local control over the exchange function, the health and independence of local economies also requires the localization of savings and investments. In today's world, locally owned and managed banks have become increasingly rare, most having been acquired or replaced by branches of huge bank holding companies that are owned and controlled by entities outside the region. Local savings deposited in those banks can and do get invested anywhere in the world, often in ways that are detrimental to the interests of the saver and the health of his or her local economy. They often leave homegrown enterprises starved for capital while funding mega-corporations, weapons, war, and projects that are socially or environmentally destructive. Structures can be created that channel temporary surpluses of both conventional money and exchange credits into enterprises that enhance local production and quality of life.

Additional support structures are suggested by the experience of the Mondragon cooperatives in the Basque region of northern Spain. Over a period of more than fifty years, the Mondragon network has grown and thrived on the basis of cooperation and social solidarity. In addition to more than 250 industrial and service cooperatives and associated companies, it has developed structures to provide finance, education, and research in support of its regional cooperative economy. The Caja Laboral Popular (CLP, or Working People's Bank), for example, is itself a cooperative that invests the savings of the local community and provides financing for the other cooperative enterprises.

STAGE V AND BEYOND: TRANSITION TO AN OBJECTIVE MEASURE OF VALUE AND ACCOUNTING UNIT

Eventually, it will become necessary to denominate local credits in some independent, objective, nonpolitical unit of account based on a concrete standard of value. This will become especially important as political currencies continue to be inflated and their monetary units are debased, and as local clearing networks become interlinked regionally and across national boundaries. Trade credit units originally defined as being equivalent to the dominant political currency unit (like dollars, pounds, euros, and yen) will shift over to a value unit that is objectively defined in terms of valuable, commonly traded commodities. Such a unit will facilitate trading across national borders by obviating the need for foreign exchange and eliminating the exchange rate risk, and will be immune to the inflationary and deflationary effects that beset national political currencies.

The remaining design details and implementation strategies can be settled upon as the program unfolds. For now, it is sufficient to say that all of the necessary monetary science is well established and all of the major system components are readily available. With a modest amount of funding or investment, programs designed along these lines can be quickly launched and a credit clearing system can quickly reach critical mass. It is expected that the success of this model in one or two local regions will inspire others to implement it, leading to a rapid proliferation of healthy and sustainable communities that might associate to form a worldwide economic democracy.

21

A RETURN TO THE VALUE OF BEING HUMAN

HARDIN TIBBS

SEEKING ESCAPE

In March 2007, the BBC broadcast in the UK a three-part documentary called *The Trap,* by the controversial British filmmaker Adam Curtis.[1] Its message was that "a simplistic model of human beings as self-seeking, almost robotic, creatures" plus an overriding belief in human selfishness have created "a cage" for human beings in modern society. The documentary argued that this predicament is in part the result of a long process by which social and personal values have become dominated by reductionist thinking. *The Trap* was pessimistic in tone and did not offer any clear solution. The question it left open, which this paper addresses, is whether it is possible to reverse this process by establishing a basis for values that would not be reductionistic, and that would offer a way out of the present trap.

REDUCTIONISM AND HUMAN IDENTITY

The root of the problem is that our picture of human beings has been gradually reshaped by the dominance of one particular mode of thinking—reductionism—as a means of generating knowledge. What this has caused us to believe and value about ourselves in turn shapes how we behave toward each other. If our picture is somehow inadequate or incomplete, our behavior will also fall short of its natural potential and serious social and other problems may develop. This can easily happen without our noticing it and is not easy to detect or correct.

Reductionism is essentially the procedure of reducing things to their component parts. The idea of taking things apart as a means of finding out more about them has been an extremely powerful way of building scientific knowledge. Early scientists began by looking at easily visible internal structures, and then we developed instruments such as microscopes for looking at parts at smaller and smaller size scales. This led us to the modern theory of the atom, and beyond that to subatomic physics, and to the paradoxes of the quantum realm.

What we lost sight of in the process is that knowing what things are made of does not necessarily help us to value them appropriately.

The basic assumption of reductionism is that a thing really is simply the sum of its parts. Each part is made of something smaller, right down to the basic building blocks of material reality, the sub-atomic particles. In this view, everything is a material construct. The properties of multiparticle things are seen as outcomes of system interactions, and thanks to computer simulations we now know these can be surprising and unpredictable. The features that appear as things get more elaborate are referred to as "emergent" properties of complex systems.

We see everyday objects around us that have internal structure and are built up from smaller parts, and this does apparently explain how their properties arise. This can be seen very clearly with simple machines. If we take a bicycle apart we are left with a collection of mechanical components and we can see exactly how they come together to form the bicycle. The fact that this approach works so well with machines made it easy to think that it could be applied to living organisms without raising any new issues.

Simple reductionism sees the properties of the whole as fully determined by the properties observed in the parts when separate. Complex systems theory refines that by saying that although the parts of complex systems determine emergent behaviors, these new properties must be studied as phenomena in their own right. But in both cases, parts are seen as primal and causal, reflecting a bias that the parts somehow exist first and then come together to form the whole.

If we ask how the parts of a living system are different from the parts of a bicycle, a somewhat deeper answer is that the parts are themselves altered by the dynamic interaction among the parts in a way that does not happen in a bicycle. When the parts are in the living system they are literally different than when they are not—we call the latter state "dead." This suggests a holistic reality in which parts and wholes are interdependent, so that in biological systems the whole can dynamically reshape the parts. An analogy would be the creative activity of engineering design, in which the parts are shaped as a means of accomplishing the concept of the whole.

Yet even this answer is still subtly framed in terms of parts, whereas a better way to see living organisms might be as patterns of resonance like holograms. Living organisms are not assembled from parts like a machine—they appear as much simpler and smaller formations we call eggs or seeds, and all their internal structure appears from nowhere as they grow. From a reductionist perspective we have trouble making sense of this, which suggests that for science to transcend its current limits, it now needs to move beyond reductionism.

Nevertheless, in reductionist biology the explanatory arrow goes from parts to wholes. Biological organisms clearly have complex internal structure, and do have parts, although these parts are bound together in a much more intimate way than the parts of a bicycle, as anyone who has attempted a dissection will know. Dissection—and sometimes vivisection—of living creatures enabled the knowledge base of biology to be built up, leading eventually to molecular biology, in which the operative parts are not bones, muscles, and nerves but the far smaller nucleic acids, proteins, and enzymes. It was quickly obvious that the internal structure of human beings is very similar to that of animals, so similar that we often talk colloquially about "the human animal."

This similarity, and the effectiveness of reductionism, led to the modernist understanding of a human being. We asked ourselves, what is a human being? And we answered by saying: human beings are advanced animals. And what are animals? They are systems of life processes. And what are these life processes? Well, they are dynamic systems of atoms and molecules. And so, in a few simple steps we reduced our idea of a human being to a set of material, atomic phenomena.

The largely unseen problem is that when we apply reductionism to living creatures, and most significantly to human beings, we inadvertently perform not one but two reductions. The obvious one is that we reduce the living creature to its material components. The other, overlooked one, is that we also reduce our appreciation of its qualities as a living being. In place of an appreciation of distinctive human qualities we are left with a perception of material qualities only. We have reduced our understanding of human beings to the same level as our understanding of material things.

There are several qualities of being human that are devalued or even lost when this happens. As humans, we are self-aware, able to choose, and the holistic experience of being human is our unique existential identity. These qualities cannot be found in the parts that make up a human, or in material constructs such as bicycles, but can only be appreciated from the standpoint of actually being human. To be able to put the appropriate value on these qualities, we must use the holistic experience of being human as our frame of reference and basis of analysis.

Instead, our modernist belief in the power of reductionism to develop knowledge led us to think that the successive steps of the reductionist definition are a disclosure of the truth about being human. We consequently came to regard the material aspect of human beings as more real or more fundamental, and therefore more important and more valuable than other qualities. But the more we see ourselves as material constructs, the more we will begin to treat each other as if this is what we value most about each other.

There are many signs that this has happened, and has become one of the distinguishing marks of modernity. We say that nothing other than materiality exists, and that this is self-evidently true. We deny nonmaterial aspects of ourselves, dissociating ourselves from our own nature. We no longer see uniquely human qualities because we do not take them seriously anymore. We do not treat them as real in themselves, or as representing primary value; we say that they only exist as a by-product of material processes. And as we become dead to various human qualities in ourselves, and in others, our society begins to be less and less accommodating to certain aspects of being human. This is the predicament described in *The Trap*.

We are living in a predominantly modernist culture that admires material and mechanistic qualities more than human ones. It places great value on the qualities of machines—their speed, precision, and efficiency—and we often see these as better than human attributes. In many contexts we aspire to be as much like machines as possible, and sometimes we actually wish to be machines, devising robotic implants and dreaming that we will be able to upload our consciousness to silicon and defy death.

The shift to this outlook has been gradual, and largely without our noticing we have ceased to appreciate fully what it is to be human. So much so that this assertion itself may seem questionable, in spite of our uneasy awareness that it does carry some kind of meaning that we cannot quite pin down. The changes, these reductions in the way we see ourselves, have crept up on us gradually. We did not see them coming and we do not notice how they alter the way we see the world and how we behave toward each other. But we do see that there are social problems we do not know how to fix, and perhaps we sense that the full depth of experiencing life has somehow been diminished.

REDUCTIONISM AND THE PROBLEM OF THE WHOLE

Reductionism has not only had an unintended social impact, but it also limits our ability to find solutions to the problem of technological impact on the natural environment. It also helped create this problem in the first place. The effectiveness of reductionism in generating practical knowledge enabled us to develop advanced technologies, which have been a major force behind the exponential growth of industrialization and the spread of modernity. We used our knowledge almost exclusively to create disrelated instances of applied technology, such as consumer products and infrastructure projects, which we put into the world without any special thought for their impact on the whole context, the larger natural and social environment.

For most of the industrial period the larger environmental context was simply not an issue. When industrialization began, it was a small development in a vast world that was patterned in ways far beyond human influence or understanding. We simply took for granted the preexisting structures and processes that organized the world. Even as we poured technology into the world, we thought the pattern of the whole would simply take care of itself.

This was true up to a point, while the scale of industrial activity compared to the rest of the world remained small, but from sometime in the 1970s onward the relentless growth of the industrial economy began to overtake the scale of the biosphere itself. After the 1970s, according to the World Wildlife Fund, we began to consume renewable natural resources faster than the global capacity to regenerate them. This vast scale of operation meant that the total collection of technologies that had been deployed began to disrupt the preexisting pattern of the whole.

The problem with reductionism is that it generates knowledge about parts that is capable of disrupting the whole, but this knowledge does not work the other way round to help us to bring order to the whole. This is illustrated by the way the structure of a living organism does not arise from its separated parts being put together to form a whole, but from the emergence of its parts in the context of a whole that exists from the outset. Yet so far almost all scientific exploration has been biased toward the parts rather than the whole. This gives us detailed knowledge of the parts, but little insight into how we might fix the disruption that is caused by the bias in our focus. To address the "problem of the whole" we need to find a way of appreciating the value of wholes as wholes. Until we can rebalance the value we put on the whole versus the parts we will not be able to heal the pathology caused by the entire system of human socio-technical organization—the disruption of the whole.

REDUCTIONISM AND SUSTAINABILITY

These two problems, our picture of human beings as material constructs, and the pathology of the whole, come together as a problem of sustainability. Disruption to the pattern of the whole is a direct threat to the sustainability of present-day human society. This means reductionist thinking is a key underlying source of *un*sustainability in the world today.

This link between reductionism and sustainability should not be surprising. There is a connection between our understanding of what it is to be human and our ability to sustain our lives. If there is a distortion in our picture of ourselves, our sense of our needs will also be distorted, and this will affect our ability to sustain ourselves.

This happens through the way we make choices to meet our needs.

One of the attributes of being human is our ability to choose. Most of us, most of the time, choose to sustain our lives, to keep them going. If our lives are in danger, we will do our best to save ourselves. On a day-to-day basis we choose to sustain ourselves by making sure our needs are met.

Our ability to do this of course depends on our being able to accurately identify and value our various needs. Because in the modernist worldview we consider the material or physical level of description to be the most real, we value our needs at this level more highly than our needs at other levels. Since we naturally make the most effort to meet the needs we value most, we then tend to neglect or ignore the remaining needs.

If we consistently and systematically fail to meet our full range of needs as human beings we are indirectly threatening our ability to sustain ourselves. This unsustainability may not be obvious immediately, because it mostly involves our nonmaterial needs, whereas a lack of basic material needs causes obvious problems faster. Nevertheless our shift from a holistic appreciation of human needs to a reduced appreciation is an underlying cause of the wider problem of systemic unsustainability.

AN ANTIDOTE TO REDUCTIONISM

Is there an antidote to our bias toward valuing the parts more highly than the whole? How can we restore our sense of the qualities of the whole, and bring ourselves back to a fuller appreciation of what it is to be human? Is there an alternative to reductionist thinking that would achieve this?

Suppose we throw the sequence of reduction into reverse. Instead of working down the sequence of levels of description and ending up with material parts as the answer to our questions about the whole, we could work our way upward toward the whole, integrating into our understanding of the whole the properties we find at each level, and crucially, giving equal value to each of the levels.

To demonstrate this approach we could take the human being as the paradigm, not least because it has more levels of qualitative reduction than any other whole system we know. We would first set out and then describe each of the levels of reduction. We would then see various human qualities revealed at each level. Our aim would be to achieve the sustainability of the whole, and to heal the pathology of the whole, and we have seen how that depends on valuing all our needs equally. We would therefore look for the needs we have at each level when our reality or our identity is considered at that level. This procedure would result in several groups of needs that are qualitatively distinct. We would then bring these sets of needs together into an integrated whole picture, giving equal value to each set.

This process would put all the steps of the reduction back together and build back up to a much more fully described sense of what it means to be human. The result would be a holistic sense of being human, with a balanced sense of all the needs we as humans value being able to meet. This integrated picture would provide a holistic sense of human value.

HUMAN NEEDS AND THE LEVELS OF REDUCTION

Here is how this process would look in practice. We start by setting out the steps of the reductionist description of a human being:

    (Level 0) The starting point: we experience ourselves as
                 human beings.
                 We ask: what is a human being?
    (Level -1) We answer by saying: human beings are
                 advanced animals.

We ask next: what are animals?

(Level -2) We answer by saying: animals are systems of life processes.

We ask next: what are life processes?

(Level -3) We answer by saying: they are dynamic systems of atoms and molecules.

This gives us four levels of description, starting at the top level with the whole human being, and ending at the bottom level with material components.

Next, we build back up from the lowest level, observing the human qualities and needs that exist at each level in turn.

At the third most reduced level (-3 above), we see the human being as an assembly of atoms. At this level our corresponding needs are the ones met by assemblies of atoms and material constructs. These include basic material requirements such as tools, clothes, and infrastructure for functions such as transport and shelter. At this level of human identity the highest meaning of things arises from their relation to our physical needs.

At the second most reduced level (-2 above), we see the human being as a set of systems of life processes. At this level our corresponding needs are ones the ones met by systems of life processes. These include a viable biosphere to provide ongoing life support, and food composed of complex organic compounds. At this level of human identity the highest meaning of things arises from their relation to our biological needs.

At the first most reduced level (-1 above), we see the human as being essentially an advanced animal. At this level our corresponding needs are the ones that we have in common only with animals. These include social contact, social organization, social reciprocity, membership of family groups, and emotional relationships. At this level of human identity the highest meaning of things arises from their relation to our social needs.

At the nonreduced or whole level (0 above), we see the human being as uniquely itself, unlike anything else we can compare it with. At this level our corresponding needs are the ones met at this level, and unique to humans. Our uniquely human qualities and attributes include reflexive awareness, abstract knowledge, and the potential for impartial judgment. Our needs include education and justice, intellectual development, and aesthetic satisfaction. At this level of human identity the highest meaning of things arises from their relation to our uniquely human needs, what might be called our "cultural" or "civilizational" needs.

We can go further and add one level beyond or "above" our experience as human beings. We could call this level (+1). This level relates to a question about our ultimate identity, about the meaning of being human. We are not able to answer this question definitively, since we cannot fathom the source of our own identity. But perhaps the best answer available to us is that we appear to be creative beings who develop an innate and open-ended individual potentiality and who therefore need to be free or unconstrained in this by other human beings. Our needs at this level are therefore for freedom of self-realization and self-actualization, in free response to the mystery of creation. At this level we might say, although it is hard to pin down an exact definition of the word, that the highest meaning of everything in human experience arises from its relation to our "spiritual" needs.

This (+1) is not a level of reduction, since it cannot be found when reducing the system we are dealing with to a description of its parts. Science will therefore be unable to find it using reductionism as the research mode. Rather than being a reduction, it is at a level of integration higher than the whole we are examining, which is why it is referred to as "plus 1." However paradoxical this may be, it is important to include it because it acknowledges something further about human beings. We are not only aware of ourselves as wholes with unique attributes, but we are also (at least from time to time) aware that there is something about us that goes beyond our everyday experience of life. At the very least we are reminded of this because we are repeatedly haunted by questions about our own identity. This (+1) level provides a way to accommodate the idea of the "spiritual" and allow for religious needs, without attempting to precisely define it. However, should we ever want to designate more complex structure in reality above the human (0) level, the "plus" notation can accommodate it by means of levels (+2), (+3) etc.

The listing of needs at each level given here is intended to be indicative or illustrative, not exhaustive. Further exploration and questioning will no doubt clarify the general or common human needs at each level, and in addition there will be many specific needs existing in particular situations, locations, and times.

REINTEGRATING A HOLISTIC VALUATION OF HUMAN NEEDS

If we now take all these groups of needs and bring them together, we can approximate a holistic picture of human needs.[2] Putting together just the needs listed above, the picture looks like this: As human beings our needs include material requirements such as tools, clothes, and infrastructure for functions such as transport and shelter; a viable biosphere to provide ongoing life support, and food composed of complex organic compounds; social contact, social organization, social reciprocity, membership of family groups, and emotional relationships; education and justice, intellectual development, and aesthetic satisfaction; and freedom of self-realization and self-actualization, in free response to the mystery of creation.

In bringing together this holistic picture we are no longer trying to define or value these needs in terms of each other. In particular we are not trying to explain the higher ones in terms of the lower ones. The aim is not to explain, but to harmonize functioning wholes, which requires appreciation of the qualities of the functioning whole and the needs related to them. This means developing the ability to perceive and value all the attributes. The quality of being fully human will only be possible if all the qualities of being human are recognized, and the needs related to them are valued equally and fully met.

We now have the necessary starting point for achieving whole system sustainability, a procedure for identifying and valuing our full range of needs as human beings. The next step is to consider how we might make use of this to meet those needs in the practical context of the world, bearing in mind that the existing pattern of the whole is increasingly disrupted, as described earlier. A more precise definition of the disruption would be that the world as a whole is no longer able to self-regulate in a manner that will meet human needs indefinitely. We are overshooting planetary limits, and the risk for us is that if we push the overshoot too far, the biospheric system may crash or instead self-regulate by sweeping us out of the picture—this is the "revenge of Gaia" scenario.[3] What we are looking for therefore is a process that enables human beings to relate to the whole system of the world in such a way that it can self-regulate and indefinitely meet (or allow us to provide for) human needs as it does so.

TOWARD A COMPREHENSIVE DESIGN PROCESS FOR SUSTAINABILITY

As individual human beings, we look to our surroundings to meet many of our needs. Our need for clean air is met by the functioning of the biosphere, while our need for human contact is met through our association with other human beings. At an earlier stage of human history our needs were directly met through the natural functioning of the larger ecosystem in which we live, just as with animals living in their natural habitat. As human societies developed, we created increasingly specialized economic and technological systems for meeting our needs—and the needs of some at the expense of others—and these operated inside and depended on the global set of natural ecosystems.

These human-technology-based subsystems, which could be classed as ecostructures along with beavers' dams and spiders' webs,[4] were developed without special thought about the functioning of the natural global ecosystem, because, as already discussed, in the early stages of industrial growth this kind of thinking simply wasn't necessary. At our current stage, however, industry has grown to span the planet, and involves physical flows of material that are as large as the flows of material within the natural global ecosystem. It is now essential that we do address the impact we have on the whole context within which we operate—the planetary biogeochemical system, or more simply the natural global ecosystem.

The "pathology of the whole" is a disturbance of the entire biosphere, as well being the social issue described in *The Trap*. Life of some kind will no doubt survive the present period despite our environmental depredations, but we as a species are far more fragile than life in general. Our practical concern as human beings is that the planet remains habitable for us, and for the highly developed ecosystems that support us, and that something close to our current civilization can continue. It is certainly not in our interest for the planetary eco-climatic conditions to break down. If Gaia "strikes back" by moving beyond the range we can tolerate, we will be in serious trouble.

In principle it should be possible to maintain human civilization, for several reasons. One is that we can now make adequate material provision for everyone because our technological capability allows us to overcome the material scarcity that existed before. Basic resources are still unequally accessible only because social belief and politics are lagging behind our actual capability. The social and psychological work of overcoming our outdated and now

dangerous belief in fundamental scarcity is one of the most important tasks of the present century. The brunt of this task is now to
master collectively the emotions of fear and greed that are fed by
the belief in scarcity and that drive much dysfunctional political
and corporate decision-making.

A second reason is that we now have a great deal of scientific
knowledge about how the world works and how our own technological activities have an impact. If we design ingeniously it is
entirely within our ability to configure our applied technologies to
coexist respectfully with the natural processes of the biosphere.

To keep the planet habitable we must now aim not only for our
own human well-being but also the well-being of the whole system
of which we are a part. This aim will mean finding ways of meeting our needs that are in line with three principles: first, that the
meeting of any one need does not compromise the meeting of any
other need; second, that the meeting of any one person's needs
does not compromise the meeting of any other person's needs;
and third, that the meeting of human needs in general does not
compromise any of the attributes of the world—such as a functioning biosphere—that enable our needs to be met.

A further reason is that the world actually or potentially contains everything we need. The reason we are able to meet our
needs at all is because there are matching attributes in the world
around us. If we recognize our needs fully and place an equal value
on meeting them all, we will be obliged to look after all the corresponding aspects of the world as a whole. If we can avoid putting all
our stress on one set of needs—as we have been doing—we should
be able to develop processes for meeting our needs that will also
bring the world into balance.

The steps in doing this are first that we develop a holistic sense
of our own needs, and second that we design integrated systems
that can meet our needs and at the same time form part of the
balance and functioning of the whole. This is essentially how the

natural ecosystem as a whole is already organized, so we could say that we are looking for an ecosystemic form of organization for human life within the planetary ecosystem. By analogy with computer operating systems, we could think of this as an ecosystemic operating system for planet earth.

Ecosystems in general are systems that meet the needs of their participants (of whatever species) through mutual interaction and reciprocity. The first part of the word *ecosystem* is derived from the Greek word for household, *oikos*. The general idea behind the word is of a system whereby the household runs. So, without going too far from its biological sense, we could think of the word *ecosystem* as representing a "home-locality needs-meeting system." The various human needs–meeting subsystems could then be thought of as subsidiary ecosystems within the natural global ecosystem. Using the word *ecosystem* signifies that these systems can meet needs and also interact cooperatively with the overall global ecosystem.

The process of designing these ecosystems would start with an assessment of human needs. The same basic needs exist everywhere, but the specifics differ in each locality and community, and for each organization in meeting the needs of its members and those it serves. Every group, community, or organization applying this approach would have to carry out its own detailed needs assessment at its own scale of operation and at each level of description (as discussed earlier). Because of the range of knowledge required—from ecology to social science—the assessment team would need to comprise individuals with expertise in the various need areas. The process would have to be open and participatory, to ensure that all the needs of everyone affected would be represented. The assessment would involve the subjective appraisal of needs by a group of people. This assessment could be based on emerging protocols such as "consensus design" in architecture as developed by Christopher Day, and the "science of qualities" being pioneered by the biologist Brian Goodwin.[5]

A locally relevant needs-meeting system—a local ecosystem—would then be designed and developed for meeting each group of needs (the rationale for a local focus is discussed below). Material-level needs (level -3) would be met by an industrial ecosystem;[6] life-support needs (level -2) by a bio-agricultural ecosystem; social needs (level -1) by a social reciprocity ecosystem; and human-level needs (level 0) by a human development ecosystem. (The ability to pursue needs at the more elusive +1 level would be assured by freedoms of individual religious and spiritual inquiry and practice, always operating within the criteria of noninterference with the meeting of other human needs.)

The design of these ecosystems would use and synthesize the existing range of human knowledge. They would mesh with each other so that the functioning of one ecosystem would not compromise the functioning of any other (through an emphasis on design ingenuity rather than trade-off, as described by Roger Martin in *The Opposable Mind*.)[7] They would also mesh with the larger surrounding or adjacent ecosystems of each type. Meshing with local and larger-scale natural ecosystems would be achieved by features that would sustain and restore natural ecosystems rather than merely exploiting or degrading them. Protocols such as The Natural Step, a Swedish sustainability method, would provide the design criteria for eco-compatibility.

EMERGENCE OF A CELLULAR ECONOMY

The integration or meshing of the four types of ecosystem would be achieved by a design synthesis of industrial ecosystems, bio-agricultural ecosystems, social reciprocity ecosystems, and human development ecosystems, coming together into a general socio-economic and governance system that is itself nested in and compatible with local and global natural ecosystems. These combined ecosystems could then be called "general ecosystems." General ecosystems would be defined as integrated systems that provide the essential needs of a human group, community, or organization in a locally comprehensive, autonomously directed, and ecologically sound way.

The focus on localness does not imply that everything would be restricted to local scale, merely that locally scaled general ecosystems would be the basic building bricks or "cells" of the larger system. The economy and society as a whole would be structured as a mosaic of these cellular subsystems, which would be the primary units of organization. These cells would be communities organized to meet the full range of human needs locally, not in a quest for self-sufficiency, but simply to ensure that all the needs are indeed met, an important distinction. An element of self-sufficiency would be needed for this, but most cells would also specialize in activities or production that could be exported to other cells, while importing other specialized offerings—somewhat like the role of cells in the body.

The prospect of trade between cells raises the question of money. In our present market economy, money is regarded as the primary means of accessing needs. A cellular economy built up from general ecosystems would be a system designed to meet needs through its intrinsic structure, so the role of money would be less dominant.

Money is a means of accounting for certain types of human interactions, so if we revalue our sense of being human, many types of relationships would be demonetized as they become less transactional. The design of general ecosystems would allow this by raising the general level of social reciprocity. This implies that the use of money for many everyday activities would be greatly reduced.

At the moment money reinforces reductionism. We increasingly think we can use it to obtain all our needs, a view encouraged by consumerism, despite the old admonition that money cannot buy happiness. Money is literally something material, and just as we have allowed our material-level needs (level -3) to dominate, we have allowed money itself to determine our sense of human needs. This is what happens when we say that something cannot be done because it is uneconomic. In a revalued cellular economy we might override such a view to assert that something should be done even though it is "uneconomic" in our current sense of the term.

In a cellular economy money is likely to be used very flexibly. For example local non-fiat currencies might be used in the design of general ecosystems to track the provision of specific needs. If trade between cells requires conversion of value from one money system to another this might well be carried out differently. At the moment exchange rates are determined by market transactions that reflect the money surplus or deficit position of different areas, in effect a value comparison based on material-level needs (level -3). A cellular economy might override this material-level dominance. For instance, exchange rates might be set by equalizing the local cost of a selection of foods that provide a day's calorie intake (say 2,000 calories) in the two different areas. This would ensure that trade was always fair in terms of its effect on nutrition, which is not the case today.

In short, money is likely to be less important in a cellular economy, but where it is present it would be used to express a human rather than a material approach to value.

APPROPRIATE SCALE

Successful general ecosystem cells would not simply grow in size by "scaling" like growing businesses. As cellular subsystems they would spread by replication, not by gigantism, through independent re-creation of the entire ecosystemic cell. If a particular general ecosystem design proved successful, other communities could reproduce it. Expansion by whole system replication while keeping the cell size small would be vital to preserve the essential feature of the general ecosystem—its ability to meet the full range of human needs by organizing locally. At larger size scales—eco-regional, national, and supranational—the society and economy would be a patchwork of similar and dissimilar but complementary ecosystemic cells linked by mutual trade.

Part of the rationale for the primacy of local scale is that a variety of factors and trends indicate that future economic and social relocalization might be both desirable and feasible. This can be seen on a variety of fronts. Socially, relatively small groups form the primary unit of structure. For example, cross-cultural studies in sociology and anthropology indicate that the maximum size of a genuine social network such as a village is about 150 members, and this is known as the "Rule of 150" or Dunbar's Number. This number may be related to the average human ability to recognize people and keep track of emotional information about all members of a group. Agriculturally, if basic foods are grown locally they are fresh and seasonal, with corresponding ecological and health benefits. Industrially, in spite of the well-known concept of economy of scale concept, recent thinking about flexible demand-led "lean manufacturing" leads to smaller plants close to consumers, rather than huge centralized plants at a distance. Technological developments such as 3-D printing are also heading in this direction, as production equipment becomes smaller and more flexible. Various economies of scale still exist, but the viable scale of manufacturing is progressively reducing in size as technology advances. In economics, the success of industrial clusters also emphasizes the value of local scale. Politically too, the smooth functioning of democratic systems depends on the vitality of local political engagement.

The exact size or scale implied by "local" is suggested by these factors but not precisely defined. A balance would need to be struck between a scale small enough for certain kinds of human interrelatedness, and large enough for certain activities to have a minimum viable size. A working definition of local could be expressed in, say, numbers of people, geographic area, or travel time, but these factors all interrelate and change over time. Historical analysis of human settlements shows that their average radius has been roughly equal to the distance that could be traveled in half an hour by the prevailing transport technology. As transport speed has increased, so has the population size of towns and cities, so they no longer offer a good social definition of local. Their ecological footprint has also vastly expanded. This scale problem inspired the "new urbanism movement," an urban planning initiative that designs village-like urban layouts clustered around rapid transit stations. The concept of general ecosystems goes beyond this, potentially being something like a localized integration of village-like urban form, economically independent production clusters, closed-loop recycling, ecologically balanced food production, intimate social scale, and civic self-governance.

The ultimate benchmark for the scale of locally focused socioeconomic organization is the individual's experience of how human needs are met. Imagine a child growing up in a community organized as a general ecosystem. Because the system would meet all the fundamental needs of the people in the community, the child would experience a high quality of life. He or she would be able to see directly, as part of everyday experience, how the entire system worked and was operated by people belonging to the community. Much of the child's education would involve witnessing how all the important parts of the system were designed, created, interrelated, and maintained. This would be much more likely to foster a feeling of personal involvement and responsibility, ecological awareness, economic autonomy, local political self-determination, and give a comprehensive insight into the way the world works. In these terms, local might be both justified and defined as whatever scale of general ecosystem allowed a child to have this kind of experience growing up.

In preindustrial times, most children grew up on farms or

in small towns and villages, where they would directly witness how things were made, how food was grown, how social order emerges among animals, and what distinguishes humans. However, they may not have experienced a high level of social justice and mobility, or the freedom to develop themselves. The modern era has made great headway toward these things, but at the cost for most people of any comprehensive sense of how the world as a whole works, and with a loss of any real sense of participation and responsibility. Some form of general ecosystemic organization might therefore be the key characteristic of a future "trans-modern era" that would combine the benefits of modernity with a restored sense of direct personal participation and the security of belonging to a coherent community.

These speculative thoughts about general ecosystems are intended as an exploration of future possibilities rather than a prediction of the future. Building on a way of revalidating the full range of human needs, the general ecosystem concept is a possible framework for organizing society to meet human needs in full.

CONCLUSION

We live in a world in which most needs of most people in most places are not fully met. The forces of modernity that shaped our world have given us unrivalled power to meet human needs, yet the shortfall persists and the general situation becomes steadily more chaotic.

We try to solve our increasingly complex problems by throwing more money at them to deploy more physical resources. Our overemphasis on the physical often actually crowds out and reduces our ability to meet other needs. Ever more money is soaked up and the problems remain. Despite our vastly increased technological capabilities we have a growing "problem of the whole" that we do not know how to address.

Before the industrial era we did not have to worry about this. The "pattern of the whole" was simply inherited from the historical past. Social and economic relationships, and the relationship of humans to their natural environment, were not things that anyone consciously thought out. The roots of these things had arisen in the immemorial past, and most people regarded them as God-given, along with nature itself.

In the modern period, scientific knowledge and technology expanded into the old unconsciously shaped world and progressively cut away its moorings. We now urgently need to respond to the growing chaos of the whole with a consciously determined repatterning, but we have no obvious pattern to follow. We have a greatly expanded view of human agency, and a repertoire of sophisticated and powerful tools. But we lack an organizing pattern that combines our scientific knowledge with wisdom about our place in the whole.

In order to resolve this impasse, it is useful to heed the admonition attributed to Albert Einstein: "We cannot solve our problems with the same thinking we used when we created them." The mode of thinking primarily responsible for creating our current predicament is the application of reductionism as a means of generating knowledge. Although successful in many ways, it has had the unwanted effect of gradually reducing our picture of human beings, changing how we value ourselves and others.

The corrective response suggested here centers on a revaluation of human beings and a corresponding reintegration of human needs. It builds on this to propose a simple but comprehensive pattern of organization that has the potential to provide a new fundamental framework for achieving socio-economic continuity and ecological sustainability.

The pattern of the whole for which we search is the same as the pattern of ourselves. Once we recognize our needs fully and place an equal value on meeting them all, we will be obliged to look after all the corresponding aspects of the world as a whole, which actually or potentially contains everything we need.

The message of *The Trap* was that our reductionist model of human beings has created a cage for human beings in modern society. Our release, and our ability to solve "the problem of the whole," now depend on rediscovering the wholeness of being human and applying it in our relationships with each other and with the world as a whole.

22

ORIGINAL WEALTH AND PEOPLE'S CAPITALISM

STEVE BHAERMAN

Not surprisingly, America's founders had a deep understanding of "natural economy," acknowledging that nature's renewable wealth was abundant and only needed tending and harvesting from humans willing to do the work. Consider the freedom this provided. In the Old World, land was held strictly by lords and hereditary landowners. Ordinary people had absolutely no chance to acquire land, and consequently could never become wealthy.

In the New World, land was everywhere. And while it could be rightfully argued that this land was being wrested from the native peoples, and parts of it yielded wealth only through the hard work of slaves, it still provided a rare opportunity in a "dominate or be dominated" world. Two centuries before Darwin, economic Darwinism was in full flower. Beginning with Columbus's journey, followed by the explorers of Spain, Portugal, Holland, and England, the New World was first of all a source of gold. That gold made Spain a wealthy nation, and indirectly led to "enlightening up" the Dark Ages.

England got into the act in 1600, when Queen Elizabeth founded the East India Company, the purpose of which, according to agrarian economist Charles Walters, was to "plunder the planet."[1] For along with the "divine right" of royalty came the divine right to everything that could be acquired. The New World was not only a source of gold, but a source of free land, free food, and "subhuman savages" who could either be harnessed to the plow or dispensed with. Here is a quote from Columbus himself that illuminates the five hundred years of history that followed his journey: "[The Indians] are the best people in the world and above all the gentlest—without knowledge of evil—nor do they murder and steal. They would make fine servants. With fifty men we could subjugate them all and make them do whatever we want." Perhaps the philosopher who first observed that the road to hell is paved with good intentions should really have said: "The road to hell is paved with *people* with good intentions—who were used as paving stones by people with *bad* intentions."

Nonetheless, there were several factors that made the North American colonies unique. First, many of the settlers were refugees from either religious or economic persecution, and in the colonies they had the freedom to experience "live and let live" as opposed to "dominate or be dominated." They were also influenced by the native peoples—particularly the Iroquois Nation—who had an advanced system for living in balance with nature and with each other. These native cultures informed the Enlightenment, and these enlightened ideas became the founding principles of what would become the United States.

In a world where England and the other European nations saw exploitation as the natural scheme of things, America's founders had a more enlightened understanding of how to thrive without exploiting or being exploited. Wrote Benjamin Franklin, "There seem to be but three Ways for a Nation to acquire Wealth. The first is by War as the Romans did in plundering their conquered Neighbours. This is Robbery. The second by Commerce which is generally Cheating. The third by Agriculture the only honest Way; wherein Man receives a real Increase of the Seed thrown into the Ground, in a kind of continual Miracle wrought by the Hand of God in his favour, as a Reward for his innocent Life, and virtuous Industry."

BIG BOX STORES, EIGHTEENTH-CENTURY STYLE

Just as the Revolutionary War was fought to overcome economic exploitation, the United States itself was founded for the specific purpose of protecting and nurturing its own wealth that came from what this new land yielded. In the period 1783 to 1789, the newly freed colonies suffered a severe economic depression. Why? Because British merchants were flooding the colonies with cheap goods made by cheap labor, sharply undercutting the growing industries here. Does this sound familiar? More than two hundred years ago, the 1700s version of big box stores was putting America's neighborhood outfits out of business!

Here were the colonies that had so recently lost blood and fortune to gain political independence, and were now being recolonized by the economic tyranny of cheap goods. While then as now, cheap goods were attractive, the bargain came with a hidden price tag. The influx of cheap goods drove prices down in the colonies, caused businesses to fail, and resulted in widespread unemployment. People without wages had little buying power, and that reinforced the market for cheap goods, "cheapening" the entire American economy. Meanwhile, in the colonies or factories where these goods were being produced, workers, natives, and land were being exploited—that is, used without fair compensation. As a result there was a loss on both ends, with only the middleman gaining from both transactions.

Consequently, the United States of America was created to protect the most unique economy in the world against "free trade" just as we might erect a fence around a newly planted garden to keep the deer from nipping it in the bud. In contrast with the predator economies of Europe that sought to take wealth from others through force and leveraged trade, here was a new nation where it was understood that wealth was on the ground and in the ground, available to all willing to work it.

The nations of Europe resented this upstart start-up nation that had the nerve to imagine it could be economically independent. When Abraham Lincoln decided to issue "greenbacks"—fiat currency without gold backing—to finance the Civil War, a London *The Times* editorial fulminated, "It will pay off debts and be without debt. ... [and] become prosperous without precedent. ... That government must be destroyed or it will destroy every monarchy on the globe." What America was founded on—and what has now been severely compromised by greed, misunderstanding, and manipulation—is what economist Carl H. Wilken called "people's capitalism." Although little remembered now, Wilken was a visionary voice in the wilderness at a time when America was making the choice once and for all to move from a generative economy to a predatory one.

Wilken's ideas were based on the simple contention that "all new wealth comes from the soil." Even in the cyber economy we find ourselves caught up in today, without the goods that come from the earth life would perish. As Benjamin Franklin understood, agriculture is "manna" from the ground up. Every year, as if by magic, edible life springs up from the ground. Cultivation of this abundant wealth—and being paid fairly for it—is the foundation of people's capitalism. Writing in the 1930s, Wilken contrasted this with two other forms of capitalism, state capitalism and international capitalism. In state capitalism—typified by socialism and communism—the state owns the means of production, and runs the system from the top down. International capitalism, typified today by international banks and multinational corporations, is concerned only with profits, and these profits are too often based on exploitation. People's capitalism meant building wealth from the land. The function of the government, at least as the founding fathers saw it, was to "protect the individual against exploitation of a more powerful neighbor." Congress and only Congress was authorized to coin money, money that was not created out of debt but which accurately represented the value of the wealth of the nation. Living in this age of multinational corporations, many of us may have developed a jaundiced view of capitalism. But Wilken saw a nation of six million capitalist farmers, all growing not just their crops, but the wealth and savings of the whole country.

THE AMERICAN DEVOLUTION: FROM ORIGINAL WEALTH TO ORIGINAL DEBT

"From 1700 to 1800," said Wilken's associate Charles Ray, "our nation's farmer-pioneers were creating the first basic capital in the wealth of [America] by raw labor out of the soil." E. H. Taylor, editor of *Country Gentleman,* called this bounty of raw materials "original wealth." And yet, two centuries later the United States, the most powerful empire in the world, has an economy so compromised it can only function through massive infusions of debt. Whereas our parents and grandparents enjoyed a high standard of living fifty years ago on one income, it now takes two-and-a-half incomes to even approach that standard of living. The money most families once put aside for savings now goes to repay debt. What went wrong?

The subtext of American history from this country's founding until 1913 was the struggle between those who wanted banks in charge of monetary policy and those who wanted the government of the people to determine how much currency was coined. The battle was decisively won by the banks in 1913, when the Federal Reserve was established, insuring that U.S. currency would be debt-based and issued through private banks.

A year later, the World War began in Europe and European bankers had loaned the Allied powers $15 billion. But by 1916, the war was going poorly for the Allies and the bankers needed two things to secure their loans. First, they needed for the United States to enter the war and shift the balance of power toward the

Allies. Second, they needed for America to loan the Allies an additional $15 billion from the U.S. Treasury. And so Woodrow Wilson,
the man who ran for president in 1916 on the platform "he kept us
out of war" (not, we should note, "he's gonna keep us out of war")
got us into war on April 6, 1917, just weeks after his inauguration.
America's "victory" in that war may have set the country on the
road to ruin. At the end of the war, the Allied powers were victori-
ous, but bankrupt. Without money, they had to repay the United
States in goods. Well, goods are good, right? Not exactly. At a
time when America was already prosperous and self-sufficient,
Congress lowered the tariffs in order to import the goods and
collect the war debts. From 1919 to 1929, America imported
$43 billion in goods—and that meant $43 billion that our own
industries weren't earning. Plants closed, and by late 1929 there
were twelve million unemployed.

Meanwhile, European banks had $3.5 billion on deposit
in U.S. banks. When they "drafted" those reserves, America's
banks were caught short. And the economic house of cards
came tumbling down.

And so by 1932—less than two decades after the establishment
of the Federal Reserve—America's economy had experienced all of
the disasters that a national bank was supposed to have prevented.
The farming community was devastated by overwhelming debt and
falling land prices. Factories were closed, and banks were going
bankrupt. National income dropped 52 percent, and one-quarter
of America's workforce was unemployed.

According to Stephen Zarlenga, director of the American
Monetary Institute, "In that horrendous climate many economists were aware that the banking system caused the problem and
major changes were needed."[2] At this challenging moment, Henry
Simons at the University of Chicago assembled the "greatest economic minds of the country." The plan they came up with became
known as "the Chicago Plan," and was circulated to a thousand

academic economists across the country. Of those who responded, 235 agreed with the plan, 40 agreed with some reservations, and only 45 disapproved.

The Plan was harshly critical of the banking system of the time, stating, "If the purpose of money and credit were to discourage the exchange of goods and services, to destroy periodically the wealth produced, to frustrate and trip those who save, our present monetary system (does that) most effectively!"

As for prescriptions, they were radical:

1. Only the government would create money. Fractional reserves—the mechanism banks had used to "create" money—would be abolished. Banks would essentially be warehousing money and charging a fee for their services.

2. Lending—the province of the banks—would be separate from money creation. This would prevent banks from "borrowing short" and "lending long," another way that banks created money out of thin air and were able to pull the rug out on ordinary people when money "tightened" again.

3. An important distinction was made between money and credit. During the early years of the Depression, defaulted loans and reduced borrowing artificially shrunk the money supply. This is why there was work to do, but too little money to pay for it. Separating money and credit would greatly stabilize the economy, possibly preventing future depressions.

The plan called for the money to flow right into the banks, many of which had had to close their doors because of "runs" when their customers demanded more cash than they had on hand. Under this plan, the banks would be paying interest to the government instead of the other way around. The banks would still be able to make reasonable profit through making loans. The Chicago Plan would have returned America to the original notion of the founding fathers—that it was the government (representing the will of sovereign citizens) that would issue the money, and this money would reflect the value of the real wealth in the economy. This money supply would not be subject to the manipulation of the "money changers" for their own benefit.

The Plan was enthusiastically supported by the "best economic minds" of the era. Paul Douglas—later a U.S. Senator from Illinois—wrote, "This proposal will of course be opposed by the bankers from whom it takes the lucrative privilege of creating purchasing power. It would however insure the safety of deposits, give large revenues to the government, provide complete social control over monetary matters and prevent abnormal fluctuations in the capital market. At the same time it would permit the allocation of productive resources … to remain primarily in private hands. All in all it seems the most promising program for the reform of our monetary and credit system …" A young Milton Friedman became a well-known advocate of the plan, writing, "… the creation of fiat currency should be a government monopoly."

So what happened? How did the Chicago Plan go the way of the Chicago Plan for the Cubs to win the World Series? Quite simply, it was an idea whose time had not yet come, and those who benefited from the old system were able to mobilize their resources to prevail. Although legislation was submitted to Congress, the legislation languished and not even its sponsors—like Senator Bronson Cutting of New Mexico—could articulate it well. No one bothered to present it to the people themselves because no one imagined they could understand it.

Meanwhile, the bankers and Secretary of the Treasury Henry Morgenthau, Jr. convinced President Franklin D. Roosevelt that the plan was unworkable and steered him to another economic guru, John Maynard Keynes, whose approach was to keep the bankers in power but soften the impact of economic vicissitudes on the public. "Keynes," writes Zarlenga, "was therefore not revolutionary except in relation to the utter backwardness of the financial establishment."

Keynes, like most economists at the time, believed that investment runs the economy. The more money made available for investment, the more the economy could grow, even if that investment money was borrowed. "We're borrowing from ourselves," the saying went. Unfortunately, what this really meant was that "we the people" would end up owing large sums of money to "we the very, very few people."

In contrast, the raw materials economists like Wilken tried to make the point that no economy could be based on debt. The foundation of a healthy economy, he argued, was "earned income based on the parity monetization of raw materials," meaning that real wealth comes from the tangible products we bring forth from the earth, *and* a fair price paid to those who do the extracting. An exacting mathematician, Wilken came up with a formula that would accurately predict America's national income fourteen years running: national income was always roughly seven times the farm income.

He explained it this way: The earth is the only producer of "original wealth," meaning that the earth gives her yield without charging interest. Each season, new wealth is infused into the economy. The farmer is the first earner and first spender of that wealth, which "reverberates" through the economy. The farmer pays the feed store owner, pays for farm equipment, and buys clothes, etc., fueling the prosperity throughout the local community. Meanwhile, as this new harvest is distributed more people make money and more communities benefit, all the way down to the local grocer or supermarket. Think of it this way. If there were no food to sell, Whole Foods would have to call themselves Whole Nothing. Food is the basic "fuel" for our economy because it is the most constantly and consistently consumed item.

Consider further that if a farmer raises one hundred bushels of corn and gets paid ten dollars a bushel, this infuses one thousand dollars into the economy. But what if—in the name of lower food prices—the farmer only gets five dollars a bushel? That means that only five hundred dollars is infused into the economy, half as much. To prove his point, Wilken pointed to the farm income in 1929—the last year before the Depression—and in 1932. Farm income dropped from $11 billion in 1929 to $5 billion in 1932, and yet production remained the same! The only difference was a loss in buying power.

As Wilken loved to point out, a bushel of corn at five dollars had just as many calories as a bushel at ten dollars. In a pamphlet called *The Key to Prosperity,* Wilken wrote that America could have any level of prosperity it desired as long as it remembered this seven-to-one ratio of national income to farm income. "A parity— or equal exchange," he wrote, "is not simply a matter of fairness to the people engaged in agriculture. It is a matter of direct self-interest to those in every other group in America."

AMERICA'S NEAR-DEBT EXPERIENCE

However, in the midst of a grave economic emergency, President Roosevelt chose a different path. He launched a massive public works campaign that may well have prevented a fascist or communist revolution during these times. Following the Keynesian model, he infused money into the system through organizations like the Works Progress Administration (WPA) and young unemployed workers helped build our national parks system and other valuable infrastructure. Young writers and photographers were also paid to do cultural history projects (such as interviews with the dwindling population of ex-slaves), and these too have added to America's collective knowledge and intelligence. But the problem with this program was the same problem we are suffering from today. They were all debt-based.

"Debt," Wilken warned, "is a mortgage against the income of future generations." But in the end, the "international capitalists" were too strong and the persistent belief system of "unregulated private business" and "free market system" prevailed, while ironically government spending skyrocketed! In a trend that began at the beginning of the twentieth century, American capitalists accelerated investment in exploitative enterprises overseas, and have used America's military might to secure these investments.

This has resulted in a geometrically multiplying loss for the United States, even as it's become the most formidable military power in the world. The losses are threefold. First, America has lost its own foundation in people's capitalism. Farming is now largely factory farming, as rural population is now 10 percent of what it was a century ago. Secondly, in its place we have a debt-based house-of-cards economy that is kept in place by our military might. That military has cost us $15 trillion since the end of World War II. And speaking of debt, our military operations—overt and covert—around the world have greatly increased our karmic debt because they have been largely and tragically in service of the interests of exploitation.

THE NURTURING ECONOMY

So, at a juncture when not just America but the world is crying out for a new economics, what have we learned? And how can this learning help us design a system that reflects nurturing rather than exploitative values?

The first thing we learn from America's experience is that borrowing to consume is unnatural. The body, for example, only has so many energy resources. Any new "investment"—repair of infrastructure or creation of new cells—must be done with available cash (food being digested) or savings (fat and nutrients stored in the body).

That's why animals do not reproduce if they're not sufficiently nourished. How do we know? Well, consider that when young women who are anorexic reach a certain level of malnutrition, their periods stop. It's nature's way of saying that unless you "pay for" your body's current operating expenses, there are no savings available to manufacture a new being. The second important learning—the really good news, in fact—is that on this planet, the source of all wealth is the energy from the sun, and the food from the earth. All else is derivative. And this is really great news because both of these resources—understood and managed properly—are infinitely renewable. As sure as the sun comes up in the morning, solar power is available, either "new" or "used." As Thom Hartmann pointed out in his book of the same title, the oil we are burning today—in ever-dwindling supply—represents "the last hours of ancient sunlight." And while we may be running out of stored sunlight, there is an abundance of fresh stuff coming our way daily. Says Dennis Hayes, former director of the U.S. Solar Energy Research Institute, says, "No country uses as much energy as is contained in the sunlight that strikes its buildings each day."

Because the sun also controls atmospheric dynamics, wind energy too is "solar," and—as long as the sun comes to work every morning—renewable as well. According to a 1997 U.S. Department of Energy report, three states—North Dakota, Kansas, and Texas—had "enough harnessable wind energy to satisfy national electricity needs." However, according to Lester Brown, that was a "misunderestimation" based on technology that existed in the 1990s. Advances in wind turbine designs now indicate that wind power in just these three states could meet America's entire national energy demand.

Furthermore, energy consultant Harry Braun suggests that because these wind turbines are so similar to auto engines, Detroit's auto industry could regear to mass-produce these on an assembly line. This could drop the cost of wind-generated electricity two cents a kilowatt hour! Lester Brown suggests that by shifting current energy industry subsidies—e.g., the current $210 billion yearly fossil fuel subsidies—this new technology can be developed.[3]

What stand in the way of this development are the same things that have kept the dominator economy in place long since it's outlived its uselessness: (1) An influential and powerful minority benefits from it; (2) The vast majority of the rest of us have been myth-led to believe that this is the way things have always been and always must be.

Part of what has kept the current economic system in place is the persistent belief in scarcity. With 6.5 billion people on the planet, how could we possible grow enough food for all? The answer is simple and natural. The goal is for each community everywhere to be sustainable, and food and energy self-sufficient. If the sun and soil are the sources of all wealth, then a healthy, wealthy commonwealth begins with every community having access to this abundance. On one end of the spectrum, it means the end of exploitive monoculture economies where resources are extracted without the proper payment, and local sustainable farming is marginal at best. On the other end—in the most urbanized and ghettoized areas of our country—food must be grown locally, as a thriving business opportunity. Consider the empty lots in cities like Philadelphia and Detroit, and the possibilities for growing food and sending it up the economic food chain as this food is sold, processed, and delivered.

If we've learned anything from people's capitalism and the laws of biology it is that when "cells" are allowed to thrive, the entire organism thrives. Those top-down attempts to force collectivism have been miserable failures. However, when individuals cooperate together voluntarily, and when they are allowed to gain a fair price for their labor, communities thrive and the commonwealth builds. The body cares for all participating cells, and so participation is key.

REGROWING YOUR GARDEN

How, then, do I participate and regrow *my* garden?

Once again, rather than answers we offer more questions for us each to ask ourselves: What is it that truly brings me happiness? What is of value, and what is worth having? Each time "I want" comes up, the next question is, And if I had that, what would it do for me? What beliefs are keeping my status quo in place? What fears or concerns? How can I downscale my footprint and upscale my life? How can I use less and at the same time increase my happiness? This is tricky because there is such a persistent invisible belief in sacrifice and deprivation. So the game is, whatever you choose *must* not just make your footprint smaller, but *must* make your life better. Self-fulfillment is far more satisfying than selfish feel-fullment.

How can I educate myself, and help educate others? In a world where we are increasingly seeing that all things are related, we can no longer discount things that are out of our comfort zones, whether those involve economics, politics, or spirituality. In these wildly transformational times, we might do better embracing our "discomfort zone" so we become more comfortable with the discomfort of change.

As we allow the "myth-perceptions" of obsolete economic thinking to fall by the wayside, we can recognize how all systems— economy, ecology, banking, health care, education, defense—are really one conversation: how do we, individually and collectively, use our resources wisely for the well-being of all? Why? Because in a healthy, caring system a "health care system" requires a fraction of the resource it currently uses, because prevention is far cheaper than cure. And that brings us to a final lesson we can learn from the natural economy. Just as surely as international capitalism (corporatism) is proving itself incapable of delivering us into a healthy new world, the same is true of state capitalism (i.e., communism). In a natural economy based on extraction, production, and distribution of real (renewable) resources, the forms of organization likewise arise from the grassroots up. Consider that in villages and rural communities the world over, some form of barn raising is commonplace. Independent entities (in this case, farmers) recognize their interdependence, and combine voluntarily to assist one another.

The future of economics, not to mention our species, involves growing a noncoercive, nongovernmental public movement of voluntary cooperation that will weave all the functional and productive aspects of economy into a true web of mass-construction that will make us all interdependently wealthy. This is already happening via the slow money movement, Transition Towns, and buy local alliances. These alliances often transcend old political polarities, and combine the most functional aspects of libertarian conservatism and progressive liberalism. Regardless of what this new economic system is called, it will involve two things: wisely using the resources of nature, and wisely using the resources of human nature. In order to maximize the renewable original wealth of the sun and earth, we will need to mobilize and apply the unique gifts our species brings to the world: love and imagination. Through imagination, we create sustainable technology. Through love, we multiply the goodness throughout the system so that we need fewer goods to feel good. We recognize that the most sustainable form of economic growth is growing happiness.

May we grow happier, as we embrace our mission to tend the garden we have been given, and fruitfully multiply the "common wealth" instead of fruitlessly scrapping over the scraps.

23

TOWARD A SPIRITUAL ECONOMICS

AMIT GOSWAMI

It does not take a genius to see that capitalist economics as practiced today is at a crisis point. Present-day capitalism is based on continuous growth and expansion that require unlimited resources; this cannot be sustained on a finite planet. (In fact, the finitude of resources may already have caught up with us.) This expansion produces higher and higher standards of living, and wages cannot keep up without producing inflation. To meet the demands of higher standards and their higher cost, people are forced to give up their other needs, such as the need of children for quality time with a parent or the need of adults for leisure time to pursue meaning. Thus, and invariably, some of the basic promises of capitalism are shortchanged by the nature of the beast itself.

Capitalism recognizes one basic need for people: the survival and security of their physical bodies. This basic ego need requires private property—and any economics that ignores this basic need of people is bound to fail. But as the psychologist Abraham Maslow pointed out, we have an entire hierarchy of needs beyond the body. One major defect of capitalist economics is the ignoring of the people's higher needs. Following Maslow, but modifying his theory according to the insights of my general approach to spirituality—science within consciousness—we can easily see what these higher needs are.

OUR REDEFINED HIGHER NEEDS AND THE RUDIMENTS OF A SPIRITUAL ECONOMICS

Consciousness is the foundation of all being, and its possibilities are fourfold: material (which we sense); vital energy (which we feel, primarily through the chakras and secondarily through the brain); mental meaning (which we think); and supramental (which we intuit). "Supramental" includes discriminating contexts, such as physical laws, as well as contexts of meaning and feeling, such as ethics, love, and aesthetics. The material aspects of experience are sometimes called "gross"; the rest make up the "subtle" domain of our experience.

When consciousness chooses the actual event of its experience out of these possibilities (material, vital, mental, and supramental), the physical has the opportunity to represent the subtle. The material is like computer hardware; the subtle is software. Our capacity for making material or physical representation of the subtle evolves. Our capacity for making representations of the vital evolved through the evolution of life via more and more sophisticated organs to represent living functions such as maintenance and reproduction. Next, the capacity of making more and more sophisticated representations of the mental evolved. This is the stage of evolution we are in right now. Our capacity effortlessly to represent the supramental has not evolved yet. However, there is evolutionary pressure on us to move in this direction; it is the primary reason some of us are attracted to spirituality.

In this way, there must be an urge to satisfy not only physical needs but also the needs of all the other dimensions of our experience. Thus a spiritual economics must address the satisfaction of emotional needs both conditioned and unconditioned (positive emotions such as love, compassion, and satisfaction itself); the pursuit of meaning, including the pursuit of new mental meaning that requires creativity; and the pursuit of spiritual and supramental (soul) needs such as altruism, aesthetics, and happiness.

And in truth, this ladder of needs is not entirely hierarchical. If one satisfies higher needs, the urge to satisfy lower needs actually decreases. But if a lower need is satisfied, the demand for satisfying a higher need increases. In this way, a strategy for an economics more suitable than capitalism would be to address all of our needs simultaneously.

Whereas capitalism is an economics of physical well-being based on the satisfaction of our conditioned physical ego-needs, idealist or spiritual economics must be an economics of holistic well-being based on the satisfaction of both our (physical) ego needs and higher needs (pertaining to the exploration of the vital, mental, soul, and spirit).

MICROECONOMICS OF THE SUBTLE

Economics is about production and consumption, supply and demand, prices and so forth. How does all of this relate to our subtle needs? Let's talk about these micro-details.

Production of positive vital energy can be accomplished in many ways: forestation (plants and trees have abundant vital energy), cultivating positive health in society (people of positive health radiate vital energy), and so forth.[1] But the best way to ensure production of vital energy is to encourage ordinary workplaces to offer facilities for their employees to practice positive health, including space for yoga, tai chi, and meditation. As for production of mental meaning, we already have some things in place in the arts and entertainment industries. Both of these industries have the capacity to produce positive vital energy (positive emotions); however, they have largely been bogged down with the negativity of a materialist culture. But we can shift the emphasis from negativity to meaningfulness and positivity.

The production of supramental and spiritual energy requires

more effort today than it used to. In the olden days, spiritual organizations like churches, temples, synagogues, mosques, and the like
cultivated and produced supramental and spiritual intelligence in
their leaders and practitioners. Nowadays, these organizations are
more interested in influencing mundane politics than in investing
in the supramental. But make no mistake about it; it can be done,
although we may have to develop new spiritual organizations to do
it. In the olden days, perhaps the most effective means of production (and dissemination) of supramental energy were travelling
monks (called *sadhus* in India; troubadours are an example in the
West). This we can revive; to some extent the many new age conferences on spirituality are already serving this purpose. Also effective
are group meditations, through which (as some of parapsychologist
Dean Radin's experiments show) people can experience nonlocal
consciousness and hence can take creative leaps to the supramental domain. This can be done even in workplaces.

Now to the question of consumption. Because the vital and
mental are mappable in us, they can be consumed both by local
and nonlocal means. For example, if we see good theater, it culti-
vates the processing of meaning in us, even new meaning. When we
partake of good, meaningful entertainment, we also feel positive
emotions; we are consuming them. As we consume, we ourselves
have the potential to become producers.

Supramental energy consumption is nonlocal, but it requires
local triggers. There are scientists who subscribe to the so-called
Maharishi effect, according to which the spiritual and supramental
energy generated by a group meditation is consumed automatically
in the local vicinity. There have been claims of crime reduction in
big cities where Transcendental Meditation groups perform such
meditation. However, this is controversial and I am not advocating
it. A purely quantum-mechanical consumption of your spiritual
energy requires that I be correlated with you by some means or
other. For example, experiments by Mexican neurophysiologist

Jacobo Grinberg suggest that if two people practice meditative intention together, they become so correlated—but it should be simpler than that. There are many anecdotes of people who have felt peace in the presence of a sage (I myself have experienced this). So just being locally present may trigger consumption.

The best part of the story of subtle energy products is that it is mostly free. The subtle dimensions have no limits; we can consume a sage's love all we wish, and the supply is not going to diminish. There is no zero-sum game in the subtle. Since there might be a bit of material cost of production, we might put a material price tag on subtle products to offset this—and that may not be such a bad idea, because it enables people to be more serious about their intentions when they consume subtle products. This would also be an opportunity for the government to subsidize the subtle industry, for example, in the form of tax exemption or research grants.

DOES SPIRITUAL ECONOMICS SOLVE THE PROBLEMS OF CAPITALISM?

But how can spiritual economics—the economics of the subtle—address the problems of capitalism I articulated earlier? First, let's look at the problem of limited resources. Capitalistic growth economics depends crucially on keeping consumer demands going; this is often accomplished by creating artificial physical needs, such as new annual fashions for women's garments. It is very wasteful and detrimental to finite resources.

In spiritual economics, when people's higher needs are met—even partially—their physical needs reduce, reducing the demand for consumption and thus reducing the wastage of limited material resources. The economy still expands—but in the higher planes, where resources are unlimited (there is no limit on love and satisfaction).

There is another, related problem with capitalism and material-expansion economics: environmental pollution. This is a tricky one. In the short term, production of pollution helps expand the economy by creating pollution cleanup sectors of the economy. Believe it or not, the Exxon Valdez oil spill disaster actually produced an economic boom in Alaska. But in the long run, environmental pollution on a finite planet is bound to end up with a doomsday of reckoning. Many environmentalists think that global warming has already reached doomsday criticality. In spiritual economics, material consumption is reduced, thus automatically reducing environmental pollution.

Next, let us consider the free market. Why isn't it free in the way Adam Smith envisioned? The truth is, a really free market has large ups and downs—but a democratic government must level out these business cycles in order to survive; voters wouldn't allow them to go unchecked. So the government intervenes, either through the Keynesian approach (tax the rich and increase government programs to increase jobs and economic movements) or the supply-side approach (reduce tax for the rich; the rich will invest, producing economic activity that will trickle down to the poor). If these steps require deficit financing, so be it. Now, nothing is wrong with government intervention per se. Adam Smith himself was quite aware of this: he suggested government intervention to reduce unjust income distribution, to ensure that the entry to the free market is really free even for the small entrepreneur (regulation against monopoly, for example), and to provide liberal education to everyone participating in the market. Governments today tinker with the free market in a few other ways that Adam Smith may not have approved of: they make bureaucratic regulations, bail out big companies from bankruptcy, and give tax incentives to segments of the economy counter to the spirit of capitalism. The problem with this kind of tinkering is the indefinite-growth economics that we seem to have become stuck on. I have already commented on how spiritual economics solves this problem.

More recently, the freedom of the market has been affected by more than this traditional sort of tinkering. Materialism has produced a wound in our collective psyche, one which has released the powerful among us from the search for mental meaning to the slavery of our instinctual greed, avarice, and competitiveness. One of the effects of this is the gross corruption of the practices that keep the market free. The current practice is to manage corruption through laws, but this has very limited success. The other effect is subtle.

There is now an active counter-evolutionary movement for taking away meaning processing from large segments of people. Right now, this is more of an American phenomenon, but it may soon spread to other developed economies with strong currencies. Americans have been in a unique situation since the gold standard shifted to the dollar standard. Americans can borrow money to buy resources and goods from other countries almost indefinitely because those countries have few options other than reinvesting their money in the American dollar and the American economy. The American government then has the capacity for large amounts of deficit financing—and it is using this deficit financing to cut taxes for the rich. This is not immediately detrimental to the economy, because the rich are the biggest consumers and they are also big investors. But the practice makes the gap between rich and poor larger and tends to eliminate the middle class. In this way, market share is becoming more concentrated in the hands of the rich, and a new class system is being created. Can traditional capitalism function when the capital becomes concentrated again as it did under feudalism or a mercantile economy?

Spiritual economics would foster a universal revival of idealist values; instead of dealing with the symptoms of the materialist wound, such as corruption, we should rather heal the wound so that the symptoms disappear. For example, take the case of deficit financing; right now it is being used to increase the wealth gap between rich and poor, contrary to the spirit of capitalism. Even worse, deficit financing removes the very important economic constraint against nations with aggressive ideas. George W. Bush's Iraq war would not have been possible if deficit financing were not permitted. So should we be against deficit financing in spiritual economics? Not necessarily. How does spiritual economics deal with a government that creates income disparity between rich and poor or starts aggressive wars? In an idealist society, the root cause for a government's actively creating income disparity or war—negative emotion—would be addressed, and attempts would be made to eliminate them by creating an oversupply of positive emotions. Through spiritual economics, we would then use deficit financing to eliminate income disparity (as Adam Smith envisioned) as far as practicable without affecting the proper functioning of the economy—nationally and internationally—so long as the deficit increase or decrease remains within a few percentage points of the increase or decrease of the Gross National Product (GNP).

Next, let's take up the subject of multinational corporations. Multinational corporations have access to cheap labor in underdeveloped economies employed by shifting manufacturing to underdeveloped countries, outsourcing, etc. The labor thus loses the leverage of wage increase through negotiations with management, since the labor laws are very different in underdeveloped countries because of economic necessities. The labor of developed countries lose leverage, too, because of increasing fear of outsourcing of jobs.

In order to subject multinationals to uniform management labor practices, we need to turn from nation-state economies to international economic unions (but not necessarily with a single currency, like the European Union). In other words, the tendency of spiritual economics would be to move toward a single international economic union within which individual democracies would function with political and cultural uniqueness and sovereignty but with increased cooperation.

Finally, there is the important subject of the other counter-evolutionary tendency of capitalistic expansion economy—loss of the worker's leisure time. Spiritual economics has a built-in constraint on expansion, as already noted, so the standard of living does not have to keep moving up at rates faster than wage increases. Even more importantly, spiritual economics values other needs and their satisfaction that require leisure time. So in this economics, "standard of living" is defined differently; increases are measured not in the material dimension but in the higher dimensions—holistic well-being—without compromising the worker's leisure time.

REDEFINING THE GNP

How can we quantify holistic well-being? For our material needs, the GNP is a fairly good indicator of progress or decline. But can we generalize the concept of GNP for spiritual economics?

Most people believe that science only relates to the material world, because only the material can be quantified, can be measured reliably. We have to eradicate this prejudice. We may not be able to measure vital energy, prana, or chi in the same sense that we can measure a quantity of rice, but it is not true that we cannot measure it at all. For example, when vital energy moves out of you, you notice certain feelings at the particular chakra; the same is true of vital energy excesses. When vital energy moves out of the navel chakra, you feel insecurity, butterflies in the stomach. When vital energy moves into the same chakra, the feeling is quite different, that of self-confidence or pride. Similarly, meaning processing gives you a feeling of satisfaction in the crown chakra because vital energy moves into the body there. So we can quantify meaning to some extent by the "amount" of satisfaction we derive from processing it.

Even the supramental can be measured. If we altruistically perform a good deed for someone, we feel happy or blissful—

not because there is any particular influx of vitality in any of the chakras, but because our separateness is momentarily gone. With love, it is even easier, because we not only feel the bliss of not being separate from the whole, but we also feel vital energy in the heart chakra. And both can be measured.

Of course, this kind of measurement is not accurate; it is indeed subjective and always a little vague. But if we remove the prejudice that only accurate and objective measurements count, what then? Then we can certainly establish criteria to judge a nation's net gain or loss of currency (feeling, meaning, and godliness) in the subtle domain. We must note that quantum physics has already replaced complete objectivity (strong objectivity) with weak objectivity, in which subjectivity is permitted so long as we make sure that our conclusions do not depend upon particular subjects.

For example, we can send questionnaires to people to keep an ongoing tab on their feelings, meanings, and supramental experiences or lack thereof. When we tally all this for the entire year, we can easily calculate an index of vital, mental, and supramental well-being. This index would then complement the GNP, which is the index for our material well-being. In the same way, we can estimate the contribution to the vital, mental, and supramental energies from a particular production organization.

Some examples will show that well-being in the subtle dimensions really does count, and we are missing something in our economics because we do not count it. In the Native American culture of old, there was so much subtle wealth that nobody even cared to own material wealth. Native Americans treated material wealth in the same way as subtle wealth: globally, collectively, and without playing a zero-sum game.

In Hindu India (before the tenth century), the country and culture were fundamentally spiritual. The economy was feudal, of course, but according to all accounts (not only of indigenous people but also of foreign visitors) people were satisfied and happy despite the prevalence of the caste system. What gives? Hindu India certainly had wealth, but no more than today's America. In a spiritual culture, lot of good vital energy, mental meaning, and spiritual wholeness is generated—that is the reason. The subtle wealth reduced the need for material wealth and more than made up for the lack of it. The same was true for Tibet until the recent takeover by China.

Of course, the Indian and Tibetan cultures are not perfect, because they did limit the meaning processing of the lower classes; so evolution of consciousness eventually caught up with them. But so much energy was generated in the subtle domains in the Indian culture that even today, at a time when there is real poverty in the material domain, the Indian poor are still able to manage, because they continue to inherit and maintain their subtle wealth. If Karl Marx had seen that, it might make him rethink whether the exploited classes are always unhappy!

HOW SPIRITUAL ECONOMICS SOLVES THE PROBLEM OF THE BUSINESS CYCLE

Earlier I mentioned the business cycle, which is commonly referred to as a boom-and-bust cycle. In the nineteenth century, after some years of growth, capitalist economies seemed to fall into a recession. An even deeper stagnation (called depression) eventually happened in the early twentieth century. It is to prevent this kind of fluctuation that the cures of Keynesian and supply-side government intervention were proposed. With these cures, recessions still happen, but they have been milder, (except for the 2007–2008 recession.) However, these cures have created a perpetual-expansion economy. Because recovery depends almost entirely on consumerism, a perpetual drain of planetary resources has been created.

In a spiritual economy, since production of subtle products is cheap, in times of recession we could soften the blow by increasing production in the subtle sector (for example, through collective production of vital energy, or meditation by a large group), so that consumption in that sector would also increase. This would reduce demand in the material sector, giving businesses time to regroup and increase material productivity. But most people enjoy the subtle and transformative practices for awhile. In a matter of a few months, they reach a plateau. By the end of a year or so, most people have had enough transformation for now, and they are ready to resume "real work."

In the same way, in "boom" times the production of material goods would increase, material consumerism would increase, and there would be fewer subtle goods produced and consumed. As the economy recovered, people's material needs would be satisfied again, and they would once again become hungry for the satisfaction of their subtle needs, whose production would then increase. This would have the effect of putting a damper on the inflationary tendencies of "boom" times in a capitalist economy. The important thing is that there would be no subtle price for the subtle goods; there would be no inflationary pressure in the subtle dimensions. Paying attention to the subtle would just enable the entire economy to soften the blow of both recessions and boom time inflationary pressure. In other words, cyclical variations of the economy would be much less severe, so mild that little or no government intervention would be needed to keep the economy in a steady state. I am convinced that spiritualizing the economy is the way to accomplish a stable economy, something that many economists have thought impossible to achieve.

The million dollar question is, How do we go about replacing capitalist economics with this spiritual economics?

IMPLEMENTATION: WHEN AND HOW?

You might think, "Spiritual economics sounds good; it brings together spiritual values with the best of capitalism. But how is it going to be implemented? By the government? By social revolution, as with Marxist economics? By a paradigm shift in the academic practices of economics?"

But let's begin with a different question: How did capitalism come to replace feudalism and the mercantile economy? Capitalism was first implemented not because of a social revolution or because academics welcomed the idea but because capitalism served the purpose of a modernist, adventurous people. During the period in which capitalism developed, people had begun to embark on new adventures of mind and meaning, as science broke free from religious authorities; and as this meaning exploration opened up, it was necessary to make capital available to innovative people and keep it available. Compared to feudalism or the mercantile economy (Adam Smith's term for the economy prevalent in England in his time), in which the pursuit of meaning is highly limited and vast numbers of people are denied it, capitalism offered larger numbers of people the economic freedom and flexibility needed to pursue meaning in their lives. Hence capitalism was inevitable.

Spiritual economics is inevitable for implementation because our society needs it, just as capitalism was once inevitable because the society of its time needed it. As our society moves beyond our competitive ego needs, as we heal the wounds created by materialism, as we begin to explore the benefits of cooperation en masse, the old competitive capitalist economics *must* give way to a new economics in which competition exists simultaneously with cooperation, each in its own sphere of influence.

To understand this, we need to look at how any economics is really implemented: businesses, of course. It is how business is done that provides the drive for the change in economics. And vice versa: the change in economics helps businesses along. Each is essential to the other.

So what will enable spiritual economics to replace capitalism?

Ultimately, it is the need of the workplace, the businesses. And there, if you look, you will find ample evidence that business is already changing its ways. Yes, competition will continue to exist; without it there would be no market economy. But in the workplace, inside how a business is run, we increasingly find a different philosophy and a different aspect of the human being at work. In many of our businesses, we have discovered the value of creativity, leisure, love, cooperation, and happiness

The modernism of Adam Smith's time has given way to postmodernism and trans-modernism. The old-fashioned exploration and expansion found in the material world are practically over in the face of finite resources and the challenges of environmental pollution. But while the old frontier is gone, there is a new frontier on the horizon, one that belongs to the subtle dimensions of the human being—and one that requires a subtler, spiritual economics.

NOTES

CHAPTER 3

1. http://en.wikipedia.org/wiki/List_of_countries_by_GDP_(PPP)
   _per_capita. For the International Monetary Fund (IMF) estimate, see: www.imf.org/external/pubs/ft/weo/2008/02/weodata
   /weoreptc.aspx?sy=2006&ey=2013&scsm=1&ssd=1&sort=country&ds
   =.&br=1&pr1.x=38&pr1.y=12&c=001&s=PPPGDP&grp=1&a=1
   (accessed April 23, 2011). For the World Bank estimate see: http:
   //search.worldbank.org/quickview?name=%3Cem%3EGDP%3C%2F
   em%3E%2C+PPP+%28current+international+%24%29&id=NY.GDP
   .MKTP.PP.CD&type=Indicators&cube_no=2&qterm=gdp (accessed
   April 23, 2011). For the CIA estimate see: https://www.cia.gov/library
   /publications/the-world-factbook/geos/xx.html (accessed April 23,
   2011). For the definition of "purchasing power parity" see: http://data
   .worldbank.org/indicator/NY.GNP.MKTP.PP.CD. For world population
   see the U.S. Census Bureau's World Population Clock at: www.census
   .gov/main/www/popclock.html (accessed April 23, 2011).
2. See Global Footprint Network, www.footprintnetwork.org/en/index
   .php/GFN/page/world_footprint (accessed April 23, 2011).
3. See Adam Parsons, "World Bank Poverty Figures: What Do They Mean?"
   at www.stwr.org/globalization/world-bank-poverty-figures-what-do-
   they-mean.html. The complete World Bank report summarized in
   the article can be found here: http://siteresources.worldbank.org
   /JAPANINJAPANESEEXT/Resources/515497-1201490097949
   /080827_The_Developing_World_is_Poorer_than_we_Thought.pdf;
   another copy can be found at: http://citeseerx.ist.psu.edu/viewdoc
   /download?doi=10.1.1.168.949&rep=rep1&type=pdf (accessed April
   23, 2011).
4. Quoted in Simon Robinson, "The Farm Fight," *Time*, November 20, 2005, available online at www.time.com/time/printout
   /0,8816,1132867,00.html (accessed April 23, 2011).
5. See Martin Ravallion, Shaohua Chen, and Prem Sangraula, *Dollar a
   Day Revisited* (World Bank Developmeant Research Group, 2008):
   3; available online at: www-wds.worldbank.org/external/default
   /WDSContentServer/IW3P/IB/2008/09/02/000158349_200809020
   95754/Rendered/PDF/wps4620.pdf (accessed April 23, 2011).

CHAPTER 6

1. Barbara Alice Mann, *Iroquoian Women: The Gantowisas* (New York: Lang,

2000): 204–37. For more on the League, see eds. Bruce Elliott Johansen and Barbara Alice Mann, *Encyclopedia of the Haudenosaunee (Iroquois League)* (Westport, CT: Greenwood Press, 2000).

2. ShanShan Du, *"Chopsticks Only Work in Paris": Gender Unity and Gender Equality among the Lahu of Southwest China* (New York: Columbia University, 2002), especially 97–106.

3. Makilam, *The Magical Life of Berber Women in Kabylia* (New York: Lang, 2007), especially 47–76.

4. Peggy Reeves Sanday, *Women at the Center: Life in a Modern Matriarchy* (Ithaca: Cornell University Press, 2002), especially 79–88.

5. Rauna Kuokkanen, "The Logic of the Gift: Reclaiming Indigenous Peoples' Philosophies," *The Australian Journal of Indigenous Education* 34 (2005): 251–71.

6. See, for instance, the anthology, ed. Genevieve Vaughan, *Women and the Gift Economy: A Radically Different Worldview Is Possible* (Toronto: Inanna Publications and Education, 2007).

7. Barbara A. Mann, "Euro-forming the Data," in Bruce E. Johansen, *Debating Democracy* (Clear Light Publishers, 1998): 160–90.

8. Barbara Alice Mann, "Blood and Breath," in *Toward 2012: Perspectives on the Next Age*, eds. Daniel Pinchbeck and Ken Jordan (New York: Penguin Group, 2008): 97–109. See, also, my scholarly discussion of this issue in Barbara Alice Mann, Native Americans, Archaeologists, and the Mounds (New York: Lang Publishers, 2003): 169–238.

9. Fractals were so named by Benoit Mandelbrot, who first published his fractal math as *Les objets fractals, forme, hasard et dimension* in 1975. The English translation came in 1977 as *Fractals: Form, Chance and Dimension* (San Francisco: Freeman, 1977).

10. The date came from *Sganyadaiyoh*, ("Handsome Lake") called "The Seneca Prophet," by Westerners. *Sganyadaiyoh* was actually his position title as a lineage chief of the Senecas, even as "Congresswoman, Ninth Congressional District," is the position title of Marcy Kaptur (my Congressional Representative). The 2010 date from the particular Sganyadaiyoh who uttered it in the early nineteenth century was recorded by Arthur Parker, a descendant of his through the male line, which, by the way, is not how the Iroquois count descent. Arthur C. Parker, *Red Jacket: Last of the Seneca* (New York: McGraw-Hill, 1952): 143.

11. Arthur Caswell Parker, "The Constitution of the Five Nations, or the Iroquois Book of the Great Law," *New York State Museum Bulletin* 184 (April 1916): 103–104. Some say that the allusion to "west" prophesied Removal; others see it as an allusion to the direction of death. Both are right, of course.

12. This is a prophecy common to all eastern woodlanders. I have seen it written down from eighteenth-century sources in John Heckewelder, *The History, Manners, and Customs of the Indian Nations Who Once Inhabited Pennsylvania and the Neighboring States,* The First American Frontier Series (1820; 1876, reprint; New York: Arno Press and *The New York Times,* 1971), 345.

CHAPTER 9

1. Luc Laevan and Fabian Valencia, "Resolution of Banking Crises: The Good, the Bad, and the Ugly," IMF Working Paper 10/146 (Washington: International Monetary Fund, 2010). www.imf.org/external/pubs /ft/wp/2010/wp10146.pdf.

2. The "Great Depression" (with capital letters) was the title of a book published by Lionel Robbins in 1934, but it became part of the general political economic vocabulary only after that black period was safely behind us. Specifically, Harry Truman used the expression in 1952, to lambast the Republicans for "having brought on the Great Depression."

3. *The Economist* (October 11, 2008): 13.

4. This expression was first coined by Schumpeter.

5. Central banks will encourage low short-term interest rates and higher longer-term ones, which makes it possible for banks to borrow at low cost from customers and the markets, and invest in long-term government bonds. This was done for instance in the U.S. during the late 1980s during the Savings & Loan debacle, and it worked as planned. It enabled the banks to rebuild their balance sheets. Notice that such a use of funds doesn't do much to motivate banks to lend to the business sector, and thereby alleviate the "second wave" effect. Furthermore, even this relatively "mild" crisis (representing a bailout of 3.7 percent of GNP) took more than six years to be absorbed.

6. Statistic from a 2009 Report by special inspector general Neil Barofsky to the U.S. Congress, which takes into account about fifty initiatives and programs set up since 2007 by the Bush and Obama administrations as well as by the Federal Reserve. This $4.6 trillion amount was actually disbursed, while the estimate of potential costs based on various guarantees could reach over $23 trillion.

7. www.bloomberg.com/apps/data?pid=avimage&iid=ioYrUuvkygWs.

8. Nomi Prins, *It Takes a Pillage: Behind the Bailouts, Bonuses, and Backroom Deals from Washington to Wall Street* (New York: Wiley, 2009).

9. www.ritholtz.com/blog/2008/11/big-bailouts-bigger-bucks.

10. See the classics in this domain, such as Charles Kindleberger, *Manias, Panics and Crashes: A History of Financial Crises* (New York: Wiley, 1996, 1978).

11. See, for instance, James K. Galbraith, "A Bailout We Don't Need," *Washington Post* (September 25, 2008): A19; Ken Silverstein, "Six Questions for James Galbraith on the Financial Crisis and the Bailout," *Harper's Magazine* (November 2008).

12. The leverage ratio is total assets/capital, which is the inverse of capital/assets ratio. The estimates for the capital to asset ratios are respectively 2.4 percent for Barclays, 2.1 percent for UBS and 1.2 percent for Deutsche Bank, according to the *Economist* (September 27, 2008): 84. See also "Briefing" in *Trends-Tendances* (October 2, 2008): 17.

13. Michael Macenzic and John Authers, "The Week that Panic Stalked the Markets," *Financial Times* (October 11/12, 2008): 2.

14. The current modus operandi provides a hidden permanent subsidy to the banking system through seignoriage. Huber and Robertson estimated this yearly subsidy to the banking system at 49 billion pounds for the UK; $114 billion per year for the U.S.; 160 billion euros for the Euro zone; and 17.4 trillion yen for Japan. These benefits would accrue to the governments in the case of nationalization of the money creation process. For further details, see J. Huber and J. Robertson, *Creating New Money: A Monetary Reform for the Information Age* (London: New Economic Foundation.2000), 79–84.

15. Modern energy concepts and flow analyses were actually formally applied to economics as early as 1951, by Nobel laureate Wassili Leontief with his input-output analyses, modeling the flow of goods and value in economic systems (Leonticf, 1951). Ecologists then applied these same flow concepts and analyses to ecosystems, only to have economists later reapply these enhanced energy understandings to economics. Odum (1971, 1984), Hannon (1973), and Costanza (1980), for example, have all used thermodynamics and flow-network analysis as the basis for understanding the activities in both economic and ecosystem networks; and Georgescu-Roegen (1971) developed an entire thermodynamic foundation for economics.

16. Kenneth Boulding, *Evolutionary Economics,* Beverly Hills, CA: Sage Publications, 1981. The misclassification of economics as a system in equilibrium is skillfully explained in E. Beinhocker, *The Origin of Wealth: Evolution, Complexity, and the Radical Remaking of Economics* (Waterton, MA: Harvard Business School Press, 2006), chapters 2 and 3. George Soros has explained the internal dynamics of why financial markets are not moving toward equilibrium in *The Alchemy of Finance* (London: Weidenfeld and Nicolson, 1988.)

17. See, for example, P. Cvitanovic, introduction to *Universality in Chaos,* (Bristol, UK: Adam Hilger, 1984); M. Eigen & P. Schuster, *The Hypercycle:*

A Principle of Natural Self-Organization (Springer Verlag, 1979); M. Estep, *A Theory of Immediate Awareness: Self-Organization and Adaptation in Natural Intelligence* (Kluwer Academic Publishers, 2003) and *Self-Organizing Natural Intelligence: Issues of Knowing, Meaning, and Complexity* (Springer-Verlagm, 2006); F. Dressler, *Self-Organization in Sensor and Actor Networks* (New York: Wiley & Sons, 2007).

18. Sally Goerner, *After the Clockwork Universe: the Emerging Science and Culture of Integral Society* (Edinburgh: Floris Books, 1999); P. Cvitanovic, introduction to *Universality in Chaos* (Bristol, UK: Adam Hilger, 1984).

19. R. M. May, "Will a Large Complex System Be Stable?" *Nature* 238 (1972): 413–14.

20. C. S. Holling, "Resilience and the Stability of Ecological Systems," *Annual Review of Ecology and Systematics* 4 (1973): 1–23; C. S. Holling, "Engineering Resilience Versus Ecological Resilience" in P. Schulze, ed., *Engineering within Ecological Constraints* (Washington, DC: National Academy Press, 1996), 31–44; B. H. Walker et al., "Exploring Resilience in Social Ecological Systems Through Comparative Studies and Theory Development: Introduction to the Special Issue," *Ecology and Society* 11:1 (2006): 12.

21. Edgar Cahn, *No More Throw Away People* (Washington, DC: Essential Books, 2004).

22. James Stodder, "Corporate Barter and Economic Stabilization," *International Journal of Community Currency Research* 2 (1998); James Stodder, "Reciprocal Exchange Networks: Implications for Macroeconomic Stability," Albuquerque, New Mexico: Conference Proceedings, International Electronic and Electrical Engineering (IEEE), Engineering Management Society (EMS), 2000.

23. Open Source means that the source code of the software is publicly available, making it possible for users to adapt the system to their own requirements. Specific parts of the C3 methodology are protected by a patent, but the conditions to get user licence are transparency and monitoring procedures to guarantee fair treatment of the network participants, as well as a small contribution to fund the spreading of such systems. This generates the benefit of additional spending opportunities for any C3 network. More information via c3@socialtrade.org .

24. James Doran, "America's Latest Export: Empty Municipal Coffers," *The Observer* (Oct. 12, 2008): 8.

CHAPTER 12

1. Andrei Codrescu, *Zombification: Stories from National Public Radio* (New York: Picador, 1994), 101.

CHAPTER 16

1. This chapter originated as a talk given at Cooper Union in New York City, April 25, 2002.

CHAPTER 21

1. http://freedocumentaries.org/film.php?id=152 (accessed 18 April 2011).
2. It would be more appropriate to refer to this as "holonocentric," a word coined by systems theorist Richard Bawden, after Arthur Koestler's concept of the "holon." Holons are systems nested within larger systems. Each holon is both a whole and a part of a whole. Holistic implies "whole centered" whereas "holonocentric" implies "centered on wholes that are part of larger wholes," which is more apt.
3. James Lovelock, *The Revenge of Gaia* (London: Allen Lane, 2006).
4. Hardin Tibbs, "Humane Ecostructure," *Whole Earth Review* (Summer 1998): 63–65.
5. Christopher Day, with Rosie Parnell, *Consensus Design* (Oxford: Architectural Press, 2003); Brian Goodwin, *Nature's Due* (Edinburgh: Floris Books, 2007).
6. Hardin Tibbs, *Industrial Ecology: A New Agenda for Industry* (Cambridge, MA: ADL, 1991).
7. Roger Martin, *The Opposable Mind* (Waterton, MA: Harvard Business School Press, 2007).

CHAPTER 22

1. Charles Walters, *Unforgiven: The American Economic System Sold for Debt and War* (Austin: Acres, USA, 1971, 2003).
2. Stephen Zarlenga, *The Lost Science of Money* (Chicago: The American Monetary Institute, 2002).
3. Lester Brown, *Plan B 2.0: Rescuing a Planet Under Stress and a Civilization in Trouble* (New York: W.W. Norton & Company, 2006).

CHAPTER 23

1. For more information, see my book *The Quantum Doctor: A Physicist's Guide to Health and Healing* (Charlottesville: Hampton Roads, 2004).

CONTRIBUTORS

STEVE BHAERMAN is an internationally known author, humorist, and workshop leader. For the past twenty-five years he has written and performed as Swami Beyondananda, the "Cosmic Comic." As the Swami, Steve is the author of *Driving Your Own Karma, Duck Soup for the Soul,* and other books. In 1980, Steve cofounded *Pathways Magazine* in Ann Arbor, Michigan, one of the first publications bringing together holistic health, personal growth, spirituality, and politics. His latest book, written with cellular biologist Bruce H. Lipton, PhD, is *Spontaneous Evolution: Our Positive Future and a Way to Get There From Here.* Steve can be found online at www.wakeuplaughing.com.

JEFF DICKEN is a Baltimore native and a graduate of City College and Northwestern University. A big-picture idealist with a background in film production and IT systems development, he has always been interested in the dynamics of economic systems. Jeff is now Director of Baltimore Green Currency Association, administrator of Baltimore's local currency, the BNote.

CHARLES EISENSTEIN is a speaker, Goddard College faculty member, and the author of *The Ascent of Humanity* and other books. His latest book is *Sacred Economics: Money, Gift, and Society in the Age of Transition.*

SHARON GANNON is the cocreator, with David Life, of the Jivamukti Yoga Method. A student of Brahmananda Sarasvati, Swami Nirmalananda, and Pattabhi Jois, she is a pioneer in teaching yoga as spiritual activism and is credited for making yoga cool and hip, relating ancient teachings of yoga to the modern world. Sharon is the author of several books, including *Jivamukti Yoga* and *Yoga & Vegetarianism.* Her writing has appeared in numerous publications including *Toward 2012, Semiotexte* and *Yoga Journal*. She writes a monthly essay called "Focus of the Month," which can be read at www.jivamuktiyoga.com.

SALLY GOERNER is the director and cofounder of the Integral Science Institute, a nonprofit research and educational center dedicated to developing the applications of Integral Science for human systems fields such as education, business, medicine, economics, and sustainability. She has lectured extensively throughout Europe, the United States, and Japan and is on the scientific advisory council of the European Academy of Evolution Research (Berlin). She has authored over fifty articles and several books, including *After the Clockwork Universe: The Emerging Science and Culture of Integral Society* and *The New Science of Sustainability: Building a Foundation for Great Change.*

AMIT GOSWAMI's life work has been to successfully integrate science and spirituality, applying the principles of quantum physics to prove that consciousness, not matter, is the foundation of all being. He is the author of numerous books, including *The Self-Aware Universe, God Is Not Dead: What Quantum Physics Tells Us about Our Origins and How We Should Live,* and *How Quantum Activism can Save Civilization.* He has appeared in the movie *What the Bleep do we Know?* and the documentary *The Quantum Activist.*

THOMAS H. GRECO, JR., is a writer, networker, and consultant, specializing in cashless exchange systems and community economic development. A former engineer, entrepreneur, and tenured college professor, he is widely regarded as a leading authority on free-market approaches to monetary and financial innovation, and is a sought-after advisor and speaker at conferences internationally. He is the director of the Community Information Resource Center, a U.S. nonprofit networking hub that provides information access and developmental support for efforts in community improvement, social justice, and sustainability. He is the author of many articles and books, including *The End of Money and the Future of Civilization, Money: Understanding and Creating Alternatives to Legal Tender, New Money for Healthy Communities,* and *Money and Debt: a Solution to the Global Crisis.* Greco's blog, www.beyondmoney.net, and his website, www.reinventingmoney.com, offer a wealth of information on the interplay of money, finance, economics, and democracy, and provide detailed explanations and prescriptions for communities, businesses, and governments.

JOHN MICHAEL GREER is a certified Master Conserver, organic gardener, and scholar of ecological history. The current Grand Archdruid of the Ancient Order of Druids in America (AODA), his widely cited blog *The Archdruid Report* (www.thearchdruidreport .blogspot.com) deals with peak oil, among other issues. He lives in Ashland, Oregon.

Born in 1948, **LARRY HARVEY** grew up on a small farm on the outskirts of Portland, Oregon. In the late 1970s he moved to San Francisco, and soon discovered the city's thriving underground art scene. In 1986 he founded Burning Man at a local beach, and has guided its progress ever since; he is currently executive director of the project and serves as chairman of Burning Man's senior staff and Black Rock City LLC, its executive committee.

KEN JORDAN is publisher and executive producer of Reality Sandwich and Evolver.net. He has been an online pioneer since leading the 1995 launch of the award-winning SonicNet.com, the web's first multimedia music zine and digital music store, which later became a property of MTV. As a consultant for start-ups, NGOs and foundations, his clients included: Amnesty International, WITNESS, the New England Foundation for the Arts, Ford Foundation,

Rockefeller Foundation, and the Democrats in Congress. He is coauthor of the influential white paper "The Augmented Social Network: Building Identity and Trust into the Next-Generation Internet;" and is coeditor of the anthologies *Multimedia: From Wagner to Virtual Reality* (W.W. Norton, 2001) and *Toward 2012: Perspectives on the Next Age* (Tarcher/Penguin, 2009). Ken collaborated with the legendary playwright and director Richard Foreman on *Unbalancing Acts: Foundations for a Theater* (Pantheon, 1992). He has written for Wired, Paris Review, Index, and First Monday, among other publications.

ANYA KAMENETZ tells stories about change. She is a journalist, nationally syndicated columnist, and author of *Generation Debt* and *DIY U*. She blogs at www.DIYUBook.com and Twitters at Anya1anya.

BERNARD LIETAER has been active in the domain of money systems for the past thirty years in an unusual variety of functions. He is currently a research fellow at the Center for Sustainable Resources of the University of California at Berkeley. While at the Central Bank in Belgium he was responsible for the implementation of the convergence mechanism (ECU) to the single European currency system and also served as president of Belgium's Electronic Payment System. He was cofounder, general manager, and chief currency trader for the Gaia Hedge Funds, one of the world's largest offshore trading funds, during which time *Business Week* identified him as "the world's top currency trader" in 1990. He is the author of fourteen books, including *The Future of Money*, which has been translated into eighteen languages. More information about the author, as well as his technical papers, are available at www.lietaer.com.

As an educator, journalist, and media producer, **ANTONIO LÓPEZ** seeks to bridge worlds—mental, cultural, ecological, and technological. López has worked in grassroots media for over twenty years and writes nationally for newspapers and magazine on issues concerning cultural diversity, arts, youth, media, and music. He is the author of *Mediacology: A Multicultural Approach to Media Literacy in the 21st Century* (http://mediacology.com).

BARBARA ALICE MANN, an Ohio Bear Clan Seneca, is an assistant professor in the Honors College of the University of Toledo. Her scholarship in Native American studies has resulted in several books, among them *The Tainted Gift: The Disease Method of Frontier Advance, George Washington's War on Native America, Native Americans, Archaeologists, and the Mounds,* and *Iroquoian Women: The Gantowisas,* as well as numerous articles and book chapters. As codirector of the Native American Alliance of Ohio, she lives, writes, teaches, and works for indigenous causes in Ohio.

PAUL D. MILLER, AKA DJ SPOOKY THAT SUBLIMINAL KID is a composer, multimedia artist and writer. His written work has appeared in *The Village Voice, The Source, Artforum* and *The Wire* amongst other publications. Miller's work as a media artist has appeared in a wide variety of contexts such as the Whitney Biennial; The Venice Biennial for Architecture (2000); the Ludwig Museum in Cologne, Germany; Kunsthalle, Vienna; The Andy Warhol Museum in Pittsburgh and many other museums and galleries. His work "New York Is Now" has been exhibited in the Africa Pavilion of the 52 Venice Biennial 2007, and the Miami/Art Basel fair of 2007. Miller's first collection of essays, entitled *Rhythm Science,* was published by MIT Press in 2004. His book *Sound Unbound,* an anthology of writings on electronic music and digital media, was recently released by MIT Press. Look out for Miller's *The Book of Ice,* a multimedia, multidisciplinary study of Antarctica, which draws from the continent's inspiring exploration and artistic endeavors.

STELLA OSOROJOS is a freelance writer and Doctor of Oriental Medicine. Her stories have appeared in *Condé Nast Traveler, Spirituality & Health, InStyle* and more and her memoir, *Star Sister,* will be published by Evolver Editions in March 2012. She maintains a private practice in energy medicine in Pennsylvania. Find out more at www.osorojos.com.

ELLEN PEARLMAN is currently a graduate student in Telematic Art, or artistic collaborations over high-speed networks. She is also a writer, curator, critic, filmmaker, new media artist and photographer who splits her time between Bushwick, Brooklyn, Beijing, Hong Kong, Calgary, Canada and the rest of the world.

DALE PENDELL is a widely published author and poet. A consultant for herbal product development and botanical surveys, he founded *Kuksu: Journal of Backcountry Writing* and cofounded the Primitive Arts Institute. The author of the acclaimed *Pharmako* trilogy, he lives in Penn Valley, California. Further thoughts on money can be found in his futuristic novel, *The Great Bay: Chronicles of the Collapse.*

DANIEL PINCHBECK is the author of *2012: The Return of Quetzalcoatl* and *Breaking Open the Head,* among other books. He is the editorial director of Reality Sandwich and cofounder of Evolver.net.

MICHAEL (TEW) RIGBY is a U.S. transplant, originally from St. Helens in the UK, and a long-time activist in the fields of hunger and poverty with a particular emphasis on innovative economic solutions. Former legislative director of RESULTS, he was responsible for the microcredit legislation in the U.S. Congress from 1987–89.

DOUGLAS RUSHKOFF is an author, teacher, and documentarian who focuses on the ways people, cultures, and institutions create, share, and influence each other's values. His books on new media and popular culture have been translated into over thirty languages. They include *Program or Be Programmed, Life Inc: How Corporatism Conquered the World, and How We Can Take It Back,* and *Coercion,* winner of the Marshall McLuhan Award for best media book. His documentaries include *Merchants of Cool* and *The Persuaders.* Rushkoff also wrote the acclaimed novels *Ecstasy Club* and *Exit Strategy* as well as the graphic novels *Club Zero-G and Testament.*

ELIEZER SOBEL is the author of *The 99th Monkey: A Spiritual Journalist's Misadventures with Gurus, Messiahs, Sex, Psychedelics and Other Consciousness-Raising Adventures; Wild Heart Dancing;* and *Minyan: Ten Jewish Men in a World That is Heartbroken,* which was the winner of the Peter Taylor Prize for the Novel. He blogs for *Psychology Today* and *The Huffington Post.* Visit his website at www.eliezerhuman.com.

HARDIN TIBBS is a futurist and strategist. Now based in England, he used to work for Global Business Network (GBN), the scenario planning firm in California, playing a role in its early development in the 1990s. Trained as an industrial designer, he is a fellow of the RSA in London, and until recently was an associate fellow at the Saïd Business School at Oxford University, where he helped create the Oxford Scenarios Programme. His writing about industrial ecology while a consultant at Arthur D. Little Inc. in the late 1980s helped to define a new way of looking at environment and technology, and his ongoing research aims to chart the future path of industrial society. His website is www.hardintibbs.com.

ROBERT E. ULANOWICZ is professor emertius of Theoretical Ecology with the University of Maryland's Chesapeake Biological Laboratory. A graduate of the Baltimore Polytechnic Institute and Johns Hopkins University, he served as assistant professor of Chemical Engineering at the Catholic University of America before joining the Chesapeake Biological Laboratory in

1970. His current interests include network analysis of trophic exchanges in ecosystems, information theory as applied to ecological systems, the thermodynamics of living systems, causality in living systems, and modeling subtropical wetland ecosystems in Florida (http://atlss.org) and Belize.

DAVID ULANSEY is a professor in the Philosophy, Cosmology, and Consciousness Program at the California Institute of Integral Studies. He received his PhD in Religion from Princeton University and has taught at Princeton, Barnard College, Boston University, University of California at Berkeley, University of Vermont, and Pacifica Graduate Institute. David specializes in the religions of the ancient Mediterranean, particularly the Mystery religions, Gnosticism, Hermeticism, ancient astronomy and cosmology, and the relationship between religion, myth, and the evolution of consciousness. David is creator and webmaster of www.MassExtinction.net, founder of the Species Alliance, and cofounder of the Planetwork Project.

PETER LAMBORN WILSON is a poet-scholar of Sufism and Western Hermeticism and a well-known anarchist social thinker. He is the author of *Sacred Drift: Essays on the Margins of Islam* (City Lights, 1993) and *Escape from the Nineteenth Century* (Autonomedia, 1998), among many other works.

EVOLVER EDITIONS promotes a new counterculture that recognizes humanity's visionary potential and takes tangible, pragmatic steps to realize it. EVOLVER EDITIONS explores the dynamics of personal, collective, and global change from a wide range of perspectives.

EVOLVER EDITIONS is an imprint of the nonprofit publishing house North Atlantic Books and is produced in collaboration with Evolver LLC, a company founded in 2007 that publishes the web magazine Reality Sandwich (www.realitysandwich.com), runs the social network Evolver.net (www.evolver.net), and recently launched a new series of live video seminars, Evolver Intensives (www.evolverintensives.com). Evolver also supports the Evolver Social Movement, which is building a global network of communities who collaborate, share knowledge, and engage in transformative practices.

For more information, please visit
www.evolvereditions.com.